Michael J. Varhola

FIRE AND ICE

THE KOREAN WAR
1950-1953

SAVAS PUBLISHING COMPANY

Fire and Ice: The Korean War, 1950-1953
by Michael J. Varhola

© 2000 Michael J. Varhola

Includes bibliographic references and index

Printing Number
10 9 8 7 6 5 4 3 2
First Edition

ISBN 1-882810-43-0 (cloth)
ISBN 1-882810-44-9 (paper)

Library of Congress Card Number: 00-104152

Savas Publishing Company
202 First Street SE, Suite 103A
Mason City, IA 50401

(515) 421-7135 (editorial offices)
(800) 732-3669 (distribution)

This book is printed on 50-lb. acid-free paper. It meets or exceeds the guidelines for permanence and durability of the Committee on Production Guidelines for Book Longevity of the Council on Library Resources

To Les Albers
and all the warrior poets who have upheld the
Republic by opposing enemies abroad
and ignorance at home

TABLE OF CONTENTS

Foreword   i

Preface and Acknowledgments   vii

I: War on the Ground   1

II: War in the Air   33

III: War at Sea   51

IV: Geography and Battlefields   69

V: U.S. Forces   81

VI: South Korean Military Forces   115

VII: Allied Forces   127

VIII: North Korean and Chinese Forces   151

IX: Weapons, Vehicles, and Equipment   165

X: Uniforms, Insignia, and Personal Equipment   187

XI: Warlords and Statesmen   203

XII: Armistice Negotiations   223

XIII: Prisoners of War and Atrocities   239

continued . . .

TABLE OF CONTENTS (continued . . .)

XIV: The Korean War in Books, Film, and on the Web   253

XV: Facts and Figures   263

Appendix I: Chronology   287

Appendix II: Acronyms and Military Terms   299

Bibliography   309

Index   311

CARTOGRAPHY AND ILLUSTRATIONS

Maps and illustrations are found throughout this book. Except as otherwise noted, all photographs were taken by the U. S. Army Signal Corps, and are included courtesy of the U. S. Soldiers' and Airmen's Home.

THE ORIGINS OF WAR

A t 4:00 a.m. on Sunday, June 25, 1950, 10 division-sized units of the North Korean People's Army (NKPA) crossed the 38th parallel at 11 points and invaded the southern Republic of Korea. The United Nations Security Council ordered an immediate ceasefire in South Korea and the withdrawal of all North Korean forces, but the invasion continued. There is evidence to suggest that the North Koreans clearly expected to capture all of South Korea before any outside power, especially the United States, could intervene.

The beginning of the Korean War marked the climax of a series of events that unfolded over the period of several generations. This initial chain of incidents culminated in the 1910 annexation of Korea by Imperial Japan, ending a long period of tension that had smoldered since 1873, when Japan had first decided upon an eventual expansion onto the Korean peninsula. Internal political and religious problems in Korea in 1894 led to the so-called "Donghak Lan" uprising, which the ineffective Korean government tried to suppress. When the effort failed, the government called upon the Chinese for assistance. Japan, without any such request for assistance, dispatched troops to Korea and, although the uprising was quickly suppressed, both Chinese and Japanese troops remained thereafter on Korean soil.

The subsequent Sino-Japanese War of 1894-1895 led to a Japanese victory that prompted Imperial Russia to seek an agreement with Japan regarding a sphere of influence in Korea. Japan agreed and suggested the 38th parallel as the logical boundary line dividing Korea into foreign protectorates. This did not satisfy Russia, which wanted hegemony over the entire peninsula, and the protectorate plan was rejected. Vladivostok, ice-bound nine months of the year, remained Russia's only port on the Pacific.

In a new initiative, Russia, backed by France and Germany, supported the Chinese rejection of the Japanese claim to the Liaotung Peninsula as a part of the peace treaty. The subsequent Japanese withdrawal of that claim left the way open for Russia to stake out its own sphere of influence in Liaotung and to construct a military and naval base at its southern tip, at Port Arthur. This action, along with a series of other events, left little doubt, especially in Japanese minds, as to Russia's real intentions in Manchuria.

The Imperial Japanese court found the Manchurian situation intolerable and the ensuing Russo-Japanese War of 1904-1095 made indelible marks on the future history of Asia and of the world. The Japanese won the war with the moral and material support of Great Britain and the United States, a point that was not overlooked in St. Petersburg. On July 29, 1905, U.S. Secretary of State William Howard Taft and Japanese Premier Prince Katsura agreed to Japanese suzerainty over Korea after Japan pledged that it would not "harbor aggressive designs against the Philippines." Thus, the Treaty of Portsmouth, signed in September 1905, gave Korea to the Japanese and helped set the stage for World War II and the Korean War.

That the Korean people had other ideas about their future and rejected Japanese hegemony was never really appreciated in the West. The Japanese had been quick in seizing control of the country's means of communications, and news of the insurgency that followed Portsmouth was cleverly suppressed. Even the fact that the emperor of Korea refused to accept the treaty proffered by Japan in November was not broadcast to the world. Three months later, in February 1906, regardless of the lack of an agreement, Prince Ito Hirobumi was appointed the Japanese governor general of Korea. In 1907, the Japanese forced the Korean emperor's abdication in favor of his son, a Japanese puppet, and then skillfully placed their people in all of the key government positions, disbanded the Korean army, and took over the police and judicial systems.

Following the 1905 annexation, the Japanese moved against the ongoing Korean nationalist agitation with gratuitous ruthlessness but were never able to completely suppress the movement for freedom. Although thousands of Koreans died—at least 14,500 Civil Militiamen were killed in the fighting between July 1907 and the end of 1908—Korean opposition to Japanese rule never slackened. Korean leaders, many of them in exile, continued their demands for a free and independent Korea. The expatriates were generally located in the United States, the USSR, China, and Mongolia, and so it followed that the political and ideological orientation of their demands took on the flavor of their surroundings. Many Koreans gained military experience during World War II fighting alongside not just the Japanese, but also alongside both the Chinese Nationalist and the Chinese Communist forces. In fact, a Korean government-in-exile was formed in Chungking in 1944.

At the 1943 Cairo Conference, the World War II Allies attempted to undo the dishonor of 1905 and promised independence to Korea "in due course" after the victory over Japan. At Yalta, in February 1945, President Franklin D. Roosevelt advocated a trusteeship for Korea that would be administered by the United States, the Soviet Union, and China. Stalin voiced his agreement but added that Great Britain should be included among the trustees. What they, or the participants at the later (July 1945) Potsdam Conference, which reaffirmed the Cairo Declaration, obviously did not consider was the fact that Stalin had no intention of abiding by the terms of any agreement that limited Soviet expansion. This was true even though, soon after Roosevelt's death, the Soviet dictator affirmed to President Harry S. Truman's representative Harry Hopkins that the USSR was bound by the four-power agreement. When the Soviet Union opened its campaign against Japan on August 8, 1945, it did so with a declaration of support for the Korean people in their quest for independence. Four days later, the first Soviet forces entered the Korean Peninsula from the north.

American forces entered Korea from the south on September 8, 1945 and established a sphere of influence that extended northward to the 38th parallel, a line chosen by the United States and Soviet Union as a military expedient for the disarming of the many Japanese troops still stationed on the peninsula. Probably, at that moment, no one could have appreciated the impact that demarcation line would have on the future of the world.

The inherent danger in the partition of Korea was quickly recognized by the Western Powers, however, and they attempted to rectify the problem at the December 1945 Moscow Conference. The solution reached at Moscow called for the U.S. and Soviet occupation commands in Korea to form a joint commission to work toward unification. By May 1946, the experiment was given up, however, because of lack of progress in forming a provisional democratic Korean government. As the various forces in the north and in the south continued to jockey for position, a Communist-inspired uprising broke out on October 1, 1946, in the central South Korean city of Taegu. About 70,000 Communist-led rioters participated in this uprising and claimed as their reason the oppressive policies of the American occupation. The revolt was poorly led, however, and never gained any real strength.

Another attempt at a more peaceful solution failed in 1947, when the USSR, continuing its intransigent stand on how the country should be governed, raised its demands far beyond acceptable levels. Unprepared for these events, the American government was slow in developing a coherent policy that would, at least in part, have dealt with the military emergencies that were developing. The failure to achieve an internal solution through negotiation prompted the superpowers to direct the question of Korean unification to the United Nations. The U.N. General Assembly, in November 1947, ordered a general election in Korea that was to select a national assembly to draft a new constitution and form a government. When the U.N. Temporary Observation Commission attempted to enter the Soviet-controlled north to observe the elections, they were refused admission by the Soviet authorities. Elections were held in the south, however, and the Republic of Korea proclaimed Syngman Rhee, one of the exile leaders, the nation's first head of state. When the new government was formally installed on August 15, 1948, the U.S. occupation ended and, by June 29, 1949, all U.S. combat forces had been withdrawn. The 500-man Korean Military Advisory Group (KMAG) did remain to assist in the development of South Korea's military forces.

Before the withdrawal was completed, however, another Communist uprising broke out in South Korea. On October 20, 1948, a Communist-controlled group of between 40 and 300 members of the 14th South Korean Constabulary mutinied in Yosu, just before the unit was to be moved to Cheju-do, an island off the southern tip of the Korean peninsula and the site of a large Communist-inspired insurgency. The mutineers seized the town of Yosu, which is located on a small peninsula on the Korea Strait and then focused on the elimination of the constabulary's leadership, killing many of its officers and NCOs. The mutineers then seized the unit's arms depot and, joined by civilian Communist sympathizers, captured the 50,000-inhabitant seacoast town of Sunchon located at the neck of the Yosu peninsula. Using this mainland town as their base, the Communist insurgents fanned out throughout the southwestern region of Korea to incite further revolt. Yosu was recaptured on October 27, and as government forces began to restore order, the Communists fled into the Paegun Mountains to the north of Sunchon where they remained a threat to the area's security until the Korean War began. In another incident in Taegu in November 1948, a two-day uprising was easily put down by government troops. The significance of this uprising, however, was that the rebels flew the North Korean flag, which appeared to indicate the support, if not the control, of the government in North Korea.

The upshot of these incidents was the establishment of a number of Communist-inspired insurgent organizations in South Korea and the positioning of sizable guerrilla bands in the rugged mountains in southwestern and in eastern Korea, less than two years before start of the war.

When the North Korean invaded the south, at least a part of the Republic of Korea's embryonic army was engaged in the suppression of this guerrilla threat.

In the north, at the same time, the North Korean People's Committee had adopted a draft constitution in July 1948, and had inaugurated the Democratic People's Republic of Korea in September with Kim Il Sung as premier. The Soviet Union announced that all of its military forces had been withdrawn from North Korea on December 25, 1948, but refused to grant the United Nations permission to verify the claim. The Korean Peninsula was now divided into two ideologically opposed nations and the future seemed preordained.

When the North Korean invasion began on June 25, 1950, the U.N. Security Council ordered an immediate ceasefire in South Korea and the withdrawal of all North Korean forces. The offensive continued, however, and the North Koreans apparently expected to capture all of South Korea before any outside power could intervene. That same day, Chiang Kai-shek offered South Korea the assistance of the Chinese Nationalist Army on Taiwan. On June 27, U.S. President Harry S. Truman directed the U.S. Far East Command in Japan to furnish naval and air support to South Korea. Gen. Douglas MacArthur, Supreme Allied Commander, Far East, recommended acceptance of the Nationalist Chinese offer, but Truman rejected the proposal. That same day, the United Nations voted to aid South Korea and asked for assistance from its member nations. U.S. ground forces were committed on June 30, and air strikes were authorized against targets in North Korea. On July 7, the United Nations recommended that all forces in South Korea be placed under one unified command. The next day, General MacArthur was appointed commander of U.N. forces. Led by the United States, a growing U.N. force was assembled from among the allies and, within three months, allied air, sea, and land power had turned the North Korean attack into a catastrophic retreat. Soon, South Korea was liberated and almost all of the People's Republic of North Korea was in U.N. hands.

What was missing, however, was a declaration of war. As the word "war" did not then and still does not exist in the U.N. Charter, there was no way to call what was happening in Korea a war. The terms "police action" and "conflict" became the keywords to describe that struggle which was, according to Michael Walzer, an "Aggression [that] justified two kinds of violent response: a war of self-defense by the victim and a war of law enforcement by the victim and international society." Korea was a forcible example of the latter in modern times.

What is now referred to as the Korean War would also become a crucible in which new military lessons would be learned by some and ignored by others. This was a period of transition between the linear warfare tactics used in World War II and a new variety of conflict in which there would be no front lines per se, and there would be great difficulty in separating the good guys from the bad. Even so, Korea was fought as a linear, conventional, non-nuclear war by senior commanders who, for the most part, knew nothing about the employment of nuclear weapons on the battlefield, knew little about the political or ideological nature of the type of struggle in which they were engaged, and knew even less about the people and the terrain in which they were required to fight. It is fortunate that the enemy generally accepted the allied rules of engagement as their own. Otherwise, the West might have faced an entirely different, more protracted type of conflict more reminiscent of the later struggle in Southeast Asia.

Some, but certainly not all, of those Americans who fought in Korea and who would lead at later times in Southeast Asia began to comprehend the subtle differences that marked Korea as a different kind of conflict. World War II was a global struggle. By comparison, Korea was, in the narrowest sense, little more than a localized civil war.

By November 1950, the North Korean army was all but destroyed and western military and political leaders alike felt a quick and glorious end to the conflict was near at hand. Moscow and Beijing were frantic over the possibility of losing an ideological ally on the Asian mainland and a decision was made that not only changed the tactical alignment of forces but, far more seriously, turned the expected victory into a near defeat. The entrance of Chinese troops in November 1950 forced a sobering redefinition of objectives upon the United Nations, the United States and its allies and, indeed, the world. New terms were coined: "surrogate warfare," "bug out," and "gook," to name but a few. Casualties mounted, careers were made and broken and the inevitable lessons learned cataloged. Only, in this case, the lessons were not learned very well and America would suffer for it a decade later in Vietnam.

Col. John Jessup
U.S. Army, Ret.

Preface

From 1950 to 1953, more than 1.7 million American military personnel served their country in and around Korea in a tedious, bloody war against the communist regimes of North Korea and China. Millions more—including Koreans, Chinese, and Russians on the communist side and people from every inhabited continent on the allied side—participated in the conflict, which killed an estimated 2 million people and harmed unknown millions of others. It was a world war in miniature, an epilogue to World War II and a prelude to the Cold War. It is also a fascinating subject of study.

In the course of writing this book, a number of people asked me questions like, "A book about the Korean War—didn't somebody write something about that already?" In fact, much less has been written about the Korean War than about other major American conflicts (notably the Civil War and World War II), but a great proportion of what has been written has been exceptionally good. So, indeed, why write another book about this conflict?

I believe that it is incumbent upon every generation to examine history in accordance with its own experiences, which helps explain why I would write it at all. In addition, with the 50th anniversary of the Korean War before us, interest in the conflict will be as high over the next few years as it will at any time in the foreseeable future, and people will be looking for materials that discuss the war in terms that are meaningful to them. And, on the eve of a new millennium, it is an opportune time to draw lessons from the last century that can help guide us through the next.

A great body of source material was available for this book, more than at any other time since the 1950 to 1953 war in Korea. This is largely because of the increased availability of official documents from the 1950s, brought about in large part by the collapse of the Soviet Union, somewhat improved relations with communist China, and the declassification of U.S. materials.

Still, substantial amounts of information are not yet available, which makes it impossible to present a complete history of the war. Quite a bit of the existing information is also conflicting. For example, various apparently reliable sources list the year that Kim Il Sung fled to the Soviet Union as 1939 and 1941. And, while the most reliable sources claim the North Korean army had a strength of about 135,000 men in 1950, a number of mostly non-American published sources set this number as high as 250,000—a number for which there is no realistic substantiation.

I did not write *Fire and Ice: The Korean War, 1950-1953* with an eye toward supplanting any of the several excellent narrative histories of the conflict now available. Rather, I intended to provide an overview of the war for people with little or no knowledge of it, and a road map for experienced students of the conflict who want to discover other avenues worthy of deeper investigation. Hopefully, readers will find it full of fascinating and useful information about the Korean War, presented in a fresh and interesting "fact book-style" format. As users will quickly discover, my effort focuses on people, places, and things strictly as they pertained to the Korean War. For example, capsule biographies of important individuals are heavily weighted toward their activities during the conflict, and not toward their full lives and careers.

Throughout this book the term "South Korea" is used synonymously with "Republic of Korea," and the term "North Korea" is used synonymously with "Democratic People's Republic of Korea." This is done largely because the north and south references are more easily and immediately comprehensible than the full, official names of the countries.

I have also made a conscious decision to use the term "Korean War" in this book rather than "Korean Conflict," which prevailed for several decades and is still used by many people today. In the 1950s, most of those Americans who were aware of the U.S. role in Korea were content to accept it as a "conflict" rather than a "war." A rose by any other name, however, smells the same, and a war is a war regardless of what euphemism is applied to it. Korea was most assuredly a war, regardless of what anyone chooses to call it.

Michael J. Varhola
Springfield, VA

ACKNOWLEDGMENTS

A number of people, groups, and institutions have provided the moral and material support needed to make this book a reality.

Foremost among the people deserving thanks is Les Albers, who drew upon his experience as a soldier and teacher both to help me select the best source material and to help ensure that what I did with it worked.

Inspiration for the title of this book comes from the excellent four-part documentary *The Korean War: Fire and Ice* (1999), produced by Lou Reda and aired on The History Channel. Lou deserves thanks both for giving his blessing to use the same title for my book, and for creating a film that served as an inspiration while I wrote it.

A group of people who deserve recognition for their encouragement are my wife, Lt. Col. Diane Waters, and the productive "core element" of the 50th Anniversary of the Korean War Commemoration Committee. Equally important are the Korean War veterans who have taken the time and effort to frankly relate their sometimes harrowing wartime experiences. Among these veterans are Bill Alli, Wayne Bjork, Harley Coon, Harvey Galloway, John Jessup, Theodore Mataxis, and Warren Wiedhan. I am also indebted to Nick Minecci and the Soldiers' and Airmen's Home, who generously allowed me access to their extensive collection of U.S. Army Signal Corps photographs. Most of the photographs in this book were drawn from their collection. Scott Price of the U.S. Coast Guard Historian's Office helped out by providing me with photographs and information about maritime operations during the Korean War.

People who encouraged me during the writing of this book, and discussed the Korean War with me more than they otherwise might have, include my mother Merrilea, my father Michael, my brother Christopher, his fiancé Laura Russell, her father Carl, and my buddy Chip Cassano.

And, finally, I would like to thank my editor and publisher, Theodore P. "Ted" Savas, who helped guide the development of this book from concept to bookshelf.

If there is anyone who has wished me well or rendered me assistance that I have forgotten to thank, I hope that they will both forgive my lapse and remind me of it.

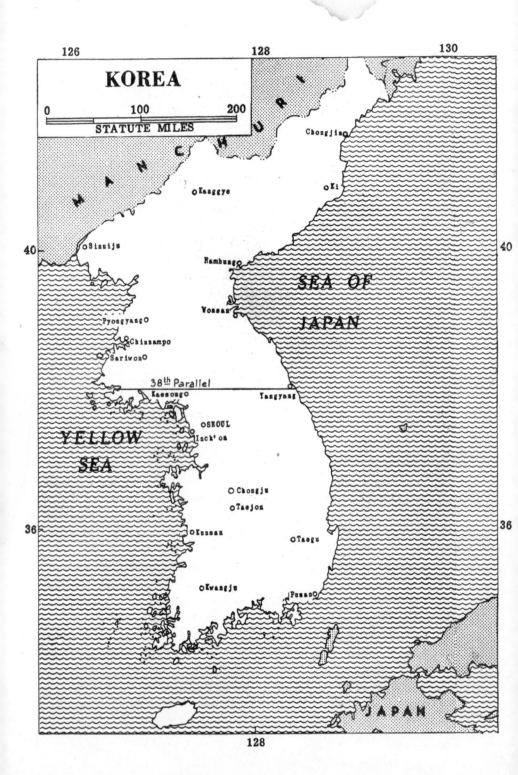

WAR ON THE GROUND

"Korea was fought mostly by infantrymen with M-1 rifles and machine guns and hand grenades and mortars. There was artillery, of course, quite good on both sides. . . . Men who fought in France in 1917 would have understood Korea; Lee's and Grant's men would have recognized it."

—James Brady, *The Coldest War*

On June 25, 1950, more than 90,000 soldiers of the North Korean People's Army swept into South Korea, overrunning its lightly armed forces and driving quickly toward the poorly defended capital city of Seoul. A United Nations force, composed mainly of Americans, intervened on behalf of the Republic of Korea, and for more than three years struggled first to resist, then eliminate, and then merely contain the communist threat.

PHASES OF THE GROUND WAR

Events during the Korean War can be divided into 10 major phases. Within each phase, both the U.N. and the communist forces launched a number of major or minor operations, military actions with specific goals, using forces as small as platoons and as large as entire armies. Actions within each phase overlapped to some extent, and the dates given could easily be shifted several days or more in either direction. For example, Chinese intervention in force began on November 22, but U.N. forces were still advancing at this point, some of them reaching the Yalu River on November 28.

Dates	Phase
June 25-Sept. 14, 1950:	U.N. Defensive
Sept. 15-Nov. 21, 1950:	U.N. Offensive
Nov. 22, 1950-Jan. 15, 1951:	Chinese Intervention
Jan. 16-April 21, 1951:	First U.N. Counteroffensive
April 22-May 19, 1951:	Chinese Spring Offensives
May 20-Nov. 12, 1951:	U.N. Counteroffensive
Nov. 13, 1951-June 19, 1952:	Second Korean Winter-Spring
June 20-Dec. 20, 1952:	Korean Summer-Fall 1952
Dec. 21, 1952-March 20, 1953:	Third Korean Winter
March 21-July 27, 1953:	Korean Spring-Summer 1953

An overall synopsis of each phase and one or more representative battles or events from them are described below. For thumbnail descriptions of additional ground battles, see Chapter XIX, Chronology.

U.N. DEFENSIVE (JUNE 25 - SEPT. 14, 1950)

During the night of June 24, elements of 10 divisions of the North Korean People's Army, a full two-thirds of its strength, finished massing along the frontier with their southern neighbor, the Republic of Korea. At about 4 a.m. on June 25, the communist forces unleashed a massive artillery barrage against South Korean military positions and then sent tens of thousands of soldiers and hundreds of armored vehicles over the border.

❏ South Korea was almost completely unprepared. Its ground forces totalled about 95,000 men, but only about one-third of them were deployed along the border with North Korea. Furthermore, these troops were lightly armed, poorly equipped, and not nearly as well disciplined or led as their adversaries. While some units made valiant stands—and were subsequently eliminated—most quickly broke and fled southward.

❏ On June 27, the United Nations Security Council called upon its members to send assistance to the quickly collapsing country. That same day, the South Korean government evacuated Seoul and relocated first to Taegu, and then to Pusan. On June 28, North Korean forces took control of the South Korean capital.

❏ Immediately after the United Nations called for its members to assist South Korea, the United States responded by sending air and naval forces to contest the communist offensive. These measures were not sufficient to stop the North Korean advance, however, and President Harry S. Truman pushed up the U.S. stake in the conflict by ordering ground troops into Korea.

❑ Detachment X, consisting of 35 men from the 507th Anti-Aircraft Artillery Automatic Weapons Battalion, arrived in Korea on June 29, 1950. These men engaged North Korean attack aircraft on the same day, shooting down a YAK fighter with their machineguns and suffering the first casualties of the Korean War—five men wounded in action.

❑ Task Force Smith, the first American infantry unit committed to the conflict, arrived in Korea on June 30. It consisted of a 406-man infantry battalion and a 134-man artillery battery from the 24th Infantry Division, the U.S. command closest to the Korean Peninsula, and was ordered to deploy to Korea and then trucked to Itazuke Air Base. This unit was named for its commander, Lt. Col. Charles B. "Brad" Smith.

❑ Few episodes exemplify the state of the U.S. military, or its underestimation of the North Korean army, than do the deployment of Task Force Smith. To this day, U.S. military planners point to it as an inevitable product of indiscriminate downsizing and lack of readiness.

Like most infantry battalions in 1950, the 1st Battalion of the 24th Infantry Division's 21st Infantry Regiment consisted of two—rather than the regulation three—rifle companies, both of which were understrength, plus one-half of a headquarters company, one-half of a communications platoon, and a heavy weapons platoon armed with six 2.36-inch bazookas, two 75mm recoilless rifles, two 4.2-inch mortars, and four 60mm mortars. Its artillery support, Battery A of the 52nd Field Artillery Battalion, was armed with one-half dozen 105mm howitzers.

Task Force Smith arrived in South Korea on July 1, 1950. Once in South Korea, it began moving north to oppose the North Korean forces. On July 4, 1950, its soldiers dug in on a pair of hills straddling the road near the village of Osan and waited to oppose the advancing North Koreans. At around 7:30 a.m. the next morning, the U.S. soldiers could see North Korean tanks advancing south toward them, and forty-six minutes later the artillerymen fired their first rounds. Lightly-armed Task Force Smith was no match for the Soviet-built T-34 tanks and accompanying North Korean division, however, and was soon overrun.

❑ By early afternoon, Task Force Smith had lost the Battle of Osan and its survivors were running for their lives. Its casualties were 20 killed in action and 130 wounded in action.

Considering its lack of men and materiel, Task Force Smith probably accomplished its mission of slowing the North Korean advance as well as was possible. And as badly as the force was mauled, the combat at Osan paled in comparison to the bloodbaths to come in the following months and years.

❏ Elements of the U.S. 24th Infantry Division, 25th Infantry Division, and 1st Cavalry Division, which continued to arrive in South Korea throughout July and the first few days of August, contested the inexorable advance of the North Korean People's Army. On July 7, the United Nations recommended all U.S., South Korean, and other U.N. forces be placed under a unified command, and on July 8 Truman appointed Gen. Douglas MacArthur to head this position.

❏ Despite their best efforts, the U.S. and South Korean forces were unable to do more than slow the communists. The allied forces were driven steadily southward, buying precious time for additional forces to arrive at the southeastern port of Pusan. For a month, desperate, mostly nameless battles, were fought in dozens of South Korean villages and towns like Chochiwon, Chonan, Pyongtaek, Hadong, and Yechon, and in the fields and roads between them.

❏ **The Battle of the Kum River** (July 1950) began July 13 and lasted until July 16, as soldiers from the 19th and 34th Infantry Regiments of the 24th Infantry Division, reinforced by supporting units, battled North Korean forces along the Kum River line. Of the first 3,401 men committed from the 19th Infantry Regiment, 650 were killed or wounded.

❏ **The Battle of Taejon** (July 1950) took place on July 19 and 20, and involved some 3,933 soldiers of the 24th Infantry Division attempting to defend the town of Taejon, site of the division headquarters, against the advancing North Korean forces. U.S. casualties were 922 men killed in action, 228 wounded in action, and many missing, including division commander Gen. William F. Dean, who disappeared when the town was overrun.

❏ **The Battle of the Notch** (August 1950) took place on August 1, when the 19th Infantry Regiment (24th Infantry Division), reinforced with other division elements, battled the North Korean People's Army, suffering 90 soldiers killed in action.

❏ The Pusan Perimeter was established by August 4, as North Korea's army steadily pushed U.N. and South Korean forces southward toward the coast and destruction. Eventually, the U.N. forces were able to establish a defensive line centered on the port city of Pusan, anchored in the hills to the north of the city and along the Naktong River to its west. To the south and east were the sea.

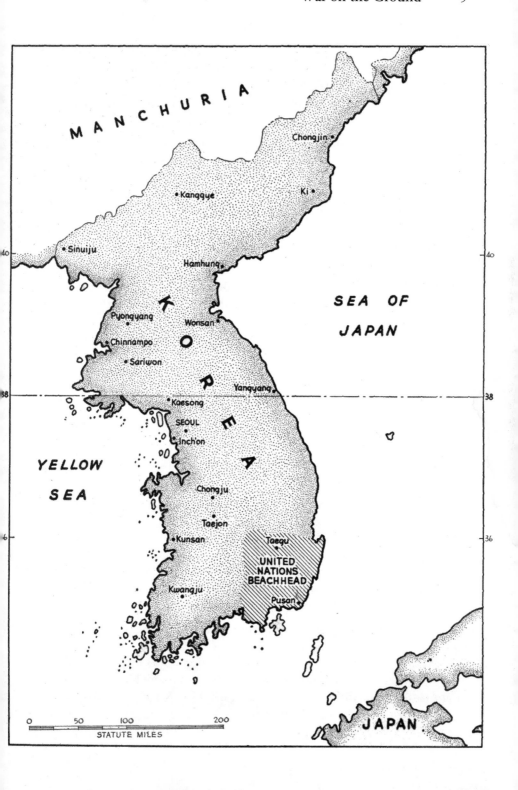

❏ Once they had established the Pusan Perimeter, the U.N. forces were able to begin drawing upon capabilities denied them when they were strung out over hundreds of miles. Units were able to support each other's flanks, reserves could be quickly deployed to fill breaches, and artillery support could be brought to bear at any point along the line.

❏ At the same time, the North Korean army had disadvantages greater than any it had faced in the previous months. Supply lines stretched down the peninsula were being torn apart by U.N. air strikes, casualties were mounting rapidly, and irreplaceable tanks and other equipment smoldered from Seoul to the edge of the Pusan Perimeter. Still, the growing U.N. forces engaged the North Koreans in some of the most brutal combat of the war during the defense of the perimeter, and their last toe-hold on the peninsula was in constant jeopardy.

❏ **The First Battle of the Naktong Bulge** (August 1950) began on August 8, when the 4th Division of the North Korean People's Army crossed the Naktong River and penetrated the Pusan Perimeter. A U.N. force consisting of the 24th Infantry Division, the 1st Provisional Marine Brigade, and elements of the 2nd and 25th Infantry Divisions counterattacked, and during a 10-day battle managed to contain the enemy salient and drive the communists back across the river.

❏ **The Battle of the Bowling Alley** (August 1950) was fought from August 15 to 20, as soldiers of the 2nd Infantry Division's 23rd Infantry Regiment and the 25th Infantry Division's 27th Infantry Regiment battled North Korean forces along a straight stretch of road that U.S. troops dubbed the Bowling Alley, inflicting heavy losses upon them.

❏ **The Second Battle of the Naktong Bulge** (August and September 1950) took place from August 31 to September 19, as U.N. forces once again battled a North Korean attack across the Naktong, committing troops from the 1st Cavalry Division, the 2nd, 24th, and 25th Infantry Divisions, and the 1st Provisional Marine Brigade. By September 10, U.N. forces had broken the momentum of the communist offensive, and for the following nine days steadily reduced the salient through close combat.

❏ **Defense of the Pusan Perimeter** (August and September 1950), between August 4 and September 16, cost the U.S. forces alone 4,599 soldiers killed in action, 12,058 wounded in action, 2,701 missing in action, and 401 taken prisoner. North Korea's forces also suffered heavy casualties in the battles along the perimeter, and, unlike the U.N. forces, each day they were growing weaker, rather than stronger.

U.N. OFFENSIVE (SEPT. 15 - NOV. 21, 1950)

Even as the North Korean People's Army attempted to smash the Pusan Perimeter and drive its defenders off of the peninsula, the U.N. forces were preparing to take the initiative and launch a two-pronged counteroffensive.

In mid-September, the newly-formed U.S. X Corps was set to conduct Operation Chromite, a landing at Inchon, about 30 miles from Seoul on the west coast of South Korea. Inchon was far behind the majority of the North Korean forces, which were preparing to launch their final offensive against the Pusan Perimeter.

After X Corps had seized Inchon, the 8th U.S. Army would rally and attempt to break out of the perimeter. Then, the two forces would move toward each other, crushing the isolated North Korean People's Army between them.

❏ **Operation Chromite** (September 1950) was intended to subdue fortified Wolmi Island, which guarded the approaches to Inchon Harbor;

U.N. troops moved north effortlessly in the weeks following the Inchon landing, encountering very little resistance from the shattered the North Korean People's Army. Peasants in villages on both sides of the 38th parallel welcomed the Americans and their allies as liberators.

capture the port and city of Inchon; seize Kimpo Airfield to the south of Seoul; and liberate the city of Seoul itself. Capture of the area would also cut supply lines to the North Korean People's Army (NKPA) operating around Pusan.

Gen. Douglas MacArthur had begun planning the operation on August 12, drawing upon his experience with amphibious operations during the Pacific island-hopping campaigns of World War II. Leaders in Washington were leery of the plan, however, and permission was granted on little more than the basis of MacArthur's reputation.

U.S. Army X Corps, under the command of MacArthur protege, Major General Edward M. Almond, was created as an amphibious assault force for the operation. It consisted of the U.S. 1st Marine Division and an attached South Korean Marine Regiment; the U.S. Army 7th Infantry Division and more than 8,000 ROK soldiers; and artillery, engineer, and a number of other support elements.

Joint Task Force 7, a nine-nation force consisting of 230 warships, 21 aircraft squadrons, and special amphibious, engineer, logistics, and underwater demolitions team units, provided naval support for the Inchon landing. On September 13, carrier-based aircraft and naval cruisers and destroyers from the task force began a devastating aerial and naval bombardment of the North Korean-held fortifications and coastal artillery positions on Wolmi Island.

Early on September 15, the 1st and 5th Marine Regiments of the 1st Marine Division landed on devastated Wolmi Island, encountering only light resistance. In less than two hours, they secured the island and sealed off the causeway leading to Inchon. Late that afternoon, two regiments of marines landed at two points in Inchon, Red Beach and Blue Beach, both of which were, in fact, high sea walls that the troops had to climb, the first units scrambling over them with scaling ladders or through holes blasted by the warships, even as amphibious warfare vessels brought in the successive waves of troops.

U.N. air forces kept North Korean aircraft from taking part in the Inchon fighting by flying interdiction missions and bombing key enemy airfields; they also attacked enemy ground forces in an area 25 miles around Inchon, while warships covered the closer approaches to the port with their big guns.

Once over the seawalls, the Red Beach marines encountered scattered pockets of enemy resistance, but reduced them fairly quickly as they moved into the city. In less than half an hour, the assault teams had captured Cemetery Hill, one of their main objectives, and by midnight had taken Observatory Hill, the other main objective. Blue Beach marines enjoyed similar success, capturing their objectives in the early morning hours of

September 16. By 7:30 a.m. that day, both forces had formed a cordon around the city and cut off the escape routes for enemy forces remaining within the city.

Casualties from the first phase of Operation Chromite were amazingly low: 20 men killed, 174 wounded, and one missing. Losses, however, would increase dramatically over the following weeks.

Additional X Corps forces landed on September 16, including parts of the 7th Infantry Division, and within 24 hours of the landing had taken the high ground east of the city, moved inland far enough to prevent enemy artillery fire from landing on the port area, and were preparing to seize Kimpo Airfield.

On September 17, X Corps troops moved quickly toward the airfield and captured it by that evening, after several hours of combat with the 400 or 500 North Korean troops holding it. Communist troops tried to counterattack during the night, but were replused with heavy casualties.

❏ Possession of Kimpo Airfield, far to the rear of the main North Korean forces, gave the U.N. command a base from which to conduct air operations against both Seoul and the communist supply lines.

❏ By September 19, the 1st Marine Division was advancing on Seoul and preparing to move into and recapture the South Korean capital. Meanwhile, most of the U.S. 7th Infantry Division began to move southward to cut off the escape and supply routes of the North Korean army, which was even then contesting the 8th U.S. Army breakout from the Pusan Perimeter.

❏ Taking Seoul was much tougher than the battle for Inchon had been. It was not until September 29, after more than a week of brutal, street-to-street fighting, that the Marines and the 7th Infantry Division units managed to take the city.

Casualties from the battle were also much higher than they had been at Inchon two weeks earlier: 427 killed, 1,961 wounded, and five missing for the 1st Marine Division, and 86 killed, 358 wounded, and 10 missing in action for the 7th Infantry Division.

❏ By October 7, North Korean forces were in disorder and those that could were retreating back across the 38th parallel. Despite the deep reservations of many U.S. leaders, Operation Chromite was a complete success and, debatably, one of the most effective amphibious operations in military history.

❏ **8th Army's Breakout from the Pusan Perimeter** was set to begin on September 16, the day after the marines landed at Inchon, but for another three days the U.N. forces still had to defend the perimeter at several points. As word of the landing at Inchon slowly began to spread through the communist ranks, however, enemy pressure abated.

❑ On September 19, the 1st Cavalry Division, the 2nd, 24th, and 25th Infantry Divisions, and various other U.N. units, advanced against the encircling North Korean People's Army and broke out of the perimeter. 8th U.S. Army moved north, routing the North Korean forces in heavy fighting as it moved forward. On September 26, northward-moving elements of the 8th Army met up with southward-moving elements of X Corps at Osan, three months after Task Force Smith had been defeated there.

Casualties from the breakout were high, as they had been along the Pusan Perimeter over the six weeks preceding the operation. U.S. Losses included 790 killed and 3,544 wounded.

❑ The U.N. advance on the Yalu River (October and November 1950) and North Korea's border with China began soon after the capture of Seoul. A shift in U.S.–U.N. policy occurred around this point, from fighting a war of defense to penalizing and overthrowing the communist regime in North Korea.

❑ Following the fall of Seoul, the two main elements of the U.N. forces in Korea remained separated, with the 8th U.S. Army advancing northward along the western half of the peninsula, and X Corps moving north along the east coast.

❑ ROK units led the advance into North Korea throughout October and November, at times engaging U.S. units in a race for key objectives. On October 19, the 1st ROK division beat the U.S. 1st Cavalry Division to Pyongyang and took control of the communist capital.

❑ On November 1, troops of the 8th Army fought the northernmost U.S. action of the war, when soldiers of the 24th Infantry Division's 21st Infantry Regiment captured the North Korean village of Chonggodo, a mere 18 miles from the Yalu River crossing at Sinuiju.

❑ **The Wonsan Campaign** (October to December 1950) began on October 2, when the X Corps began reembarking at the port of Inchon. It was transported around the Korean Peninsula to its east coast and the North Korean ports of Wonsan and Iwon. Mines delayed the amphibious landing for two weeks, however, while naval units worked to clear them. It was not until October 25 that the 1st Marine and the 7th Infantry Divisions made an anticlimactic administrative landing, to the jeers of ROK troops who had captured the city on October 10.

❑ South Korean forces were already moving northward up the east coast road, so X Corps headed first north to Hamhung and then northwest, toward the Chosin Reservoir, from which they would make their last thrust to the Chinese border. 1st Marine Division units advanced up the west side of the reservoir, while 7th Infantry Division units moved up its east side.

CCF INTERVENTION (NOV. 22, 1950 - JAN. 15, 1951)

Although 15 divisions of Chinese communist troops had entered the Korean Peninsula in mid-October 1950, their attacks upon the advancing U.N. forces had been limited, and after each one had disappeared back into the mountainous interior of the country. This made it very easy for MacArthur in Tokyo to dismiss the Chinese presence as insignificant and exhort his commanders to move northward as quickly as possible.

When the 260,000 soldiers of the Chinese People's Volunteers Army struck near the end of November, it was in numbers and with a fury that came as a complete surprise to the largely unprepared American, South Korean, and other allied forces. U.N. commanders paid for that lack of preparation with the blood of their men and a humiliating defeat.

By November 1950, U.N. troops had advanced into North Korea and were approaching its border with China. American soldiers and Marines celebrated Thanksgiving within site of the Yalu and looked forward to being home for Christmas, unaware that the Chinese were about to enter the war with a vengeance.

On November 21, the 17th Infantry Regiment (7th Infantry Division) reached the Yalu River at Hyesanjin, near its headwaters. Strung out behind it throughout North Korea were all seven of the U.S. combat divisions—the 1st Cavalry, 1st Marine, and 2nd, 3rd, 7th, 24th, and 25th Infantry Divisions—along with their attached ROK and allied units.

On November 25, the Chinese launched their counteroffensive, decimating the U.N. forces around the Chosin Reservoir in the west and around the village of Kunu-ri in the east.

❑ **The Battle of the Chosin Reservoir** (November and December 1950) erupted on November 27, when Chinese forces assaulted U.N. units on both sides of the lake, an attack that continued for about two weeks.

Task Force Faith, composed of elements of the 31st and 32nd Infantry Regiments (7th Infantry Division), was deployed east of the Chosin Reservoir in late November, getting ready to make the final push toward the Yalu. The Chinese hit this 3,200-man force on November 27, and by December 1 had practically annihilated it; a mere 385 of its soldiers survived the carnage.

On the other side of the reservoir, the 1st Marine Division was strung out along a narrow road that led from the coast up through the villages of Koto-ri, Hagaru-ri, and Yudam-ni at the north end of the Chosin Reservoir. Its commanders had slowed the advance as much as possible, however, despite exhortations from MacArthur to move more quickly, and as a result was less spread out than it otherwise might have been.

Chinese troops took control of the road from the coast at several points and encircled the various elements of the 1st Marine Division. Unwilling to either surrender or stand their ground and die, the marines began a fighting withdrawal back down the road toward the port of Hungnam. Heavily armed, resolute, and supported at every leg of their two-week retreat by attack aircraft, the marines battled sub-zero temperatures and Chinese roadblocks and flank attacks during their grueling march to Hungnam.

By December 9, the 1st Marine Division made it to Hungnam, where it established a defensive perimeter under the protective fire of U.N. warships. Casualties for the division were 718 killed, 3,508 wounded, and 192 missing, plus 7,313 casualties from frostbite and illness. Remnants of the 7th Infantry Division straggled into Hungnam as well, their advance north turned into a precipitous retreat. By December 10, most of the division's units had made it back to the coast, having suffered casualties of 2,657 killed and 354 wounded.

As the communist forces closed in on Hungnam, the broken elements of X Corps began to embark on transports, warships, and chartered civilian vessels and sail out of North Korea. By December 24, the U.N. flotilla had

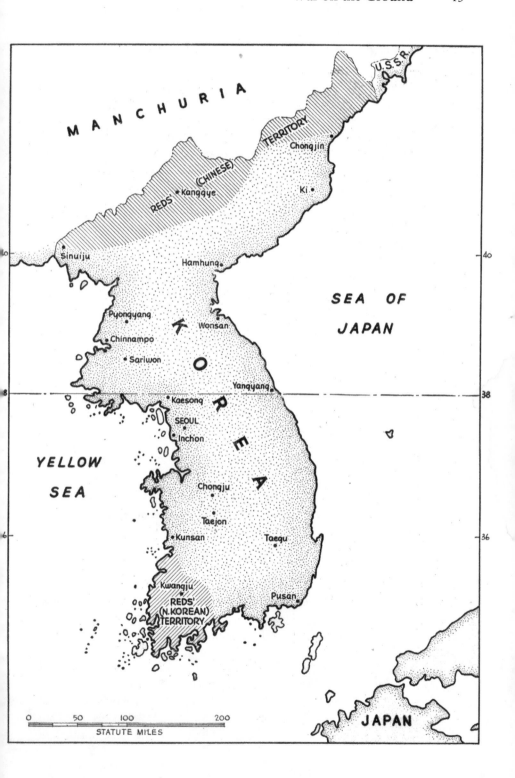

evacuated 105,000 military personnel and nearly 100,000 North Korean refugees.

❏ **The Battle of Kunu-ri** (November and December 1950) erupted in western North Korea on November 29. Chinese forces surrounded, overwhelmed, and almost completely destroyed the U.S. 2nd Infantry Division, and by December 1 the command had lost virtually all of its vehicles and heavy equipment, as well as 4,940 men killed or missing.

❏ **The Longest Retreat in U.S. Military History** (November and December 1950) began in late November, as units of the 8th U.S. Army collapsed and their soldiers started to "bug out," abandoning weapons and equipment and withdrawing back toward South Korea in disorder. Commanders were, for the most part, unable to slow the rout, and Americans, South Koreans, and other allied troops straggled back across the 38th parallel singly and in small groups. By December 15, 8th U.S. Army commanders had managed to regain control of their units and to establish the Imjin River defensive line south of the 38th parallel and north of the city of Seoul.

Even as they dug in and prepared to face the coming Chinese onslaught, however, the U.N. Forces suffered yet another casualty: On December 24, 8th Army commander Gen. Walton H. "Johnnie" Walker was killed in a traffic accident when his jeep was struck by a ROK Army truck. Hard-edged Gen. Matthew B. Ridgway arrived in Korea the day after Christmas and assumed command of the shattered 8th Army and immediately began to reorganize it.

❏ **The Third Chinese Phase Offensive** (January 1951) began on New Years day, when 500,000 communist troops advanced on the U.N. lines in an attempt to keep the U.N. off balance and to once again capture the South Korean capital. This offensive succeeded in driving the already beaten U.N. forces even farther southward, 50 miles below the 38th parallel, and allowed the communists to capture Seoul for the second time. Primitive supply lines were the bane of every Chinese offensive, however, and while the communist forces regrouped and began once again to build up the materiel they would need for their next thrust, the U.N. forces under Ridgway began to prepare a counteroffensive.

Throughout late winter and early spring of 1951, U.N. forces struggled toward the South Korean capital of Seoul in an attempt to liberate it once again. This time, however, they faced a determined Chinese and North Korean defense.

FIRST U.N. COUNTEROFFENSIVE
(JAN. 16 — APRIL 21, 1951)

At the southern end of the peninsula, the 1st Marine Division spent January and part of February routing out North Korean forces and partisans hiding in the hills along the Strait of Korea coast. This operation, known as the "Great Pohang Guerrilla Hunt," was conducted around the southern Korean towns of Pohang, Andong, Masan, Sondong, and Uisong and succeeded in virtually eliminating the North Korean 10th Division.

Along the line of contact in the middle of the peninsula, Ridgway had been eager, since assuming command of the U.N. ground forces in Korea, to launch an immediate counteroffensive against the communist forces. U.N. troops were still exhausted and demoralized from their recent retreat, however, and it was not until mid-January that Ridgway was able to launch Operation Wolfhound, a probe-in-force of the solidifying communist lines. A series of operations geared toward recapturing Seoul and establishing a defensive line north of the 38th parallel soon followed.

Significant engagements fought during this period include the Battle of the Twin Tunnels, in which the U.S. 23rd Infantry Regiment and the French Battalion killed at least 1,300 Chinese troops; the Battle of Hoengsong, where the American forces suffered their single largest loss of life during the war; and the Battle of Chipyong-ni, the largest engagement during a Chinese counteroffensive.

❑ **Operation Wolfhound** (January 1951) was a limited, probing operation by elements of the 8th U.S. Army's I Corps against communist forces deployed along the southern banks of the Han River, south of Seoul. It was named for the 27th Infantry "Wolfhound" Regiment, which led the attack. Reports received in early January described the buildup along the Han, but were vague as to the exact strengths and dispositions of the enemy forces. By mid-January, the 8th Army had advanced northward from Osan toward Seoul and had nearly reached Suwon, just 30 miles south of the ROK capital.

Ridgway wanted more information before deciding whether to establish defensive positions around Osan or advance further toward Seoul, and on January 14 ordered Operation Wolfhound, which began two days later.

27th Infantry Regiment forces met little opposition until reaching Suwon itself, where it engaged communist units and inflicted heavy losses on them, suffering few casualties in the process. At the same time, pressure from communist forces in other 8th Army sectors was alleviated. Fearing that the 27th Infantry Regiment might be cut off and mauled, Ridgway decided to end Wolfhound on January 25 and withdraw his forces to defensible positions south of Suwon. Before the U.N. forces could withdraw, however, the communists themselves retreated eastward, to positions in the hills around Wonju and Yoju, just south of the capital.

These apparent successes led Ridgway to believe that the communist forces did not yet have enough men or materiel to either launch or withstand a general offensive. Wanting to act before they could become stronger, he ordered Operation Thunderbolt.

❑ **Operation Thunderbolt** (January and February 1951) was a general offensive by the I, IX, and X Corps of the U.S. Eighth Army against communist forces south of Seoul and was an operational precursor to the recapture of the capital itself. Ridgway ordered the operation on January 23 and it began two days later.

On January 25, the three commands began advancing northward on either side of the Han River, I Corps on the west side, X Corps on the east of the river, and IX Corps in between them, straddling the river with elements on both sides of it.

I Corps was tasked with recapturing Kimpo Airfield and Inchon, west of Seoul. Moving north, it captured Suwon on January 27, MacArthur's birthday (which the supreme commander called the best birthday gift he had ever received). I Corps fulfilled its mission by February 1 and established a defensive line centered six miles southwest of Seoul.

X Corps was tasked with advancing through the town of Wonju and into Hoengsong and its environs. Its forces completely destroyed Wonju and moved on to their ultimate objective, capturing it on February 2. IX Corps was tasked both with capturing Chipyong-ni, southeast of Seoul, and supporting the corps to either side of it. Its forces encountered heavy resistance from Chinese forces dug into the hilly country around Chipyong-ni, and by February 2 IX Corps was still bogged down in combat.

Hoping to relieve pressure on the area around Chipyong-ni and Seoul and to divert the enemy to the east as much as possible, on February 5, Ridgway ordered X Corps to launch Operation Roundup.

❏ **Operation Roundup** (February 1951), a followup to Operation Thunderbolt, was a limited X Corps offensive intended to move the U.N. lines northward and, perhaps, force the communists to abandon the South Korean capital of Seoul. Ridgway hoped that Roundup, even if it failed, would disrupt any counteroffensive planned by the communists and reveal their dispositions and intentions. Before the operation jumped off, Ridgway reinforced X Corps and the ROK III Corps with troops from the western, more secure sector, of the U.N. line.

On February 5, the U.N. forces advanced northward from Hoengsong toward Hongchon. Enemy resistance increased as they neared the town, however, and after several days the allied advance began to slow.

While U.N. forces were advancing on Hongchon, one North Korean and two Chinese divisions left Seoul and moved to block them. Despite the fact that intelligence reports warned of the possibility of this counterattack, however, X Corps commander Lt. Gen. Edward M. Almond ordered his troops to continue advancing.

On February 11, the communists launched a powerful nighttime counterattack, smashing through the U.N. lines and setting up roadblocks to hinder any allied attempt to retreat. Although X Corps was able to fight its way back to Wonju, communist forces annihilated the ROK 8th Infantry Division, killing or capturing some 7,500 men and all of the unit's equipment. Ridgway ended the retreat by ordering his forces to dig in and prepare a defense against the counterattack. One of its most apocalyptic battles of that offensive was fought out around Chipyong-ni and Wonju.

❏ **The Battle of Chipyong-ni** (February 1951) began February 13, when 18,000 Chinese troops, the main thrust of the communist counteroffensive, attacked positions controlled by elements of the U.S. 2nd Infantry Division.

A U.N. force consisting of the U.S. 23rd Infantry Regiment, the 1st Ranger Company, the 37th Field Artillery Battalion, Battery B of the 82nd Antiaircraft Artillery Battalion, and the French Battalion, stood their ground, however. U.N. forces were almost overrun a number of times, with gunners firing their howitzers into advancing Chinese regulars at nearly point-blank range, and infantry resolutely holding their ground, forcing the Chinese to advance foxhole by foxhole. With the help of artillery, armor, and air support, the defenders of Chipyong-ni managed to withstand and ultimately shatter the Chinese advance during three days of heavy fighting.

U.S. casualties from the Battle of Chipyong-ni included 94 killed and 259 wounded, compared to much higher Chinese casualties. More significantly, this battle was China's first tactical defeat during the war, and served to bolster the flagging morale of the U.N. troops.

From February 12 to 21, other prongs of the Chinese counteroffensive were launched against sectors held by the 1st Cavalry Division, the 7th Infantry Division, and other elements of the 2nd Infantry Division. Although U.S. troops suffered nearly 2,000 casualties during these attacks (615 killed and 1,296 wounded), the Chinese did not accomplish much more than they did in the bloody attack at Chipyong-ni.

With the communist counteroffensive broken, U.N. forces launched a number of operations intended to recapture the South Korean capital of Seoul and reestablish the defensive lines along the 38th parallel.

❏ **Operation Killer** (February and March 1951) was a general offensive launched on February 21 by the U.S. 1st Cavalry Division, the 2nd, 7th, and 24th Infantry Divisions, and the 1st Marine Division to drive the Chinese communist forces north of the Han River. Squeamishness in Washington led to some criticism of the name "Killer" being used for the operation. Ridgway saw no reason to mince words, however, and the name was retained.

Bad weather and problems with logistics and supplies impeded the operation, however, and the only troops it ended up killing or forcing across the Han were rearguard elements left behind to cover the Chinese withdrawal. By the time Operation Killer ended on March 1, it had not succeeded in inflicting massive casualties upon the communist forces; it did, however, improve U.N. positions and set up allied forces for the next step in their offensive: Operation Ripper.

❑ **Operation Ripper** (March 1951), a general offensive involving all seven of the divisions in the 8th U.S. Army, was launched on March 7 and lasted about two weeks. It succeeded first in surrounding and isolating the city of Seoul, then recapturing it, and finally in driving the communist forces back to the 38th parallel.

Airborne troops of the 187th Regimental Combat Team and the 2nd and 4th Ranger Companies supported the offensive on March 23 by jumping into Munsan-ni, 20 miles northwest of Seoul. Dubbed Operation Tomahawk, it was the last airborne operation of the Korean War. Casualties included 84 injured in the jump, one killed in action, and 18 wounded. Overall U.N casualties during Operation Ripper were fairly high, and included 566 men killed and 3,220 wounded.

❑ **Operation Rugged** (April 1951) launched on April 3, was the general 8th Army advance to what would eventually be called the Kansas-Wyoming Line, just north of the 38th parallel along most of its length. By April 6, the U.N. forces had crossed the 38th parallel and reestablished themselves along the Kansas Line. Allied casualties included 156 killed and 901 wounded.

❑ **Operation Dauntless** (April 1951) was launched on April 11 by the U.S. 3rd, 24th, and 25th infantry divisions to establish the Utah Line, an extension of the main defensive line. It achieved its objectives by April 22, with U.S. Army casualties of 95 killed and 1,056 wounded.

With the conclusion of Dauntless, U.N. forces had once again liberated Seoul and had retaken and improved their positions along the Kansas Line. With that, they began to dig in and prepare to defend the new line.

CHINESE SPRING OFFENSIVES (APRIL 22 - MAY 19, 1951)

In April 1951, President Truman relieved MacArthur from command and made Gen. Matthew B. Ridgway overall commander of the U.N. forces a mere four months after he had assumed command of the 8th U.S. Army. Seasoned veteran Gen. James Van Fleet replaced Ridgway as commander of the U.N. ground forces. Unlike MacArthur, Ridgway was in full accord with sentiments in Washington, which were against making another attempt to conquer North Korea or expand the war beyond the peninsula.

Soon after these changes in command, Chinese forces launched two major offensives in a final attempt to destroy the U.N. forces and achieve a decisive military victory in Korea. When the attack came, the Americans, South Koreans, and their allies were as ready as they could be to meet it.

❏ **The Chinese First Spring Offensive** (April 1951) began on April 22 when, after extensive preparations, Chinese communist forces launched what they called their Fifth Phase Offensive. An estimated 486,000 Chinese troops moved toward Seoul and Kapyong, in the I Corps and IX Corps sectors of the Kansas Line, while North Korean forces launched a limited supporting offensive on the east end of the front. The resulting general engagement was the largest single battle of the war.

While Chinese tactics had been effective during the winter against isolated U.N. units strung out across North Korea, they were quite costly and largely ineffective when utilized against well-prepared defenders supported by artillery and attack aircraft.

Still, Chinese forces managed to break through the U.N. lines at Kapyong, mauling the ROK 6th Division and compelling the allied forces to gradually fall back under the weight of their onslaught. For the most part, however, U.N. forces conducted a fighting withdrawal, and some units, especially the 1st Commonwealth Division, helped to break the momentum of the communist offensive and inflict heavy casualties in the process.

After withdrawing from the Kansas Line, the U.N. forces moved about 35 miles to the south, where they dug in and established the No Name Line, just north of Seoul. By this time, however, Chinese supplies were spent and their tactics had exhausted and bloodied their troops. As a result, the Chinese First Spring offensive was unable to crack the new U.N. line and the fighting came to an end.

U.S. casualties suffered during the Chinese First Spring Offensive included 314 killed and 1,600 wounded. ROK and Chinese casualties are uncertain, but were much higher.

❏ **The Chinese Second Spring Offensive** (May 1951) began on May 16, when the communists sent 21 Chinese and nine North Korean divisions against the No Name Line, unexpectedly shifting the weight of their attack eastward. As they did during their First Spring Offensive, the Chinese targeted ROK units. And, as during the previous month, the South Korean units cracked and broke under the weight of the communist advance. For the most part, however, other U.N. forces held their ground and contained the penetrations of their lines.

On the section of the line held by the U.S. 2nd Infantry Division, along the Soyang River, the communists suffered such heavy casualties from May 16 to 21 that the battle was referred to as the "May Massacre."

While the earlier offensive had at least managed to dislodge the U.N. forces, the second spring offensive did not achieve any of its objectives. By May 20, seven divisions of the 8th U.S. Army were moving into position for a counterattack, and by May 22 the Chinese and North Koreans broke off their attempt to force the allied lines and fell back in disorder. U.N. casualties from the Chinese Second Spring Offensive included 333 killed and 888 wounded. Although exact Chinese casualties are impossible to determine, they were the highest suffered by the communist nation during the entire war.

Like North Korea's attempts the year before, the Chinese spring offensives demonstrated that China, too, could not prevail over the U.N. forces. Their failures ultimately led to the communists' decision to seek a negotiated peace. Fear that the U.N. forces might begin to advance on the Yalu River also contributed to this new-found Chinese interest in negotiation.

U.N. COUNTEROFFENSIVE (MAY 20 - NOV. 12, 1951)

Beginning in late spring 1951, U.N. forces launched a series of division-level operations intended to retake positions lost during the preceding communist offensive and to secure improved positions. While intensive combat would continue at various points along the front until the last day of the war, this phase was the last in which such large scale operations were conducted. At the end of November, U.N. forces settled into an "active defense" of the front.

Also during this phase, the United States rejected the option of a total war with China, and resolved to ensure that the hostilities remained confined to the Korean Peninsula.

❑ Major U.N. ground operations conducted from late spring to early fall 1951 were all geared toward retaking or establishing defensive lines. These operations included Operation Detonate, designed to resecure the Kansas Line, which had been taken by the communists in April 1951; Operation

Having survived the Chinese spring offensives, the U.N. forces launched a large-scale counteroffensive in the summer of 1951 to regain territory lost during the previous months."

Piledriver, intended to secure the Wyoming Line and take control of the Iron Triangle; Operation Commando, a multinational offensive launched to establish the Jamestown Line; and Operations Nomad and Polar, to secure what was eventually called the Missouri Line.

❏ Battles waged during this period, typically fought over hilltops held by one side or the other, include the Battle of Taeusan, the Battle of Bloody Ridge, and the Battle of Heartbreak Ridge.

❏ **Operation Piledriver** was the first part of the U.N. counteroffensive during this phase, while the Battle of Bloody Ridge was a typical but especially gruesome struggle for three hills along the line of contact.

Operation Piledriver (June 1951) was a U.N. attempt to strengthen its position on the Kansas-Wyoming Line and to seize control of the Iron Triangle. It began on June 1, when the U.S. I Corps advanced into the triangle. By June 13, the U.N. forces had captured the remnants of the three towns that marked the corners of the Iron Triangle—Chorwon, Kumhwa, and Pyongyang (not the North Korean capital). Chinese forces controlled the high ground over the latter village, however, prompting I Corps to abandon it almost immediately.

Operation Piledriver succeeded in driving communist forces out of the Iron Triangle and breaking their hold on it. Neither side was able to exert control over it for the balance of the war, however, and the demilitarized zone established by the armistice ran right through the middle of it. Casualties for the four U.S. divisions participating in Operation Piledriver were 231 killed and 1,787 wounded.

❏   **The Battle of Bloody Ridge** (August and September 1951) began when U.N. forces launched an attack against Hills 773, 940, and 983 and their connecting ridges, an area running parallel to the line of contact that earned its name from the resulting engagement. While Bloody Ridge itself had little strategic value, operations to take it were intended to both keep U.N. forces in fighting trim and to keep pressure on the enemy in order to influence the armistice negotiations.

On August 18, the ROK 36th Infantry Regiment (ROK 7th Division), backed up by the U.S. 72nd Tank Battalion, 2nd Infantry Division artillery, and U.N. air support, attacked Bloody Ridge. After a week of heavy fighting, the ROK troops managed to take the ridge. On August 26, however, they were forced to relinquish it under heavy pressure from North Korean forces. The next day, on August 27, the 2nd Battalion, U.S. 9th Infantry Regiment (2nd Infantry Division) attacked Hill 983, but its attack was broken by the entrenched North Korean troops. Later in the day, the regiment's 3rd Battalion was sent against Hill 773, but it, too, was repulsed before it reached its initial objective. When night fell, the communists counterattacked.

U.N. forces resumed the attack on August 30, bombarding the ridge with 451,979 rounds of artillery and assaulting it frontally with the 1st and 2nd Battalions of the 9th Infantry Regiment. The heavily entrenched North Korean units survived the bombardment, however, and the U.S. infantrymen had to fight their way across the ridge, reducing the defenders' positions with machine guns, grenades, and flamethrowers. These U.N. attacks continued until September 5, when they finally succeeded in driving off the North Korean defenders. The communist troops did not move far, however, merely relocating to nearby Heartbreak Ridge, about 1,500 yards to the north.

Both sides suffered high casualties during the Battle of Bloody Ridge. Losses for the U.N. forces participating in the offensive were 326 killed, 2,032 wounded, and 414 missing. Communist casualties were more than 15,000, including at least 1,389 killed.

SECOND KOREAN WINTER
(NOV. 13, 1951 - JUNE 19, 1952)

By the second winter of the Korean War, the U.N. and communist lines of battle had solidified. The opposing forces dug in from one coast to the other on a line running across the entire Korean peninsula.

This situation has often been likened to the trench warfare of World War I, but in reality was very different. In the Great War, opposing divisions controlled relatively narrow but very deep sections of the line of contact and had friendly units on either side of them. In Korea, however, divisions controlled broad sections of the battle line, but their regiments were frequently dug in on isolated hilltops and separated from other units by hundreds of meters or more.

Air strikes, artillery bombardments (the communists fired 102,000 artillery rounds against U.N. positions in May alone), and raids by small units of heavily armed soldiers continued, punctuated by a handful of larger, generally unsuccessful operations. One of these was Operation Clam-Up, which demonstrated how frustrated the U.N. command was becoming with the stalemate.

Other engagements included a raid by nine tanks of the 245th tank Battalion (45th Infantry Division) against communist-held Agok, in retaliation for three raids against the division's sector; an ambush by two Chinese companies of a patrol from the 179th Infantry Regiment (45th Infantry Division); Operation Counter, a series of attacks by the 45th Infantry Division to establish 11 patrol bases around Old Baldy (Hill 266); and a series of Chinese assaults against U.N. outposts on Snook Hill, Pork Chop Hill, and Old Baldy.

❏ **Operation Clam-Up** (February 1952) was intended to make the communists believe that the U.N. forces had withdrawn from the front. To accomplish this, from February 10 to 15 U.N. soldiers did not patrol, fire artillery, or conduct air strikes in an area 20,000 yards from the line of contact. Allied commanders hoped that the communists would respond by sending a force to investigate the ostensibly abandoned lines, so they could ambush the enemy and capture a large number of troops. Communist leaders were not drawn in by the ploy, however, and took advantage of the break in the fighting to reinforce their own defenses.

KOREAN SUMMER - FALL 1952
(JUNE 20 - DEC. 20, 1952)

Little activity occurred throughout most of the summer and fall of 1952, the opposing armies remaining entrenched across from each other on their fortified hilltops. Assaults on isolated positions, sieges of U.N. outposts, and especially heavy artillery bombardments characterized this phase. ROK troops demonstrated that, when properly trained and supported, they could go head-to-head with the communist forces.

Engagements during this period included fighting between the 7th Marine Regiment and parts of the 7th and 45th Infantry Divisions against Chinese forces at various points along the front in early July; repeated communist assaults on Old Baldy (Hill 266); the Battle of Bunker Hill, the first U.S. Marine ground action in western Korea; a 51-hour siege of Marine-held Outpost Bruce (Hill 148); a Chinese siege of Outpost Kelly, in which the 65th Infantry Regiment (3rd Infantry Division) suffered 350 casualties; an attack by the 245th Tank Battalion (45th Infantry Division) against Chinese positions; and Chinese attacks against the western and central sectors in early October.

It was in mid-October, however, that each side launched operations intended to once again improve their defensive lines, leading to the battles of White Horse Hill and Triangle Hill, the worst fighting of the year.

❏ **The Battle of White Horse Hill** (October 1952) took place when Chinese forces launched heavy attacks against a pair of U.N-held hills in the IX Corps sector. White Horse Hill (Hill 395), the most important of these points, had been heavily contested in 1951 and guarded the western approaches to Chorwon. Its loss would give the communists easy access to the area around Chorwon and deny U.N. forces the use of the area's main road networks. U.N. forces learned of the planned attack from a Chinese deserter three days before it took place. As a result, they reinforced White Horse Hill, held by the ROK 9th Infantry Division, with artillery, tanks, and antiaircraft weapons.

On October 6, two battalions of the 340th Regiment, 114th Division, Chinese 38th Field Army, attacked White Horse Hill from the northwest. They made several assaults on the hill but were driven back each time by the South Korean forces. The next day, the Chinese received reinforcements and attacked Hill 395 again, managing to drive the ROK forces off the hilltop. Two hours later, however, the South Koreans counterattacked and recaptured the hill. On October 8, the Chinese assaulted the White Horse

Hill yet again, supporting their attack with heavy artillery fire and sending in reinforcements almost as quickly as their troops fell. Soldiers of the ROK division fought back vigorously—the hill changed hands twice during the day—inflicting heavy casualties on the Chinese.

From October 9 to 11, waves of Chinese troops continued to attack White Horse Hill, determined to capture it. IX Corps responded with heavy artillery bombardments and air strikes. On October 12, the ROK 30th Infantry Regiment launched a heavily reinforced counterattack and inflicted massive casualties on the Chinese forces. After that, the battle dragged on for another three days, but gradually came to an end. During the 10 days of the battle for White Horse Hill, the Chinese suffered nearly 10,000 casualties and, ultimately, failed to take their objective.

Simultaneous with the October 6 attack on White Horse Hill, a Chinese infantry battalion launched a diversionary attack against Arrowhead Hill (Hill 281) two miles away in the U.S. 2nd Infantry Division sector. It was

During most of 1952, soldiers in hilltop positions stood ready to repel enemy attempts to dislodge them. Pictured are two soldiers of the 25th Infantry Division (Company F, 14th Infantry Regiment), Pfc. James Studer (standing) and Pfc. William Smith.

occupied by the French Battalion, which stubbornly held its ground. Hoping to keep the French pinned down and the 2nd Infantry Division busy, the Chinese launched additional attacks on October 9 and 12, but did not succeed in capturing the hill.

❑ **Operation Showdown** (October to November 1952) was a limited U.N. offensive intended to improve the IX Corps defense lines by capturing a complex of four hills—Triangle Hill, Pike's Peak, Jane Russell Hill, and Sandy Hill—northeast of Kumhwa in the Iron Triangle.

Eighth Army commander Gen. James Van Fleet said IX Corps risked heavier casualties by remaining entrenched than by attacking. Also, peace talks at Panmunjom had been suspended on October 8, and Van Fleet wanted to show the communists that recalcitrance at the armistice table could be costly on the battlefield. It was.

On October 13, the 1st and 3rd Battalions of the U.S. 7th Infantry Division's 31st Infantry Regiment, supported by fighter-bombers, moved toward their objective—the right and left arms of Triangle Hill—expecting Showdown to be a routine operation. An elite regiment of the Chinese 15th Field Army entrenched on Triangle Hill reacted vigorously, however, and the operation disintegrated into the heaviest combat since the previous year. An expected five days of air strikes, more needed than ever, were cut back to two because air support was desperately needed at White Horse Hill.

On October 15, the U.S. forces were reinforced by two fresh battalions. After heavy mortar and artillery bombardment of the objective, they captured Triangle Hill. The next day, the Americans attacked and captured Jane Russell Hill, and it appeared as if Operation Showdown was back on track.

Soldiers of the 3rd Battalion stormed and captured Pike's Peak on October 18, but Chinese forces counterattacked the following night and retook it. U.S. troops managed to withdraw from the area under cover of massed artillery fire. On October 23, the Chinese forces rallied and attempted to drive the Americans out of the hill complex. Heavy fighting ensued, as the U.S. forces tried to retake Pike's Peak and the Chinese attempted to drive them off of Jane Russell Hill. On October 25, the ROK 2nd Division moved into the complex and relieved the battered U.S. 7th Infantry Division. Fighting continued, and on October 30, the Chinese drove the South Koreans first off of Triangle Hill and, on November 1, off of Jane Russell Hill.

For four days ROK troops counterattacked, attempting to retake the lost hills. After suffering heavy casualties and failing to retake the positions, however, their attacks were called off. By November 5, four U.S. infantry battalions, a ROK infantry division, 16 artillery battalions, and 200 fighter-bomber sorties had been poured into the fray. U.N. forces, however, held almost none of the terrain they had attempted to take and had suffered about 9,000 casualties in the process. Communist forces had taken a beating as well. Trading men for terrain and once again demonstrating their willingness to balance U.N. firepower with blood, the Chinese suffered heavy casualties, including 19,000 killed and wounded on Triangle Hill alone.

❑ While Operation Showdown accomplished little on the ground, it did reinforce the ineffectiveness of limited operations and led to the intensification of pressure in the air, rather than on the ground, in the following year.

THIRD KOREAN WINTER (DECEMBER 21, 1952 - MARCH 20, 1953)

By the last winter of the Korean War, U.N. forces were dug in across from more than 250,000 Chinese and North Korean troops, and soldiers on both sides were hoping for a ceasefire. Most combat consisted of artillery duels, platoon-sized raids, ambushes, and skirmishes between heavily armed patrols.

A handful of larger engagements were fought during this phase, including a Chinese assault against T-Bone Hill, held by the 38th Infantry Regiment (2nd Infantry Division); a heavy attack by North Korean People's Army units against Hill 812, held by soldiers of the Oklahoma National Guard (K Company, 3rd Battalion, 179th Infantry Regiment, 45th Infantry Division); a raid by elements of the 5th Marine Regiment against Hill 101, near the village of Ungok; and an assault by Chinese forces against Little Gibraltar (Hill 355), held by the 9th Infantry Regiment (2nd Infantry Division).

Operation Smack was one of the larger, and more futile, limited offensives launched by the U.N. forces during the final winter of the war.

❑ **Operation Smack** (January 1953) was a combined arms experimental "scenario" launched against a troublesome enemy position on Spud Hill, facing the U.S. 7th Infantry Division sector of the battle line. A high-profile failure, it created a backlash in the United States against the war.

High ranking Army and Air Force officers, along with members of the media, were invited to watch the operation and given colored brochures describing what was supposed to happen. On January 25, a force of three infantry platoons, closely supported by tanks and aircraft, advanced against Spud Hill. Unfortunately, almost everything that could go wrong did go wrong. Air Force and Marine aircraft, for example, missed their targets. An infantry platoon was blocked and pinned down in a defile, all of its leaders were wounded, and automatic weapons and flamethrowers jammed. Well before the end of the day the operation was deemed a failure and the troops withdrawn.

Throughout the operation, U.N. forces used 224,000 pounds of bombs, more than 12,000 rounds of 105mm and 155mm artillery ammunition, 10,000 rounds of 40mm and .50 caliber ammunition, 2,000 rounds of 90mm tank ammunition, and 650 grenades against Spud Hill. Despite the high hopes for the operation and the huge amounts of materiel used to support it, U.N. forces inflicted a mere 65 enemy casualties during Smack. Communist forces, on the other hand, with far less ammunition and no air support, inflicted 77 U.S. casualties.

KOREAN SPRING - SUMMER (MARCH 21 - JULY 27, 1953)

Armistice negotiations at Panmunjom dragged on throughout the spring and early summer of 1953, slowed, for the most part, by the failure of the two sides to reach an agreement over the issue of involuntary repatriation of prisoners of war.

Battles during this phase of the war tended to be fought out between a few companies on each side, rather than the multiple battalions, regiments, divisions, and corps committed earlier in the war. At each step in the U.S. chain of command, leaders had become so sensitized to criticism over high casualties that the decision of whether to commit more than a company or so of troops was frequently kicked all the way up to the U.N. Command in Tokyo.

Intense fighting blazed at a number of points along the front during this period, usually ignited by Chinese assaults on U.N. hilltop outposts, as each side made efforts to demonstrate to the other their resolve and to improve their final positions before a ceasefire could permanently solidify the line of contact. Chinese forces launched their last offensive, resulting in the Battle of the Kumsong River Salient, and U.S. forces fought their final ground battle in the "Boulder City" section of the Berlin Complex, held by the 1st and 7th Marine Regiments.

During this period, heavy fighting also occurred at Old Baldy, held by the Colombian Battalion; at the "Nevada cities" outposts of Carson, Reno, and Vegas, points held by the 5th Marine Regiment; at Outpost Harry, a point held by the 15th Infantry Regiment (3rd Infantry Division) and the 5th Regimental Combat Team, which withstood an assault by the Chinese 74th Division; and at Outposts Berlin and East Berlin, which were attacked early in July while the 1st Marine Division was relieving the 25th Infantry Division and then overrun later that month.

Many of the engagements fought out during this final phase of the war are exemplified by the back-and-forth struggle over Pork Chop Hill.

❏ **The Battle for Pork Chop Hill** (March 1953) began on March 23, when elements of the Chinese 67th and 141st Divisions bombarded Pork Chop Hill (Hill 234) with heavy mortar and artillery fire and then made a nighttime assault upon it, driving off a company of the 31st Infantry Regiment (7th Infantry Division) dug in on top of it. After being reinforced by elements of the 32nd Infantry Regiment, the Americans counterattacked the hill and recaptured it early the next morning.

A little more than three weeks later on April 16, however, the Chinese attacked Pork Chop Hill again and managed to kill, drive off, or force into hiding most of the U.S. forces occupying it. Both sides responded on April 17 by sending reinforcements onto the hill and by blasting it with concentrated artillery fire. A company of U.S. troops launched a pre-dawn

Once the battle lines between the opposing forces solidified, combat took the form of raids, artillery duels, and concentrated assaults against specific sectors. By this stage of the war, North Korean army units had been completely reformed and rearmed.

attack upon the hill. Fighting the Chinese throughout the day with small arms, grenades, and a bayonet charge, they moved successively through the trench systems crisscrossing the peak and finally took control of it. In the early morning darkness of April 18, the Chinese assaulted the hill again but, after a bloody, close-quarters battle, were driven back off by an arriving company of U.S. reinforcements. During the three-day battle, the U.N. forces expended more than 77,000 artillery rounds (and the Chinese probably fired nearly as many), setting a record for fire support on such a small front.

Throughout the summer, however, the Chinese continued to bombard Hill 234, even as the American defenders attempted to rebuild collapsed bunkers and trenches. On July 6, after heavy artillery preparation, a numerically superior force of Chinese infantrymen launched another attack on Pork Chop Hill. Combat on rocky terrain escalated dramatically over the following days, as the U.N. forces sent in successive companies of reinforcements and the Chinese matched each one with an additional battalion. Each side continued to bombard the hill with concentrated artillery and mortar fire while the steadily increasing infantry forces battled each other over it. By July 11, five U.S. battalions were dug in on the company-sized outpost, while a full Chinese division attempted to dislodge them. Believing more forces would be needed to hold the hill and that a ceasefire was near, 8th Army Commander Gen. Maxwell D. Taylor decided to withdraw the Americans from Pork Chop Hill and have demolition crews destroy its defensive positions. Chinese forces took control of Hill 234, which, after the ceasefire was declared and the demilitarized zone established, ended up partly in the DMZ and partly in North Korea.

❏ **End of the Korean War** (July 1953). On July 26, elements of the 1st and 7th Marine Regiments fighting on Hills 111 and 119, together with units of the 3rd Infantry Division fighting on Sniper Ridge, were the last U.S. forces to engage in ground combat during the war. With the signing of the armistice agreement the following day, July 27, 1953, the Korean War came to an end.

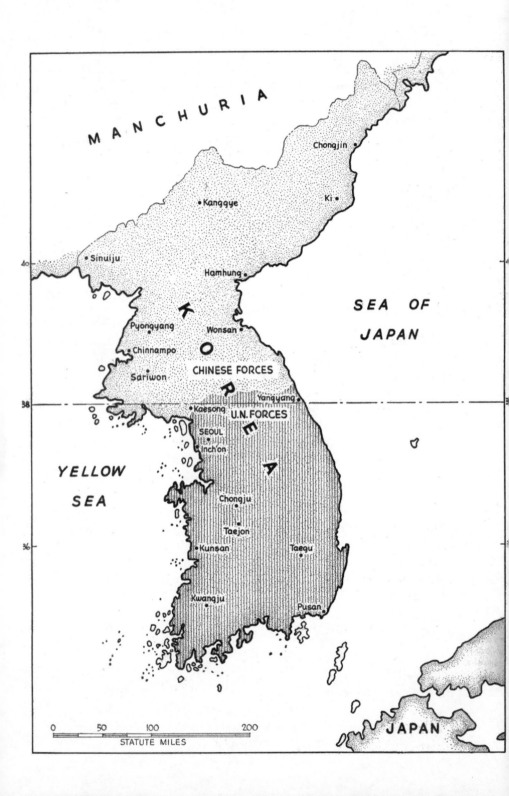

II

WAR IN THE AIR

"The next war may well start in the air, but in all probability it will wind up, as did the last war, in the mud."

—Report of the President's Board to
Study Development of Aircraft for the National Defense, 1925

During the conflict in Korea, ground forces used weapons developed during the previous war and tactics that would have been familiar even during World War I. Above Korea, however, technologically advanced fighters, bombers, and reconnaissance aircraft sped across the skies, attacking enemy ground forces and engaging each other in one-on-one combat over a wedge of territory that became known as MiG Alley.

❑ When war broke out in Korea, the U.S. Air Force was called upon to provide security for American civilians and military dependents being evacuated from Korea. Soon after, however, its role was extended to direct attacks against the advancing North Korean People's Army, in an attempt to slow and maul it as much as possible during its inexorable drive into South Korea.

❑ Initially, U.S. President Harry S. Truman hoped that air and naval forces would be adequate to smash the North Korean invasion and that ground forces would not be needed. It soon became obvious, however, that air forces could blunt, but not stop, the communist offensive.

❑ As the war progressed, aircraft and personnel from allied countries augmented those of the United States. These included South Korean fighter squadrons, fighter squadrons from the Australian and South African air forces, pilots from the British and Canadian air forces attached to American fighter squadrons, and carrier-borne aircraft of the British Royal Navy.

❑   U.S. Navy and Marine Corps pilots also participated in the war. They both flew aircraft from their own services, which were often deployed from carriers cruising off the Korean coast, and were assigned as individuals to the various Air Force squadrons.

❑   Both piston-engine and jet aircraft were used extensively throughout the Korean War, propeller aircraft for the critical close support of ground forces and jets, to a large extent, to protect this air support from the predations of communist jets. Altitude advantage became the determining factor in jet-to-jet combat, and dogfights were fought in the realm of the stratosphere, far removed from the action on the ground.

U.S. AIR FORCE

In September 1947, the U.S. Air Force (USAF) became an independent military service and replaced the U.S. Army Air Forces (USAAF), which had been a subordinate arm of the U.S. Army. Thus, the Air Force was less than three years old when it entered its first conflict in June 1950.

While the U.S. Air Force had suffered the same kinds of budget, equipment, and personnel cutbacks as the other armed services in the years following World War II, it was nonetheless ready for action when war broke out in June 1950 and began to take part in operations immediately.

❑   Air defense of U.S.-occupied Japan was the responsibility of the Far East Air Forces (FEAF), a service composed of the U.S. Fifth, Thirteenth, and Twentieth Air Forces. Of the three FEAF components, the Fifth Air Force, stationed in Japan under the command of Maj. Gen. Earle E. "Pat" Partridge, bore the brunt of the combat over Korea, while the Thirteenth and Twentieth, spread across the western Pacific, played lesser roles.

❑   At the beginning of the war, FEAF consisted of 16 groups, 44 squadrons, 657 aircraft, and 33,625 officers and airmen. Just a year later, it reached a peak strength of 20 groups, 70 squadrons, and 1,441 aircraft, and by July 1953 had a strength of about 112,200 personnel.

❑   Throughout the war FEAF squadrons dropped or fired 476,000 tons of bombs, rockets, and ammunition during 720,980 sorties. (A sortie is a mission flown by an aircraft; pilots often flew multiple sorties in a single day, landing only to refuel and re-arm.) FEAF estimated that these actions

American-made F-86 Sabre jets (foreground) and Soviet-made MiG-15s became the quintessential aircraft flown by the pilots battling for control of the skies over Korea. *Courtesy U.S. Air Force*

destroyed some 900 enemy aircraft in aerial combat and many more on the ground, 1,100 tanks, 800 bridges, 800 locomotives, 9,000 railroad cars, 70,000 motor vehicles, and 80,000 buildings. They also inflicted nearly 150,000 North Korean and Chinese casualties.

❏   FEAF lost some 1,466 planes during the war, 750 of them destroyed by the enemy (about 10 percent of them in air-to-air combat). Total FEAF casualties during the war were 1,200 killed, 368 wounded, and 273 missing.

❏   During the Korean War, FEAF constructed or improved upon some 55 airfields throughout Korea, many of which had been built by the Japanese prior to and during World War II. Each was numbered and many became better known by their numbers than by their names. Among the most important were the following:

K-1 Pusan West
K-2 Taegu
K-3 Pohang-dong
K-5 Taejon

K-6 Pyongtaek
K-8 Kunsan
K-9 Pusan East
K-10 Chinhae
K-13 Suwon
K-14 Kimpo
K-16 Seoul
K-18 Kangnung
K-40 Cheju Island
K-46 Hoengsong
K-47 Chunchon
K-55 Osan

COMMUNIST AIR FORCES

When North Korean ground units invaded the south in June 1950, they were supported by a small force of piston-driven aircraft that was quickly eliminated by the U.N. forces. By the end of the year, however, modern jet aircraft from both sides were battling each other in the skies over Korea.

❏ Apparently anticipating a possible need for aerial intervention in Korea, in early 1950 the Soviet Union deployed to China two regiments of MiG-15s, its newest and most advanced fighter.

❏ Soviet pilots were flying missions against U.N. air forces by November 1, 1950, flying sorties out of Manchurian bases at locations like Andong and Fencheng. Throughout the war, Russian pilots carried the burden of air combat for communist forces.

❏ Soviet units active in the Korean War included the 324th Fighter Air Division (FAD), made up of the 176th Fighter Air Regiment (FAR) and the 196th FAR.

❏ Up to 90 percent of the pilots in some of the Soviet regiments were veterans of Russia's Great Patriotic War against fascism, and many of the commanders were elite pilots. For example, top-scoring Russian ace Ivan Kozhedub, who had claimed 62 victories in World War II, commanded the 324th FAD; Russian ace Eugeny Pepelyaev, with 19 victories in World War II, commanded the 196th FAR.

❏ In order to keep direct Soviet participation in the war a secret, Russian pilots operating out of Manchuria wore Chinese flight overalls and flew jets bearing Chinese and North Korean markings. Soviet pilots were also forbidden from flying too far south or over the sea, in order to prevent capture if they were shot down.

❑ The Soviet pilots communicated with each other and their flight control in Russian, and some of these transmissions must have been intercepted by U.N. forces. However, despite this and other evidence, both the USSR and the United States strove to keep the Russian fliers a secret, fearing that public knowledge of direct combat between the two superpowers would lead to an escalation of the conflict.

❑ By the end of 1950, North Korean and Chinese pilots were being trained on the MiG-15s, but it was not until Summer 1951 that they were proficient enough to enter combat.

MAJOR FEAF OPERATIONS

FEAF proved itself superior to enemy air power from the first days of the war. By mid-July, within three weeks of the start of the war, FEAF had obliterated North Korea's small and obsolete air force and achieved air supremacy.

❑ Early in the war, FEAF played a defensive role. One of its primary responsibilities was guarding the ships and aircraft being used to evacuate civilians (many of them Americans) from Korea.

❑ Throughout the course of the war, FEAF aircraft attacked the infrastructure of North Korea, bombing bridges, warehouses, railroads, and other critical targets. Allied air forces stayed active right up until the end of the war.

❑ In an attempt to destroy the communist transportation system, FEAF launched three major interdiction operations against it, two labeled Strangle and one called Saturate. Inclement weather and an inability to maintain continuous night attacks, however, impeded these efforts. Nonetheless, a campaign of "air pressure" from FEAF played a large role in coercing the Chinese into accepting a cease fire agreement that was acceptable to the United States.

FEAF opened this campaign in June 1952 with highly successful air raids against hydroelectric complexes at Suiho, Chosin, Fusen, and Kyosen. North Korea suffered an almost complete loss of electric power for two weeks (and

Manchuria lost a quarter of its electrical supply) and did not regain its full generating capacity until after the end of the war.

These attacks were not enough to force an armistice upon the Chinese, but worse was to come. In May 1953, the allied air forces destroyed three of North Korea's 20 irrigation dams, a move that damaged the enemy's ability to feed its people. Floods resulting from the shattered dams destroyed railroad tracks, roads, and thousands of acres of rice fields. Although the communists were able to repair the damage, they were forced to reduce the water levels behind all their dams to prevent flooding in case they were again destroyed. This reduced the water available for irrigating their rice crops.

AIR-TO-GROUND COMBAT

Throughout the course of the war, FEAF fighters and bombers provided close air support for the troops on the ground, roaring in to unload bombs, rockets, napalm, and machine gun and cannon fire on enemy forces, sometimes within 75 yards of friendly ground forces.

❑ An advantage possessed by the U.S. Marine Corps—but not the U.S. Army—was the capability to utilize marine aviation units for dedicated close air support, resupply, and medical evacuation of marine units. For example, the 1st Provisional Marine Brigade was able to count on direct air support from Marine Air Group 33.

❑ Although the age of jet aircraft had arrived, propeller driven fighters like P-51 Mustangs and F-4U Corsairs, many of the flown by Navy, Marine, and non-American pilots, continued to make their presence felt upon the communist forces.

❑ On August 4, 1950, allied aircraft attacking NKPA positions in Kimchon, just outside of the Pusan Perimeter, dropped a 500-pound bomb directly on the North Korean command headquarters in the basement of an abandoned meat-packing plant. This bomb damaged, but did not destroy, the command center. U.N. forces never knew how close they had come to eliminating the NKPA front commander, Gen. Kim Chaek, and his staff.

❑ Effective close air support depended upon the relatively slow, piston-driven ground attack aircraft being defended from marauding communist MiGs. Such protection, by allied jet aircraft, led to combat high above, and largely divorced from, the war on the ground.

AIR-TO-AIR COMBAT

In the years following World War II, many military analysts predicted that the age of the dogfight, direct air-to-air combat between aircraft, had come to an end. Reasons cited for this presumption included that human beings could not withstand the gravity and stresses of high-speed battles; that jet aircraft moved too quickly to allow pilots to effectively use their machine guns against other jets; and that modern missiles would be able to destroy any jets that were employed in combat. The Korean War demonstrated, however, that even in the age of jet aircraft, the role of the individual pilot was as important as it had ever been.

❏ FEAF inflicted its first losses against North Korea on June 27, when some of its F-82 Twin Mustang fighters intercepted and shot down three North Korean YAK fighters as they tried to interfere with civilian evacuations. Later the same day, FEAF F-80 jet fighters shot down four more enemy planes.

❏ Air combat moved into a new and lethal phase in November 1950 when Chinese forces entered the war and MiG-15 jet fighters, superior to anything FEAF could put in the air at that time and piloted largely by veteran Russian pilots, joined in the conflict.

❏ On November 8, 1950, the first all-jet battle in history took place over Sinuiju between eight USAF F-80 Shooting Stars of the 51st Fighter Interceptor Wing and six MiG-15s. In a 30-second dogfight, 1st Lt. Russell Brown outmaneuvered and shot down one of the superior enemy aircraft.

❏ FEAF countered the MiG-15 initially with the F-86A, and later with the F-86E/F Sabre. On December 17, 1950, Lt. Col. Bruce Hinton became the first Sabre pilot to shoot down a Mig-15 in aerial combat.

❏ On July 22, 1953, Lt. Sam P. Young of the 51st Fighter Wing claimed his first victory, the last over a MiG during the Korean War. Five days later, on the last day of the war, Capt. Ralph S. Parr claimed the final aerial victory of the conflict, shooting down an Il-12 transport plane, his tenth victory in the skies over Korea.

❏ While most of the enemy jets shot down fell prey to Sabre pilots, about two dozen were shot down by the pilots of piston-driven Corsairs, Mustangs, and Sea Furies. Such kills were a marked exception to the rule, however.

❏ Sabres flew nearly twice as many sorties as did MiGs during the war, exceeding them in every month except for the period October 1951 through

February 1952. When the MiGs were in the air, however, they appeared in great strength, frequently 50 or more.

❏ During the war, a single battle occurred between American pilots and jets openly bearing Soviet markings. On November 18, 1952, U.S. Navy F9F-2 Panthers attacked targets near Hoeryong, near the Soviet border. MiG-15s from Vladivostok scrambled to intercept them, two of them being shot down before the American planes departed southward.

❏ Advantages the U.N. pilots had over their communist opponents were g-suits and flight helmets, which helped to drastically reduce the incidence of blackout during high-speed maneuvers. Russian pilots, in turn, were much less likely to black out than their North Korean and Chinese counterparts, who were less well nourished.

❏ Combat experience in World War II definitely played a role in the success both U.S. and Russian pilots enjoyed in the skies over Korea. U.N. pilots who shot down at least one enemy plane had flown an average of 18 missions each during the earlier conflict.

❏ Throughout the course of the Korean War, U.N. air forces claimed 900 enemy aircraft shot down, some 818 of which were MiG-15s. USAF pilots shot down 829 of the U.N. total, 811 of them MiGs.

❏ Russian sources acknowledge the loss of 354 MiGs flown by Soviet pilots, a number that is likely accurate, as Chinese and Korean pilots flew a preponderance of the communist MiGs that were shot down (i.e., around 464).

❏ U.S. records acknowledge the loss of about 130 fighters in air-to-air combat throughout the course of the war, and about 2,000 U.N. aircraft in total, most of them shot down by ground fire.

❏ Soviet pilots claimed victories over more than 1,300 U.N. aircraft during the war. As U.S. records show total losses of only about 2,000 planes, mostly to ground fire, it would seem that the Soviet claims are a bit high.

MIG ALLEY

By summer 1952, while war on the ground had bogged down into fighting from fixed positions, the skies over northwestern Korea became a perpetual battleground, where communist MiG-15s met Allied F-86 Sabres, F-84 Thunderjets, and F-80 Shooting Stars and engaged them in aerial duels on a daily basis. This area became known as "MiG Alley," and remained a hot spot throughout the war.

❏ Early in the war, allied B-29 Superfortresses conducted daytime bombing of targets in northwest Korea, but after MiG-15s shot down five of them during a single week in October 1951, the bombers began attacking only at night.

❏ Headquartered in Chinese bases just across the Yalu River in Manchuria in towns such as Andong, the MiGs were off limits to allied forces while on the ground. FEAF fighter jets, however, sometimes strayed over the Yalu in close pursuit of enemy MiGs.

❏ Even as combat on the ground settled down into static combat along fixed lines during the last two years of the war, air-to-air combat in MiG Alley continued unabated. In June and July 1953, the last two months of the conflict, the communist air forces increased their sorties into MiG Alley. In a single savage battle on June 30, Sabres gunned down 16 MiGs, setting a record for the number of enemy aircraft destroyed in a single battle involving F-86s.

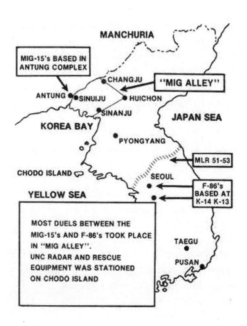

ACES

A number of pilots on both sides qualified as aces during the war, shooting down five or more enemy aircraft in air-to-air combat. In the following descriptions "half," and in one case "third," kills are those that were shared with the pilots of one or more other aircraft.

AMERICAN ACES

❏ Some 38 USAF pilots, one U.S. Marine Corps pilot, and one U.S. Navy pilot became aces during the war. Many of these top scorers, listed below, had claimed victories over enemy aircraft during World War II. Their ranks, when available, are listed.

Capt. Joseph C. McConnell Jr. claimed 16 enemy aircraft
Maj. James Jabarra claimed 15 enemy aircraft (plus 1 1/2 in WW II)
Capt. Manuel J. Fernandez claimed 14 1/2 enemy aircraft
Maj. George A. Davis Jr. claimed 14 enemy aircraft (plus 7 in WW II)
Col. Royal N. Baker claimed 13 enemy aircraft (plus 3 1/2 in WW II)
Maj. Frederick C. "Boots" Blesse claimed 10 enemy aircraft
Lt. Harold E. Fischer claimed 10 enemy aircraft
Lt. Col. Vermont Garrison claimed 10 enemy aircraft (plus 7 1/3 in W WII)
Col. James K. Johnson claimed 10 enemy aircraft (plus 1 in World War II)
Capt. Lonnie R. Moore claimed 10 enemy aircraft
Capt. Ralph S. Parr Jr. claimed 10 enemy aircraft
Lt. James F. Low claimed 9 enemy aircraft
Robinson "Robbie" Risner claimed 8 enemy aircraft
Clifford Jolley claimed 7 enemy aircraft
Leonard Lilley claimed 7 enemy aircraft
Lt. Henry Buttelman claimed 7 enemy aircraft
Maj. Donald Adams claimed 6 1/2 enemy aircraft
Col. Francis S. "Gabby" Gabreski claimed 6 1/2 enemy aircraft (plus 28 in WWII)
Maj. James P. Hagerstrom claimed 6 1/2 enemy aircraft (plus 6 in World War II)
George Jones claimed 6 1/2 enemy aircraft
Winton "Bones" Marshall claimed 6 1/2 enemy aircraft
Robert Love claimed 6 enemy aircraft
Maj. John F. Bolt claimed 6 enemy aircraft (plus 6 in World War II)
James Kasler claimed 6 enemy aircraft
Maj. William T. Whisner claimed 5 1/2 enemy aircraft
Robert Baldwin claimed 5 enemy aircraft
Capt. Richard S. Becker claimed 5 enemy aircraft
Maj. Stephen L. Bettinger claimed 5 enemy aircraft (plus 1 in World War II)

Lt. Guy B. Bordelon claimed 5 enemy aircraft
Richard Creighton claimed 5 enemy aircraft
Clyde Curtin claimed 5 enemy aircraft
Cecil Foster claimed 5 enemy aircraft
Ralph Gibson claimed 5 enemy aircraft
Capt. Robert Latshaw claimed 5 enemy aircraft
Robert Moore claimed 5 enemy aircraft
Dolphin Overton claimed 5 enemy aircraft
George Ruddell claimed 5 enemy aircraft
Col. Harrison Thyng claimed 5 enemy aircraft (plus 5 in World War II)
William Westcott claimed 5 enemy aircraft

❏   A single U.S. Marine became an ace during the war. Maj. John F. Bolt, who was attached to the 51st Fighter Wing, gunned down six MiGs, adding them to the six-and-a-half victories he claimed during World War II while flying with Pappy Boyington's "Black Sheep" squadron.

❏   Other American pilots who became aces during the war include Maj. William T. Whisner, who became the first jet ace of the 51st and Col. Harrison R. Thyng, commander of the 4th Fighter Wing, who shot down pilots of more nationalities than any other American ace, claiming victories against German, Vichy French, and Japanese aircraft in World War II.

❏   One-third of the 39 U.S. pilots who became aces during the Korean War had scored at least one aerial victory during World War II, and some achieved ace status in both wars (two of whom appear in the list above).

❏   In addition to the pilots who became aces in Korea, a dozen who had become aces during World War II scored one or more victories during the Korean War. Among these were Maj. Walker M. Mahurin, who shot down 21 enemy aircraft in World War II and another 3 1/2 over Korea before being shot down and taken prisoner, and Col. John C. Myer, who scored 24 kills in World War II and two in Korea.

❏   There were also two pilots who did not become aces in either conflict, but who achieved overall ace status by shooting down five or more enemy planes in both wars combined.

❏   In June 1953, 24-year-old Lt. Henry Buttelmann shot down five enemy aircraft in 12 days, becoming the youngest ace of the Korean War.

❏   America's 39th and last ace of the Korean War was Maj. S. L. Bettinger, who shot down his fifth enemy plane on July 20, 1953. He was subsequently shot down himself and taken prisoner; his score remained unconfirmed until his release.

❑ No pilots from allied nations other than the United States became aces during the Korean War, but several performed well and claimed victories against enemy aircraft. Among these were Royal Canadian Air Force Flight-Lt. Ernest A. Glover, who was credited with shooting down three MiGs. Two Canadian aces from World War II, squadron leaders James D. Lindsay and J. McKay, also fought in the Korean war and claimed victories over enemy aircraft.

❑ For their actions during the war, four USAF pilots were given the nation's highest award, the Medal of Honor, all posthumously. American ace Capt. George A. Davis, who was shot down and killed on February 10, 1952, just minutes after he achieved his 13th and 14th victories over communist aircraft, was the sole Sabre pilot to earn this distinction.

COMMUNIST ACES

Russian and Chinese records indicate that there were three Chinese, at least 26 Russian, and probably no North Korean aces during the Korean War. Some of the Russian claims may be exaggerated, a product of a mortal fear of failure during the Stalinist era. Ranks of the communist aces are not available in most cases.

CHINESE ACES

Chao Bao Tun claimed 9 allied aircraft
Kim Tsi Oc claimed 9 allied aircraft
Fan Van Chou claimed 8 allied aircraft

RUSSIAN ACES

Eugeny Pepelyaev claimed 23 allied aircraft
Nikolai Sutyagin claimed 21 allied aircraft
Dimitri Oskin claimed 15 allied aircraft
Lev Schukin claimed 15 allied aircraft
Aleksandr Smurchkov claimed 15 allied aircraft
Serafim Subbutin claimed 15 allied aircraft
Mikhail Ponomarev claimed 14 allied aircraft
A. Sherberstov claimed 14 allied aircraft
Sergei Kramarenko claimed 13 allied aircraft (plus 12 in World War II)
Stepan Bakhaev claimed 11 allied aircraft
Nikolai Dokaschenko claimed 11 allied aircraft

Mikhail Mikhin claimed 11 allied aircraft
Grigory Okhay claimed 11 allied aircraft (plus 6 in World War II)
Dmitri Samoylov claimed 10 allied aircraft
Arkady Boytsov claimed 10 allied aircraft
Grigory Ges claimed 9 allied aircraft
V. Alfeev claimed 8 allied aircraft
L. Inanov claimed 8 allied aircraft
Grigory Pulov claimed 8 allied aircraft
B. Bokach claimed 7 allied aircraft
Muraviev claimed 7 allied aircraft
Fedor Shebanov claimed 6 allied aircraft
Nikolai Zameskin claimed 6 allied aircraft
I. Zaplavnev claimed 6 allied aircraft (plus 6 in World War II)
Boris Abakumov claimed 5 allied aircraft
Anatoliy Karelin claimed 5 allied aircraft

❑ As with the U.N. pilots, there were a number of Soviet aces from World War II who flew in Korea but did not achieve ace status there. Among these were Gen. Georgey Lobov, who flew 15 missions over Korea and claimed four victories (plus 19 in World War II); and Ivan Kozhedub, the USSR's top scoring ace from World War II, who did not add appreciably or at all during the Korean War to his impressive score of 62 kills.

❑ U.N. pilots referred to the most dangerous communist pilots as "honchos," and believed them to be instructors or veteran formation leaders. It is now clear that many of these pilots were indeed quite experienced, and were often Russian veterans of World War II.

❑ It was a Chinese MiG pilot named Chiang Chi-Wei who locked onto USAF Capt. Davis' tail and fatally shot him out of the air as he attempted a third consecutive victory against a MiG.

AIRCRAFT

While the ground weapons used throughout the Korean War differed little from those used during World War II, significant advances were made in aircraft technology during the Korean War.

❑ By the time World War II ended, the capabilities of piston-engine, propeller-driven aircraft had nearly peaked. Even as such planes approached their practical limits, however, jet aircraft were rapidly being improved and becoming the standard. As a result, the Korean War was the first conflict in which jets were used by both sides.

❏ In the following descriptions, "bomber" refers to planes used primarily to bomb targets on the ground, "fighter" refers to planes designed to combat other aircraft, and "attack" refers to planes intended for combat against ground forces. "Ceiling" refers to the maximum practical altitude a plane could reach, and "range" to the greatest distance it could fly before needing to be refueled.

ALLIED AIRCRAFT

U.N. pilots flew many sorts of fighter, bomber, and transport aircraft during the Korean War, most of them of American manufacture. Some of the most representative aircraft of the conflict are described here. U.N. forces used a wide variety of other aircraft as well, including B-26 Marauder bombers, Australian-made Meteor 8 jet fighters, and various reconnaissance-fighters.

❏ When war broke out in Korea, F9F-2 Panther carrier-based fighters and F-80 Shooting Stars were the only type of jet aircraft the United States had in the theater of operations, followed soon afterwards by F-84 Thunderjets. None of these aircraft were adequate for facing the Russian-made MiG-15s being used by the communist forces.

❏ **F-86A "Sabre."** This single-pilot, American-made plane, which first saw action over Korea in December 1950, became the standard fighter aircraft for the U.N. forces during the war. It was manufactured by North American Aviation Inc., starting in 1950.

The F-86A was equipped with a General Electric J47-GE-13 turbojet (5,200 pound thrust), had a wingspan of 37 feet 1.25 inches, a length of 37 feet 6 inches, a height of 14 feet 9 inches, a weight of 16,375 pounds when loaded, maximum speed of 675 miles per hour at 2,500 feet, a rate of climb of 7,470 feet per minute, a ceiling of 48,000 feet, and a range of 675 miles. It was armed with six .50 caliber machineguns.

The F-86A was much more stable and maneuverable in flight than its main opponent, the MiG-15, but was inferior to it in both climb and armament. Improvements to the latter, however, were not long in coming. During the war, the United States introduced the improved F-86F. It differed from the F-86A in that it had a wingspan of 39 feet 1.5 inches, a length of 37 feet 6.5 inches, and weighed about a half ton less. Its J47-GE-27 turbojet had

5,910 pounds of thrust and allowed it to climb at 9,300 feet per minute, faster than any fighter employed during the war.

❏ **B-29A "Superfortress."** Developed during World War II for use against stationary targets like factory complexes, the B-29 was used in Korea both against static targets and against formations of advancing communist troops, especially in the first six months of the war. It was manufactured by the Boeing Aircraft Company starting in 1944. Outweighing the Soviet-made Tupolev Tu-2 bomber by more than four times and operated by a crew of 10, the piston-driven Superfortress was by far the largest aircraft used by either side to any extent during the Korean War.

The B-29 had four Wright R-2250-57 Cyclone 18-cylinder radial air-cooled 2,200 horsepower engines and was capable of speeds of 358 miles per hour at 25,000 feet. It had a wingspan of 141 feet 3 inches, a length of 99 feet, a height of 29 feet 7 inches, a weight of 141,000 pounds when loaded, a ceiling of 31,850 feet, and an impressive range of 4,100 miles. It was armed with one 20mm cannon and 10 .50 caliber machineguns, and could carry up to 20,000 pounds of bombs.

❏ **C-54A "Skymaster."** This American-made transport plane was one of the cargo workhorses of the Korean War, carrying men and equipment to airstrips throughout the Korean Peninsula. Introduced in 1942 by the Douglas Aircraft Company for use in World War II, the Skymaster had a crew of six and could carry from 30 to 50 passengers.

The C-54A was equipped with four Pratt & Whitney R-2000-7 Twin Wasp, 14-cylinder radial air-cooled 1,290 horsepower engines, had a wingspan of 117 feet 6 inches, a length of 93 feet 10 inches, a height of 27 feet 6 inches, a weight of 62,600 pounds when fully loaded, a ceiling of 22,000 feet, and a range of 3,900 miles. It was unarmed.

❏ **P-51 "Mustang."** One of the most prevalent American fighters of World War II, the single-pilot Mustang saw continued service in Korea, notably as one of the aircraft flown by pilots from the allied nations, including Australia and South Korea. The P-51 series was introduced by North American Aviation Inc. in 1943 (the P-51D variant in 1944). By the time of the Korean War, this aircraft was frequently referred to as the F-51.

The P-51D had a Packard V-1650-7 12 -cylinder V liquid-cooled 1,510 horsepower engine and was capable of speeds of up to 437 miles per hour at 25,000 feet. It had a wingspan of 37 feet, a length of 32 feet 3 inches, a height of 13 feet 8 inches, a weight of 11,600 pounds, a ceiling of 41,900 feet, and a range of 950 miles. It was armed with six .50 caliber machineguns and could carry up to 2,000 pounds of bombs.

❑ **F-4U1 "Corsair."** Made famous as the aircraft flown by Pappy Boyington's "Black Sheep" squadron during World War II, the single-pilot Corsair fighter was flown by U.S. Navy and Marine pilots throughout the course of the war, being deployed from aircraft carriers off the coast of Korea to the battlefields when needed. It was manufactured initially in 1943, by the United Aircraft Corporation.

The F-4U1D, the Corsair variant used during the Korean War, was equipped with a Pratt & Whitney R-2800-8W Double Wasp 18 cylinder radial air-cooled 2,000 horsepower engine and was capable of speeds up to 425 miles per hour at 20,000 feet. It had a wingspan of 41 feet, a length of 33 feet 4.5 inches, a height of 15 feet 1 inch, a weight of 14,000 pounds fully loaded, a ceiling of 37,000 feet, and a range of 1,015 miles. Corsairs were armed with six .50 caliber machineguns and could carry up to 2,000 pounds of bombs.

❑ **F-82G "Twin Mustang."** One of the more unconventional looking aircraft of the era, the American-made F-82 was a two-pilot, twin-fuselage plane that looked like a pair of F-51 Mustangs joined together, with a pilot in one and a navigator/gunner in the other. It was manufactured by North American Aviation Inc. starting in 1945, and its later variants, the F-82F and F-82G, were introduced in 1946 and configured as night fighters.

Twin Mustangs saw intensive service in the first months of the Korean War, primarily as night fighters. As the presence of jet aircraft increased in the Korean theater of war, however, they were relegated to a secondary status and were removed from service at the end of the war in 1953.

The F-82G night fighter was equipped with a pair of Allison V-1710-143/145 V-12 liquid-cooled, 1,600 horsepower engines, had a wingspan of 51 feet 3 inches, a length of 42 feet 5 inches, a height of 13 feet 10 inches, a weight of 25,591 pounds, a maximum speed of 461 miles per hour at 21,000 feet, a ceiling of 38,900 feet, and a range of 2,240 miles. It was armed with six .50 caliber machineguns and could carry up to 4,000 pounds of bombs.

❑ **F-80C "Shooting Star."** Used in the first months of the war, this single-pilot, American-made fighter-bomber was soon outclassed by the Soviet-made jet aircraft employed by the communist forces. It was manufactured by Lockheed Aircraft Corp. starting in 1948.

The F-80C was equipped with a General Electric J33-A-23 turbojet (4,600 pound thrust), had a wingspan of 39 feet 11 inches, a length of 34 feet

6 inches, a height of 11 feet 4 inches, a weight of 16,856 pounds, a maximum speed of 580 miles per hour at 7,000 feet, a climb rate of about 5,000 feet per minute, a ceiling of 46,800 feet, and a range of 1,380 miles. It was armed with six .50 caliber machineguns.

COMMUNIST AIRCRAFT

During the Korean War, the Soviet-made MiG-15 became the primary jet fighter used by the communist forces. In addition to the aircraft described here, communist forces in Korea also used a number of other aircraft, including the Lavochkin La-9 and the Yakolev Yak-9D piston-driven fighters.

❏ **Mikoyan-Gurevich MiG-15.** This single-pilot, Soviet-made fighter was the predominant jet aircraft used by the communist forces in Korea. It was produced by Soviet State Industries starting in 1947. The West knew about this aircraft in 1948, but assumed it was of inferior design. However, armed with a deadly array of weapons and superior in rate of climb to most American-made fighters, it outmatched allied aircraft early in the war.

The MiG-15 was equipped with an RD-45F turbojet (5,005 pound thrust), a copy of the Rolls-Royce Nene, and capable of speeds of 664 miles per hours at 40,000 feet. It had a wingspan of 33 feet 1 inch, a length of 36 feet 3 inches,

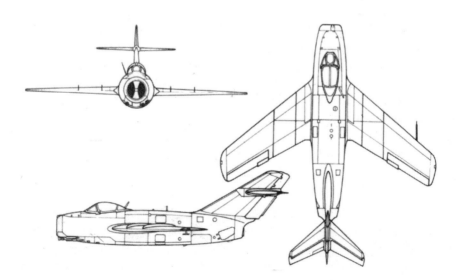

a height of 11 feet 2 inches, a weight of 12,566 pounds when fully loaded, a climb rate of 8,265 feet per minute, a ceiling of 48,817 feet, and a range of 1,220 miles. It was armed with a pair of 23mm cannon and a single 37mm cannon and could carry up to 1,100 pounds of bombs.

During the war, the Soviets introduced the MiG-15bis, a variant of the fighter equipped with a VK-1 engine with 5,952 pounds of thrust and capable of an improved climb rate of 9,055 feet per minute. This rate greatly exceeded that of the F-86A, but fell somewhat short of the F-86F's climb rate of 9,300 feet per minute.

❑ **Ilyushin Il-10.** Produced by the USSR starting in 1944 for its "Great Patriotic War" against Germany, this piston-driven attack aircraft had a crew of two, both a pilot and a rear-facing machine-gunner. It was used off-and-on throughout the war in Korea, but fell easy prey to almost anything the U.N. forces could put in the air.

The Il-10 was equipped with a Mikulin AM-42, 12-cylinder V, liquid-cooled, 2,000 horsepower engine and was capable of speeds of up to 311 miles per hour. It had a wingspan of 43 feet 1.5 inches, a length of 36 feet 9 inches, a height of 11 feet 6 inches, a weight of 14,409 pounds, a ceiling of 24,606 feet, and a range of 621 miles. It was armed with three 20mm cannon.

❑ **Tupolev Tu-2.** This twin-engine, piston-driven bomber was used only sparingly during the war in Korea (e.g., for attacks against U.N. garrisons on islands off the North Korean coast) and did not fare well when allied jets were scrambled to oppose it. It was manufactured by the USSR's State Industries beginning in 1943.

The Tu-2 had a pair of Shvetsov M-82, 14-cylinder radial air-cooled, 1,850 horsepower engines and could fly at up to 342 miles per hour at 17,720 feet. It had a wingspan of 61 feet 10.5 inches, a length of 45 feet 3 inches, a height of 13 feet 11 inches, a weight of 28,219 pounds when fully loaded, a ceiling of 31,200 feet, and a range of 1,243 miles. It had a crew of four and was armed with a pair of 20mm cannon and three machineguns and could carry up to 6,614 pounds of bombs.

III

WAR AT SEA

"Navies do not dispense with fortifications nor with armies, but when wisely handled they may save a country the strain which comes when these have to be called into play."

—Alfred Thayer Mahan, *The Influence of Sea Power upon the French Revolution, 1892*

Duincluding the Korean War, the United States sent four battleships, eight cruisers, 13 aircraft carriers of various sizes, some 80 destroyers, and hundreds of support ships to the Korean theater of operations. In addition, 10 allied nations sent ships to support the war effort.

President Harry S. Truman hoped that U.S. naval and air forces alone would be able to stop the communist invasion, and that it would not become necessary to deploy ground forces to the Korean peninsula. It was soon clear, however, that naval and air forces could contain but not stop the North Korean offensive.

Traditional naval operations against a similar foe had no place in the Korean War, and for the first time in U.S. history the navy had to tailor its operations almost exclusively to supporting ground forces.

NAVAL POWER IN 1950

❏ In the years following World War II, the United States emerged as the world's foremost naval power, seizing the position Great Britain had held just a decade before, and for the 125 years before that.

❏ After World War II ended, the United States decommissioned more ships than it had built and many of its personnel returned to civilian life. Care had been taken to modernize the fleet as much as possible immediately before World War II, however, and between 1945 and 1950 the U.S. Navy worked to adjust its materiel and strategy to both incorporate and defend against enemy atomic weapons, jet aircraft, and helicopters.

❏ Political as well as technological changes contributed to the strengthening, if not the enlargement, of the U.S. Navy in the post-WWII period. Foremost among these were the emergence of the Soviet Union as a threat rivaling that posed by the Axis just a few years before, and the need to fill the vacuum left by Great Britain.

❏ Indeed, by 1948, Great Britain's active fleet strength worldwide consisted of eight aircraft carriers, four battleships, 17 cruisers, 52 destroyers, 34 submarines, and 147,000 personnel (down from 863,000 in 1945). By 1950, its forces in the Pacific were so weak that all the great maritime power could contribute to the U.N. mission in Korea was a single small aircraft carrier.

❏ On the other hand, when the Korean War broke out, the United States had thousands of ships in service, including more than 500 destroyers, and was able to deploy the entire 7th Fleet to the waters around Korea.

U.N. NAVAL OPERATIONS

Even as U.N. ground forces were struggling, often futilely, to contain the North Korean invasion of South Korea, U.N. naval forces were quickly seizing control of the waters around the peninsula. Once control of the coasts had been established, U.N. naval forces could use their big guns against enemy troops, supplies, and lines of communications and transportation; use carrier-borne aircraft to provide close support to allied troops or attack enemy targets anywhere on the peninsula; and land or pick up troops and materiel at any point on the Korean coast.

Naval supremacy was critical to the successes enjoyed by the U.N. forces in Korea. Allied forces would probably have been forced off the peninsula long before the armistice if they had not enjoyed the benefits of naval supremacy, and if the communists had a similar naval advantage.

U.N. warships provided critical fire support for ground forces throughout the war. Here the light cruiser *USS Toledo* fires the 8-inch guns of its number three turret at North Korean military targets ashore.

❑ On June 25, 1950, the same day North Korea invaded its southern neighbor, President Harry S. Truman ordered the U.S. 7th Fleet, under the command of Vice Adm. Arthur Struble, into the Straits of Taiwan in order to prevent Chinese invasion of the island and contain the conflict to the waters around the Korean Peninsula.

❑ Task Force 77, a combined force of U.S., Australian, Canadian, and New Zealand warships, initiated their first shore bombardment of the war on June 29, 1950, when the light cruiser USS *Juneau* fired at communist targets on the east coast of Korea.

❑ On July 1, 1950, Truman ordered a blockade of North Korean ports in order to deny the communists access to the sea for either war or commerce.

❑ The next day, on July 2, 1950, a U.N. force that included USS *Juneau* engaged in the only naval battle of the war, destroying three of four attacking North Korean torpedo boats in the waters off the east coast town of Chumunjin.

❑ On July 3, 1950, warplanes from USS *Valley Forge* attacked North Korean airfields around Pyongyang and Chinnampo, the first of many carrier-based airstrikes against communist targets carried out during the war.

❏ By September 1950, the U.N. naval forces had eliminated North Korea's small coastal navy and achieved naval supremacy. China did not commit sea forces even after it entered the war, leaving the U.N. naval forces largely uncontested.

ASSAULT ON INCHON

❏ The famous landing at Inchon on the west coast of Korea—Gen. Douglas MacArthur's masterstroke—would not have been possible without the support of the U.N. naval forces, which transported the attacking X Corps and provided supporting gunfire before and during the assault.

❏ From September 14 to 24, the U.N. naval forces engaged in their first major ship-to-shore bombardment, in support of the amphibious assault at Inchon. Gunfire from the battleship USS *Missouri*, three cruisers, and five destroyers ravaged North Korean positions on Wolmi Island and Inchon harbor.

❏ U.S. ships deliberately drew shore fire from North Korean positions on Wolmi-do, a fortified island guarding the approaches to Inchon. Once the positions had been pinpointed by their muzzle flashes, the destroyers moved in to a mere 1,000 yards from the shore and, along with the other ships, used their big guns to blow apart the enemy positions.

❏ The next day, the allied warships provided covering fire for the 1st Marine Division as it assaulted the seawall guarding the port of Inchon.

MINESWEEPING OPERATIONS

❏ Following the example of its Soviet mentor and with no warships of its own at risk, North Korea made liberal use of naval mines in the waters around the peninsula, especially in shipping lanes and the approaches to its port cities.

❏ Such weapons—magnetic mines detonated by the presence of metal-hulled ships and contact mines that exploded when touched by a target—were capable of severely damaging or destroying ships, and they inflicted a number of allied losses.

❏ In the years after World War II, a tiny force of U.S. minesweepers were assigned the dreary duty of clearing mines from the waters around Japan. When the Korean War broke out, these minesweepers were deployed to the waters around Korea to support the U.N. naval operations.

❏ Mines began to take a toll on U.N. vessels early in the war. On September 26, 1950, USS *Brush* hit a mine in the waters off of Tanchon, suffering nine killed and three wounded. On September 30, USS *Mansfield* struck a mine, with casualties of 27 wounded and five missing.

❏ In October 1950, the X Corps amphibious landing at the North Korean port of Wonsan was delayed for a week in order to clear mines blocking the harbor. Minesweepers were only one method used to clear mines during this operation, and other measures included using scuba divers to clear mines, aircraft to spot underwater mine fields, and naval gunfire to detonate them. Most of these methods did not work very well, however, and the tedious but tried-and-true methods of the minesweeping crews proved most effective.

Losses from mines were especially high as a result, however. On October 1, 1951, the minesweeper USS *Magpie* was destroyed by a mine near the North Korean town of Chuksan, suffering 20 killed and 12 wounded. On October 12, USS *Pirate* and USS *Pledge* were both sunk by mines, suffering total casualties of 13 killed and 87 wounded. On February 2, 1951, a mine sank the minesweeper USS *Partridge*, killing 20 and wounding 12. Four months later, the U.S. Navy suffered its greatest single loss of the war when the destroyer USS *Walke* struck a mine on June 12, 1951, taking casualties of 26 killed in action and 35 wounded in action.

❏ Enemy mines inflicted the last loss of a U.S. Navy vessel during the war on August 30, 1952, when the ocean-going tug USS *Sarsi* struck a mine off the North Korean port of Hungnam and sank, suffering four killed and four wounded.

OTHER NAVAL OPERATIONS

❏ Allied naval forces supported the U.N. mission throughout the course of the war in a number of other ways, including transportation of men and materiel to Korea from the United States and Japan; deployment of helicopters to rescue pilots downed at sea or behind enemy lines; reconnaissance and patrol operations; and bombing raids against communist targets.

❏ From August to December 1950, U.N. ships bombarded communist forces along the east coast of the Korean Peninsula, providing support for South Korean troops as they fought their way into North Korea and toward the Chinese and Soviet borders.

❏ In early December 1950, the warships of Task Force 90 (Amphibious Force Far East) provided covering fire for U.N. troops retreating toward the North Korean port of Hungnam after being stopped and driven back by six Chinese field armies.

❏ From December 3 to 6, 1950, U.N. ships evacuated more than 105,000 military personnel and 100,000 civilian refugees from Hungnam and, after it was abandoned, helped to destroy the port with a devastating barrage of naval gunfire.

❏ On February 16, 1951, Task Force 95, a U.N. blockade and escort force, established a blockade of Wonsan harbor. This blockade lasted 861 days until July 27, 1953, the last day of the war, making it the longest effective siege of a port in U.S. Navy history. Songjin was another important port that was besieged by U.N. naval forces during the Korean War.

❏ Task Force 77 suffered its worst one-day casualties of the war on May 18, 1951, when six of its aircraft were shot down and four of its pilots killed in action.

❏ On April 21, 1952, 30 men were killed when a powder fire broke out on the cruiser USS *St. Paul* while it was providing gunfire support from the waters off of the North Korean town of Kojo.

❏ Carrier-based aircraft participated, along with FEAF warplanes, in a major raid against nine hydroelectric plants in North Korea on June 23, 1952.

❏ On August 29, 1952, U.N. carrier-based aircraft collaborated with FEAF in the largest single-day air attack of the war, a 1,403-plane bombing raid on the North Korean capital of Pyongyang.

❏ On September 1, 1952, the U.N. naval forces launched the biggest all-Navy air raid of the war, sending 144 planes from three aircraft carriers to bomb the oil refinery at Aoji in North Korea.

❏ On October 21, 1952, artillery fire from a communist shore battery near Wonsan struck the USS *Lewis*, killing seven.

❏ U.N. naval forces unleashed the heaviest shore bombardment of the war against Kosong on March 20, 1953.

❏ June 15, 1953, was a big day for carrier-based air attacks. USS *Princeton* set the record for most offensive sorties flown from a single carrier by launching 184 air attacks, contributing to a total of 910 sorties flown by Navy and Marine pilots, their greatest one-day combined total during the war.

❏ Total U.S. Navy casualties during the Korean War were 458 killed and 1,576 wounded.

U.S. COAST GUARD OPERATIONS

❏ Although it is a service usually associated with operations in domestic waters, the U.S. Coast Guard, like the other branches of the military, was active in the Korean War.

❏ Soon after World War II, the service's presence in Korea began when a U.S. Coast Guard advisory detachment helped to develop and train the Korean Coast Guard, a force that eventually became the Republic of Korea Navy.

❏ After the conflict in Korea began in 1950, 24 U.S. Coast Guard cutters served in the theater of war, serving tours of duty at remote outposts and taking part in a wide variety of military and humanitarian operations. These operations included serving as plane guards, rushing to help aircrews that went down at sea, and as communication support platforms. Coast Guard cutters were also ready to provide support to troop and supply ships on their way to or from Korea and to help in the event of emergencies. Cutters also served on meteorological duty at two open-ocean weather stations near Korean waters, Sugar and Victor, from which they provided U.N. ground, air, and naval forces information about weather patterns that could affect military operations.

❏ In the nearby Philippines, Coast Guard aircraft stood ready to rescue U.N. personnel in need of help, like the aircrews of reconnaissance planes shot down over the China Sea.

❏ U.S. Coast Guard Cutters (USCGCs) eligible for the Korean Service Medal were *Bering Strait, Chautauqua, Durant, Escanaba, Falgout, Finch, Forster, Gresham, Ironwood, Iroquois, Klamath, Koiner, Kukui, Lowe, Minnetonka, Newell, Planetree, Pontchartrain, Ramsden, Richey, Taney, Wachusett, Winnebago,* and *Winona.*

❏ In 1952, the Coast Guard reached a strength of 35,082 officers and enlisted men (including 1,600 reservists), nearly double its strength just five years before.

Nearly two-dozen U.S. Coast Guard vessels, including the USCGC *Richey*, shown here, supported the U.N. war effort during the conflict in Korea.

OTHER COAST GUARD ACTIVITIES

❏ Coast Guard crews also manned and operated Long Range Aids to Navigation (LORAN) stations in the Pacific, nine of which provided direct navigational support to U.N. aircraft and ships taking part in the conflict in Korea. Throughout the course of the war, a pair of Coast Guard cutters serviced these LORAN stations, one of which was based in southeastern Korea, near the port city of Pusan.

Nine Coast Guard Loran Stations (LORSTA) and two shore units were also eligible for the Korean Service Medal by virtue of their wartime activities. These were LORSTA Bataan, LORSTA Elmo Number 4 (Pusan), LORSTA Ichi Banare (Okinawa), LORSTA Iwo Jima, LORSTA Matsumae (Hokkaido), LORSTA Niigata (Honshu), LORSTA Oshima (Honshu), LORSTA Riyako Jima, LORSTA Tokyo (Honshu), the Far East Section (Tokyo), and the Merchant Marine Detachment (Japan).

❑ In the United States, Coast Guard proficiency in activities like cargo and ammunition handling, port security, and prevention of sabotage helped ensure the flow of supplies to the Korean theater of war.

U.S. NAVY SHIP DESIGNATIONS

All U.S. Navy ships have an alphanumeric designation in addition to any proper name they have been given. For example, the designation for the battleship USS Missouri *was BB63. During the Korean War, many smaller vessels had only alphanumeric designations and no proper names.*

Designations for some of the ship types used during the conflict follow. Other letters can identify various other characteristics of a particular ship or watercraft. For example, the prefix "E" indicated that it is experimental, and the prefix "T" indicated that it is assigned to the Military Sea Transportation Service.

Following are examples from the types of combatant ship in use during the Korean War. In addition, there were also Auxiliary Ships (e.g., destroyer tenders), Auxiliary Vessels (e.g., hospital ships), and Service Craft (e.g., garbage lighters).

Aircraft Carriers
Attack Aircraft Carrier: CVA
Small Aircraft Carrier: CVL
Support Aircraft Carrier: CVS

Amphibious Warfare Ships
Amphibious Force Flagship: AGC
Attack Cargo Ship: AKA
Amphibious Transport Dock: LPD
Amphibious Assault Ship: LPH
Dock Landing Ship: LSD
Tank Landing Ship: LST

Battleships
Battleship: BB

Command Ships
Tactical Command Ship: CLC

Cruisers
Heavy Cruiser: CA
Light Cruiser: CL

Destroyers
Destroyer: DD
Frigate: DL

Mine Warfare Ships
Minelayer, Destroyer: DM
Minesweeper, Coastal: MSC

Patrol Ships
Escort Vessel: DE
Motor Gunboat: PGM

Submarines
Submarine: SS

Auxiliary Vessels
Destroyer Tender: AD
Ammunition Ship: AE
Hospital Ship: AH
Cargo Ship: AKD
Light Cargo Ship: AKL
General Stores Issue Ship: AKS
Cargo Ship and Aircraft Ferry: AKV
Oiler: AO
Transport: AP
Repair Ship: AR
Submarine Tender: AS
Auxiliary Ocean Tug: ATA
Fleet Ocean Tug: ATF

TYPES OF SHIPS

U.N. forces used a wide variety of ships during the Korean War, from aircraft carriers and battleships to tiny minesweepers and tugboats.

In the following descriptions, "displacement" refers to the total weight of a vessel and her contents; "beam" refers to the overall width of a vessel; and "draft" refers to vertical distance from a vessel's keel to the waterline (i.e., the minimum depth of water it would need to operate). Speed is expressed in knots, or nautical miles, each of which is equivalent to 1.1515 statute miles.

Each type of ship was named according to certain criteria (e.g., battleships are named after states). Smaller craft might have simply an alphanumeric designation and no given name at all. In any case, a U.S. Navy ship is never named in honor of a living person.

LARGE COMBATANT VESSELS

AIRCRAFT CARRIERS are mobile bases for planes and are capable of moving them within striking distance of areas that might otherwise be inaccessible. Aircraft from allied aircraft carriers flew missions against communist forces throughout the Korean War.

❑ A typical World War II-era, *Essex*-class aircraft carrier had a displacement of 38,500 tons, a length of 888 feet, a beam of 93 feet, a draft of 30 feet, shaft horsepower of 150,000, an angled flight deck with an extreme width of 154 feet, and a complement of 1,950 men. Armament consisted of various combinations of 5-inch guns on twin and single mounts, 3-inch guns on twin mounts, and 40mm guns on quad mounts.

❑ An aircraft carrier's commanding officer, executive officer, operations officer, navigator, and air officer all had experience as naval aviators.

❑ Aircraft carriers were named for former Navy ships, major battles, and U.S. bays, islands, and sounds (e.g., *Valley Forge, Coral Sea, Block Island*).

BATTLESHIPS, second in size among combatant ships only to the largest aircraft carriers, are heavily armed and armored ships designed to operate both offensively and defensively against surface vessels. During the Korean War, their most important function was using their big guns to support amphibious assault and ground forces.

❑ USS *Missouri* (BB63), an *Iowa*-class battleship, had a displacement of 57,400 tons, a length of 888 feet, a beam of 108 feet, a draft of 37 feet, shaft horsepower of 212,000, and a maximum speed of 33 knots. It was armed with nine massive 16-inch guns and 20 5-inch guns and had a complement of more than 2,000.

❑ Battleships were named for states (e.g., *Iowa, Missouri*).

CRUISERS at the time of the Korean War were general utility ships, capable of operating alone, in groups, or as part of a battle fleet. They served as scouts, aircraft carrier guards, screens against enemy destroyers and aircraft, and leaders of destroyer flotillas and attack groups.

❑ *Baltimore*-class heavy cruisers, USS *Boston* and USS *Canberra,* had a displacement of 13,600 tons, a length of 673 feet, a beam of 71 feet, a maximum draft of 26 feet, and shaft horsepower of 120,000. They were armed with various combinations of guns, typically 8-inch, 5-inch, and 3-inch, and had a complement of more than 1,600. Light cruisers were somewhat smaller (e.g., 10,500 tons for *Cleveland*-class cruisers) and had guns of 6-inch size maximum and a complement of around 1,200.

❑ Cruisers were named for U.S. cities and towns and for capitals of U.S. possessions and territories (e.g., *Baltimore, Boston*).

DESTROYERS are multipurpose ships used in nearly every kind of naval operation and represent a good combination of speed, mobility, and offensive and defensive capabilities. Destroyers led the September 1950 attack at Inchon, bombarding sentinel Wolmi island prior to the troop assault. Frigates are a specialized type of destroyer used for antisubmarine operations.

❑ A *Gearing*-class destroyer had a displacement of 3,479 tons, a length of 390 feet, a beam of 40 feet, a draft of 19 feet, shaft horsepower of 60,000, a maximum speed of 32 knots, and a complement of 257. Typical armament included three 5-inch guns on twin mounts, three 3-inch guns on twin mounts, two 3-inch guns on single mounts, and four 40mm quad mounts.

❑ Destroyers were named for distinguished U.S. Navy, Marine, or Coast Guard personnel; secretaries and assistant secretaries of the Navy; members of Congress closely associated with naval affairs; and inventors (e.g., *Decatur, John Paul Jones, Walke*).

U.N. domination of the waters around the Korean Peninsula gave the allied forces ready access to supplies and denied the enemy the same benefit. Here *Kukui*, a U.S. Coast Guard transport vessel, loads supplies bound for shore onto landing craft

---

SMALL AND SPECIALIZED COMBATANT VESSELS

A variety of relatively small combatant vessels were used during the Korea War, minesweepers being among the most important.

❏ Minesweepers were small, shallow draft vessels used for detecting enemy naval mines, for conducting mine clearing operations, and for marking mine fields, mine dumping areas, and swept areas with special buoys. In order to reduce the chance of detonating magnetic mines, they were built with nonmagnetic wooden or stainless steel hulls. Of the many varieties of minesweeper, the two most important during the Korean War were coastal minesweepers and ocean minesweepers.

❏ A typical coastal minesweeper had a displacement of 400 tons, a length of 144 feet, a beam of 28 feet, a draft of 8.5 feet, was driven by a pair of propellers, had a maximum speed of 14 knots, and was armed with twin 20mm guns. Ocean-going minesweepers were a bit sturdier, and typically had a displacement of 735 tons, a length of 172 feet, a beam of 36 feet, a draft of 11 feet, a maximum speed of 15 knots, and were armed with a single 40mm gun.

❏ Minesweepers were named for birds and for logical and euphonious words (e.g., *Magpie, Sagacity*).

❏ Submarines were used primarily for reconnaissance, sinking enemy shipping, and combatting enemy submarines. They played only a limited role in the waters off the coasts of Korea.

❏ A typical Korean War-era submarine had a displacement of 1,525 tons, a length of about 312 feet, a maximum beam of about 27 feet, a surface draft of about 15 feet, and was driven by four 1,600 horsepower diesel engines and four 1,100 kilowatt generators on the surface and battery-driven electric motors when submerged. A typical complement consisted of seven officers and 70 enlisted men.

❏ Submarines were named for fish and other oceanic creatures (e.g., *Albacore, Seawolf, Wahoo*).

AMPHIBIOUS SHIPS

A wide variety of specialized amphibious vessels were used during World War II and the Korean War to land the thousands of men and vast quantities of equipment, ammunition, and supplies needed to secure a foothold on an enemy beachhead.

❏ Amphibious Force Flagships were used as command ships and communications centers during amphibious operations and provided accomodations and command-and-control facilities for the various commanders involved in the operation (e.g., Army, Navy, Marine Corps), as well as centralized facilities for processing and distributing operational intelligence information.

❑ Most amphibious force flagships were converted cargo vessels, but could be easily identified by the radio cage masts rising from their superstructures. In addition to crew members, such ships could quarter about 250 officers and 900 enlisted men, were equipped with about a half dozen landing craft, and could carry a small amount of cargo and a few vehicles.

❑ Tank Landing Ships (LSTs) were used for landing troops, vehicles, and other cargo directly on enemy shores, via bow doors and a ramp that led into a huge hold called a "tank deck." An LST could also be used to transport and launch a utility landing craft (LCU) or pontoon causeway section. LSTs were critical in the execution of the Inchon Landing, one of the greatest amphibious operations in history.

❑ A typical LST had a displacement of 3,200 tons (5,800 tons when fully loaded), a length of 384 feet, a beam of 55 feet, a draft of 17 feet, four diesel controlled-pitch propellers with a total horsepower of 6,000, and a complement of 120. Weapons usually consisted of three 3-inch guns.

❑ Tank Landing Ships are named for counties and parishes, with the word "county" or "parish" in the name (e.g., *Stark County, York County*).

❑ Utility Landing Craft (LCU) were open-decked, barge-like craft with a bow ramp, and could transport up to 50 tons of vehicles, equipment, and cargo from ship-to-shore. They could also be used for seaborne transportation under suitable conditions, but were generally transported to the site of an amphibious assault in the well of a dock landing ship (LSD).

❑ LCUs typically had a displacement of 395 tons, a length of 119 feet, a beam of 35 feet, a maximum draft of 6 feet, a speed of 10 knots, and a complement of 14. Armaments were limited to a few machineguns.

❑ Dock Landing Craft (LSD) were the largest type of landing vessels, and were actually self-propelled floating drydocks that could transport and launch smaller amphibious vessels and vehicles. Such ships could also render limited docking and repair services to small ships.

❑ A *Thomaston*-class LSD had a displacement of 6,880 tons (12,150 tons when fully loaded), a length of 510 feet, a beam of 84 feet, a maximum draft of 19 feet, a pair of steam turbine engines with shaft horsepower of 23,000, and a complement of 280. Equipment and armaments included a pair of 50-ton cranes and eight twin mounts for either 3-inch guns or .50 caliber machineguns.

AUXILIARY VESSELS

While operating far from their home ports, as in the waters around the Korean Peninsula, ships constantly needed to be supplied with food, fuel, munitions, men, mail, repair parts, and a great many other things. Such goods were delivered to the warships by a wide variety of auxiliary vessels, including replenishment vessels (e.g., ammunition ships, some cargo ships, oilers), designed to transfer men and materiel from themselves to other ships while underway. Some of the most important auxiliary vessels are described here.

❏ Cargo ships were used to carry vehicles, equipment, munitions, and limited numbers of troops. Many were designed to perform special functions, such as general stores issue ships, used to replenish ships at sea; light cargo ships, which carried small quantities of general cargo, used to transport materiel from port-to-port; and aircraft ferries, often converted older aircraft carriers, used to transport aircraft.

❏ Cargo ships were named for astronomical bodies (e.g., *Antares, Mirfak, Betelgeuse*).

❏ Transports were used for rapid transportation of troops and limited quantities of cargo from port-to-port, and could also be used to evacuate casualties, troops, and refugees, as they were from the North Korean port of Hungnam in December 1950, and to provide medical care to wounded personnel. Because they were designed for use with port facilities, they did not carry large numbers of landing craft, as did amphibious warfare ships like LSTs.

❏ A typical transport had a displacement of 17,980 tons, a length of 623 feet, a beam of 76 feet, a maximum draft of 26 feet, and a maximum speed of 20 knots. It could carry more than 3,000 men under normal conditions.

❏ Transports were named in honor of commandants and other officers of the U.S. Marine Corps, U.S. counties, sites of historical interest, signers of the Declaration of Independence, famous women, and men of foreign birth who fought for American independence (e.g., *Cambria, Fremont, Rockbridge*).

❏ Tenders, including destroyer and submarines tenders, provided maintenance and supply services for the combatant vessels to which they were assigned. Such ships usually had chaplains aboard, could provide some medical and dental services, and sometimes had recreational facilities, especially in the case of submarine tenders.

❑ Destroyer tenders were named for areas of the United States (e.g., *Dixies, Everglades, Yellowstone*).

❑ Oceangoing tugs were ships used for hauling, towing, fire-fighting, and salvage operations and included a number of different varieties. Such vessels were extremely versatile, and could be put to many nonconventional uses, including patrolling, rescue operations, laying smokescreens, pulling stranded landing craft off of beaches, or towing damaged warships back to their home ports.

❑ Oceangoing tugs were named for American Indian tribes (e.g., *Apache, Navajo, Paiute*).

❑ Repair ships were floating workshops with skilled mechanics, electricians, and other technicians aboard that performed repair and maintenance services that were beyond the capabilities of damaged vessels or their crews. Tasks such ships could perform included underwater cutting and welding, engine and hull repairs, and machine and electrical work. Facilities aboard such ships included foundries, forges, and carpentry shops, instrument shops, machinery shops, and boat and boat-engine repair shops.

❑ Several specialized varieties of such ships existed, including heavy-hull repair ships, battle-damage repair ships, internal combustion engine repair ships, landing craft repair ships, and aircraft repair ships. Some repair ships were built from converted LSTs.

❑ A typical repair ship had a length of about 530 feet, a beam of about 73 feet, a maximum speed of about 19 knots, a complement of up to 1,100 personnel, and armament of four 5-inch guns in a main battery and four sets of twin 40mm antiaircraft guns.

❑ Repair ships were named for mythological characters (e.g., *Ajax, Vulcan*).

❑ Ammunition ships operated with groups of other replenishment vessels to deliver munitions to ships at sea. They were given names suggestive of fire or explosions (e.g., *Nitro, Mauna Kea*).

❑ Oilers carried black oil, gasoline, and other petroleum products and operated with groups of replenishment vessels to deliver their cargo to ships at sea. Oilers were named for rivers with American Indian names (e.g., *Brazos, Platte, Rapidan*).

❑ Hospital ships were used for transporting casualties and for providing temporary medical care to them en route to hospital facilities ashore. Care of the wounded fell to a complement of doctors, nurses, orderlies, and chaplains appropriate to the size of the vessel, which was treated in all other respects like a normal navy ship, albeit one with an enlarged sick bay; sailing, maintenance, and other functions of the ship itself were handled by line officers and crew.

❑ Hospital vessels were painted white and clearly marked with numerous crosses, and, under the provisions of the Geneva Convention, were supposed to be immune from attack. They were not immune to accidents, however. On August 25, 1950, USS *Benevolence*, recommissioned for service after the Korean War began, collided with the SS *Mary Luckenbach* while on a trial run in the waters near San Francisco. It sank with a loss of 18 lives.

❑ Hospital ships were given names descriptive of their caregiving mission (e.g., *Consolation, Haven, Repose*).

IV

GEOGRAPHY AND BATTLEFIELDS

"Unless you know the mountains and forests, the defiles and impasses, and the lay of the marshes and swamps, you cannot maneuver with an armed force."

—Sun Tzu, *The Art of War*

Korea's rough, mountainous terrain and its climatic extremes played an important role in how and where the Korean War was fought, and the names of its hills, rivers, reservoirs, and villages will forever be associated with the hundreds of battles fought during the 37 months of the conflict.

When World War II ended, the allied powers occupied the Korean Peninsula, a former colony of the Japanese Empire. Soviet forces occupied the north and U.S. forces occupied the south, their zones of control separated by the 38th parallel of northern latitude.

Since that time, the area south of the 38th parallel has been known as South Korea and, since 1948, it has been known officially as the Republic of Korea. Similarly, since 1945 the area north of the 38th parallel has been known as North Korea, and officially since 1948 as the Democratic People's Republic of Korea.

With the conclusion of the armistice in 1953, the official border between the countries was no longer the 38th parallel, but rather the 150-mile long demilitarized zone (DMZ) that was based upon the final line of contact when the ceasefire was declared.

TERRAIN

❑ Korea is a peninsula about 575 miles in length from north to south and an average of about 150 miles across from east to west. To the north are China and, along a very narrow border, Russia; to the east and south are the Sea of Japan and the Korean Straits and, beyond these waters, Japan itself; to the west is the Yellow Sea.

❑ Total land area of the Korean Peninsula, including islands, is about 85,270 square miles. About 45 percent of this land, some 38,030 square miles, constitutes the territory of South Korea, while the remaining 55 percent, 47,240 square miles, constitutes the territory of North Korea.

❑ Mountains, hills, and highlands constitute most of the peninsula's land area, some 70 percent of South Korea and 80 percent of North Korea. From south to north, the mountainous country grows progressively higher and more rugged.

❑ In the south, the principal ranges are the Taebak Mountains, the Sobaek Mountains, and the Chirri Massif. The highest mountain in South Korea is Mount Halla, a 5,347-foot volcanic cone on Cheju Island. All of the peninsula's highest peaks are in North Korea, including 7,524-foot Mount Paektu. Major plateaus in North Korea are the Chaeryong Plain and the Pyongyang Peneplain, around the capital city.

❑ Principal rivers in the south are the Naktong, the Han, and the Kum. Principal rivers in the north are the Taedong, the Yalu, and the Tumen. Many rivers played a role in the war's various battles and helped determine where defensive lines were established during the conflict.

CLIMATE

❑ Extending from 34 to 43 degrees north latitude, Korea is subject to climatic extremes that made living, moving, and fighting difficult for the troops on the ground, and equipping and managing those troops a logistical nightmare for the leadership on each side. Korea's climate is dominated by very hot, humid (and usually wet) summers, and extremely cold, but fairly dry, winters.

❑ Monsoon rains and flooding characterize the summers, which tend toward either heavy rains or high temperatures and extreme humidity.

Two-thirds of the annual precipitation of about 40 inches a year falls from June through September, and an average of five typhoons rip across the Korean Peninsula every year. Droughts parch the peninsula approximately every eight years, however, and the summer of 1950—the first season of the war—was an aberration in that it was both very hot and very dry.

❑ Despite the summer heat, the Korean War is more often associated with cold winters. Korea's freezing winters are exacerbated by arctic winds sweeping down from the steppes of Siberia.

GEOGRAPHICAL SITES

Below are a number of locations and geographical features that were significant during the Korea War. Islands are signified by the suffix "-do" after the name of the island. Hills are identified in most case by both their numerical designations and the name by which U.N. troops came to know them.

❑ *Armistice Line*: see Demilitarized Zone.

❑ *Bloody Ridge*: A stretch of high ground formed by Hills 773, 940, and 983 that was part of what was called the Punchbowl. This area was the scene of heavy combat in late summer 1951, when elements of the U.S. 7th Infantry Division, including South Korean forces, attacked the ridge to keep the troops on either side from becoming complacent and to demonstrate U.N. resolve to the negotiators at Panmunjom.

❑ *Capitol Building* (Republic of Korea): A Western classical style structure completed by the Japanese in 1926 and used as the seat of their colonial government in Korea until 1945. It became a symbol of the Republic of Korea in 1948 when President Syngman Rhee stood upon its steps to announce the establishment of the new nation. Many South Koreans had ambivalent feelings about the structure, however, among them Rhee, who refused to use it. From 1961 until it was torn down in 1996, it served successively as government offices and a national museum.

❑ *Cease-fire Line*: See Demilitarized Zone.

❑ *Changjin Reservoir*: Korean name for what is more often called the Chosin Reservoir.

❏   *Cheju-do*: Island off the south coast of Korea that was the site of a major communist uprising in 1948. Its climate is significantly warmer and milder than the rest of South Korea.

❏   *Chinnampo*: Port city at the mouth of the Taedong River on the west coast of North Korea. It is about 30 miles southwest of the capital Pyongyang and serves as its port (similar to the relationship between Inchon and Seoul). In December 1950, U.S., Canadian, and Australian naval forces used Chinnampo to evacuate U.N. troops retreating before the Chinese advance into Korea, and inflicted major damage to enemy shore positions during the operation. Chinnampo is known today as Nampo.

❏   *Chipyong-ni*: Village in South Korea near the middle of the peninsula that U.N. troops defended against overwhelming numbers during the Chinese offensive in mid-February 1951. After three days of heavy fighting, the completely surrounded U.N. force both withstood and broke the momentum of the communist assault.

This aerial view of the Chosin Reservoir, taken just before U.S. forces in North Korea were overwhelmed and forced to retreat by the Chinese People's Volunteers Army, hints at the rugged and unforgiving nature of the terrain.

❏ *Chosin Reservoir*: Chosin was the name of this North Korean reservoir as it appeared on the Japanese maps drafted during the imperial occupation of Korea that the U.N. forces were using. Its Korean name was Changjin. In November 1950, elements of U.S. X Corps, particularly the U.S. 1st Marine Division, were deployed along both sides of the reservoir and preparing to move north to the Yalu River when Chinese communist forces launched a major offensive, breaking the U.N. drive and forcing a retreat.

❏ *Demilitarized Zone (DMZ)*: A strip of land about 2.5 miles wide stretching entirely across the Korean Peninsula and separating the Republic of Korea from the Democratic People's Republic of Korea. This zone is based on the line of contact between the opposing forces that existed when the ceasefire was declared in July 1953, and stretches from a point south of the 38th parallel on the west coast to a point north of it on the east coast.

❏ *Farm Line*: The line in South Korea behind which farming could again be undertaken after the July 1953 ceasefire.

❏ *Formosa*: Another name by which the island of Taiwan was known.

❏ *Han River*: A 278-mile-long river flowing north to south through Seoul and forming a barrier on its west.

❏ *Hill 303*: Hill near Waegwan, in South Korea. During the defense of the Pusan Perimeter in summer 1950, troopers of the 5th Cavalry Regiment counterattacked onto the hill and discovered 26 American mortarmen who had been bound and executed by North Korean soldiers.

❏ *Hill 314*: Steep, mile-long hill overlooking the town of Taegu that was considered to be the key to its defense. On September 12, 1950, the 3rd Battalion of the 7th Cavalry Regiment (1st Cavalry Division) drove enemy forces off of this ridge after a determined assault.

❏ *Huichon*: Village in North Korea, in the rugged mountains east of Kunu-ri.

❏ *Hungnam*: North Korean port on the east coast of the peninsula that was the site of a major U.N. evacuation in late December 1950. By December 24, some 105,000 U.N. personnel and nearly 100,000 North Korean refugees had embarked on warships, transports, and chartered civilian vessels and were evacuated from the city, which was subsequently destroyed by naval gunfire and demolitions.

❏ *Imjin River*: A river flowing north-south that crosses the 38th parallel just north of Seoul.

❑ *Inchon*: Port city in South Korea, 30 miles west of Seoul. Site of a massive U.N. amphibious landing on September 15, 1950.

❑ *Iron Triangle*: A triangular area in the middle of the Korean Peninsula just north of the 38th parallel, its three corners consisting of Pyongyang (not the capital city) in the north, Kumhwa in the east, and Chorwon in the west. This area gained its name from the fact that it was heavily defended by communist forces and was the site of heavy fighting from Spring 1951 through the end of the war. When the ceasefire was declared in 1951, the line of contact, and as a result the DMZ, ran through this area.

❑ *Itazuke Airbase*: Airbase in Japan from which Task Force Smith was deployed to Korea.

❑ *Kaesong*: City just south of the 38th parallel, about 35 miles northwest of Seoul. A South Korean city from 1945 to 1950, it was the first city captured by North Korea when its forces invaded in June 1950. Kaesong was north of the line of contact when the armistice was signed in 1953 and thus remained in North Korea.

In the summer 1951, the communists proposed and the United Nations accepted Kaesong as the site for armistice negotiations, despite the fact that it was in the communist zone of control, and talks began July 8. Although the negotiation site was designated neutral ground, the communists used their control of the area to intimidate the U.N. negotiators and control access of Western journalists. Problems continued even after a neutral zone was established around the site, and the U.N.'s chief negotiator, Vice Adm. C. Turner Joy, broke off talks on August 23.

Talks were resumed in October 1951 in Panmunjom. For the balance of the war, however, the communist negotiators were headquartered in Kaesong. As a result, U.N. forces continued to treat it as a neutral city and, in December 1952, decided against bombing Kaesong when it was suspected that the communists were using it as a staging area for an attack.

❑ *Kansas Line*: U.N. defensive line north of the 38th parallel that was established in April 1951 after U.N. forces counterattacked against the Chinese forces. This line ran northeastward from the junction of the Han and Imjin Rivers in the west to Yang-yang in the east.

❑ *Kapyong*: A small town about 30 miles northeast of Seoul. In April 1951, during the fifth Chinese offensive, Kapyong was the site of combat between attacking Chinese troops and the 27th British Commonwealth Brigade. After heavy fighting, British, Australian, Canadian, and New Zealand troops succeeded in breaking the attack of an entire Chinese division before being forced to withdraw.

Hundreds of Korean cities, towns, and villages—especially those in the middle of the peninsula—were devasted by the violence of the Korean War.

❑ *Kum River*: A major 216-mile-long river in South Korea.

❑ *Kunu-ri*: A village in North Korea at the junction of the north-south road from Sunchon and an east-west road that connected it with Huichon, to the east. Shown as "Kunmori" on some maps.

❑ *Kwangfu*: Village in South Korea, southwest of Seoul. Location of the ROK 5th Division when North Korea invaded.

❑ *Kynonju*: Village in southeastern Korea, used by the North Koreans as a route of attack against the Pusan Perimeter.

❑ *Manchuria*: Mountainous, industrialized region of China bordering North Korea and separated from it by the Yalu River. Historically important as the principal land route into and out of Korea, it served as the staging area for Chinese troops before their entry into the Korean War and throughout the conflict as a safe haven for communist air bases. Known to the Chinese as *dongbei*, or "eastnorth," it consists of three provinces: Heilongjiang, Jilin, and Liaoning.

Because many ethnic Koreans lived throughout the region, Manchuria served as a base of anti-Japanese Korean guerrilla activity from 1910 until the end of World War II. In 1932, Japan moved into Manchuria from northern Korea and established a puppet state, known as Manzhouguo, under the last emperor of China. This puppet state collapsed in the final weeks of World War II, when it was captured by troops from the Soviet Union, who pillaged it of industrial equipment before withdrawing.

Still used in the West as a name for the region, "Manchuria" is no longer used as an official designation by the People's Republic of China.

❏ *MIG Alley*: Area in northwestern Korea where communist MiG-15s, flying out of their bases in Manchuria intercepted U.N. bombers´on their way to bomb the Yalu River bridges. Scene of heavy air-to-air combat, the skies over MiG Alley were the only place in Korea where the U.N. did not enjoy unqualified air superiority.

❏ *Miryang*: Village in southeastern Korea that was used as an attack route against the Pusan Perimeter by the North Korean army.

❏ *Naktong Bulge*: A bulge on the western side of the Pusan Perimeter, caused by a North Korean assault across the Naktong River in August 1950 and again, briefly, in September 1950. In both cases, 8th U.S. Army forces were able to contain the communist attack and, after bloody combat, reduce the salient and drive the North Koreans back across the river.

❏ *Naktong River*: This 281-mile-long river, the longest in South Korea, originates in the Taebak Mountains and flows south, entering the sea in a delta west of Pusan. Along with its tributaries, the Naktong comprises the primary river system of southeastern Korea and the second largest river system in the Republic of Korea.

In summer 1950, the Naktong formed much of the western edge of the Pusan Perimeter. In August and September 1950, North Korean troops attacked across the Naktong in an attempt to penetrate the perimeter. U.N. and communist forces engaged in heavy fighting along the river until the communist forces were too depleted to continue. After U.N. forces landed at Inchon on September 8, U.N. forces broke out of the Pusan Perimeter and crossed the Naktong against the North Korean forces.

❏ *No Name Line*: A defensive line established by the U.N. forces in April 1951, after they were forced from the Kansas Line during the Fifth Chinese Phase Offensive.

❏ *North Korean People's Republic*: Official name for communist North Korea.

❑ *Old Baldy (Hill 266)*: A hill west of Chorwon that was a scene of heavy fighting from summer 1952 until spring 1953. In June 1952, Old Baldy was selected as one of several outposts for the U.S. 45th Infantry Division. After heavy fighting, the outpost was established, but was subsequently overrun by both sides a number of times over the ensuing months.

❑ *Ongjin Peninsula*: This small peninsula on the west coast of Korea, south of the 38th parallel, was originally part of South Korea but was completely cut off from it by land and could only be reached by sea or air. It was the scene of cross-border fighting from 1948 onward, and was probably the first part of South Korea invaded by North Korean forces in June 1950. The communists captured it almost immediately (June 26, 1950), and today the peninsula is part of North Korea. According to the official communist history, the Korean War began when South Korean forces attacked across the 38th parallel from the Ongjin Peninsula, prompting North Korean forces to counterattack into the Republic of Korea.

❑ *Osan*: Village in South Korea that was the site of the first battle between U.N. and North Korean ground forces. On July 5, 1950, the 406-man Task Force Smith was routed by a much larger force of North Korean infantry and tanks. After the mid-September 1950 landing at Inchon and breakout from Pusan, elements U.S. X Corps moving south and 8th U.S. Army moving north met, ironically, at Osan, the site of America's first military defeat on the peninsula.

❑ *Panmunjom*: Village near the middle of the Korean Peninsula on the line of contact that was the site of armistice negotiations from October 25, 1951, to July 27, 1953. A neutral zone was established around Panmunjom to make it accessible to both the U.N. and communist parties. It is in the center of the DMZ that was established by the ceasefire.

❑ *Pork Chop Hill (Hill 234)*: This hill changed hands several times during the war and was the scene of especially heavy fighting during the last four months of the war. Even as the armistice negotiations were nearing their conclusion at Panmunjom, U.N. and Chinese forces drove each other off the hill repeatedly in what has often been characterized as a struggle by each side to demonstrate their moral resolve.

❑ *Punchbowl*: A circular complex of hills in the middle of the Korean Peninsula near the line of contact of the last two years of the war. From 1951 onward, it was a site of heavy combat, including the Battle of Bloody Ridge and the Battle of Heartbreak Ridge.

❑ *Pusan*: This city is located on the southeast coast of the Korean peninsula. In August 1950, U.N. forces were driven south and lost all of the peninsula except for a narrow perimeter around Pusan. A major seaport, troops and material arrived at Pusan throughout the war. In September 1950, it was used as a staging area for the 8th U.S. Army's counterattack against the NKPA.

❏ *Pusan Perimeter:* A roughly rectangular defensive line established in late July 1950 by U.N. forces around the port of Pusan, in the southeast corner of the peninsula. Its northern boundary ran about 50 miles from Sanju on the Naktong River, east to Yongdok on the Sea of Japan. Most of its western boundary was formed by the Naktong River itself, running about 80 miles from Sanju south to the Korean Strait at Chindong.

For a month, the communists had driven the U.N. forces steadily southward, and the perimeter was a final attempt by the 8th U.S. Army to dig in and keep from being driven out of Korea or destroyed. U.N. forces held the perimeter through the heaviest combat of the war, until mid-September 1950, when U.S. X Corps landed at Inchon. 8th Army forces then broke out of the perimeter and headed north.

❏ *Pyongyang:* Capital of North Korea. Captured by the U.N. forces in October 1950, but recaptured by the communists just a month later, when the Chinese and North Korean forces counterattacked and drove the allies southward once again.

❏ *Republic of Korea:* Official name for South Korea.

❏ *Seoul:* Capital of South Korea. It was captured four times by the opposing sides during the Korea War, first by the North Korean forces, just a few days after the war began.

❏ *Sobaek Mountains:* An extension of the larger Taebak Mountains and one of South Korea's three mountain ranges.

❏ *Sunchon:* Village north of Pyongyang that, along with Suwon, was the site of an allied airborne operation in October 1950.

❏ *Suwon:* Village north of Pyongyang that U.N. airborne forces jumped into in October 1950.

❏ *Taebak Mountains:* Foremost of South Korea's three mountain ranges, running north to south along the east coast near the middle of the peninsula. This range separated the 8th U.S. Army and the U.S. X Corps during the U.N. advance into North Korea in the fall of 1950.

❏ *Taiwan:* Island off the southern coast of mainland China that became the seat of the ousted Chinese Nationalist (Kuomintang) government in 1949, the last year of the Chinese Civil War.

❏ *38th parallel*: Line of latitude that divides the Korean Peninsula roughly in half and that served as the border between North Korea and South Korea until June 25, 1950, when forces from the north crossed it and invaded the south. From 1945 to 1948, the 38th degree of north latitude as it bisects the Korean Peninsula (the "38th parallel") served as an arbitrary line of demarcation between North and South Korea, and from 1948 to 1950 as the border between the Democratic People's Republic of Korea (north) and the Republic of Korea (south).

❏ *Tokyo*: Capital of U.S. occupied Japan and location of the U.N. Command during the Korean War.

❏ *Tumen River*: River in North Korea that formed that country's short northern border with the Soviet Union.

❏ *Wake Island*: U.S.-held Pacific island, about one-third of the way between Korea and the continental United States, that was the site of an October 5,

Two soldiers of the 7th Infantry Division, near Hyesanjin on November 21, 1950, gaze across the Yalu River toward the mountains of Manchuria. A temple and bridge set afire by air forces still burn in the valley below.

1950, conference between President Harry S. Truman and Commander--in-Chief of the U.N. Troops, Gen. Douglas MacArthur.

❏ *Wolmi-do*: Island guarding the approaches to Inchon harbor. Held by the North Korean army in early September 1950, capture of this island was considered crucial to the success of the Inchon landing. It was successively bombarded by U.N. warships and aircraft, and then assaulted by a force of marines on September 15.

❏ *Wonsan*: North Korean port on the east coast of the peninsula. Site of a major but uncontested amphibious landing by U.S. X Corps in November 1950, and of a forced U.N. amphibious withdrawal in December 1950 (much smaller, however, than the withdrawal at Hungnam).

❏ *Yalu River*: Major river that formed most of North Korea's northern frontier and its border with the Chinese region of Manchuria.

❏ *Yellow Sea*: Major body of water to the west of the Korean Peninsula.

❏ *Zone of the Interior (ZI)*: Term used during the war in official military documents to refer to the continental United States.

V

U.S. FORCES

"The soldiers insensibly forgot the virtues of their profession, and contracted only the vices of civil life. .... They were either degraded by the industry of mechanic trades, or enervated by the luxury of baths and theatres. They soon became careless of their martial exercises, curious in their diet and apparel; and while they inspired terror to the subjects of the empire, they trembled at the hostile approach of the Barbarians."

—Edward Gibbon, *The History of the Decline and Fall of the Roman Empire, Chapter XVII*

Most of the soldiers who came to Korea to fight under the banner of the United Nations were American. Indeed, U.S. forces, second in numbers only to those of the Republic of Korea during the conflict, were about 10 times larger than all 16 of the other U.N. contingents combined.

U.S. ARMY ORGANIZATION

❏ In the years after 1945, the American military leadership strove to reform and restructure the Army based upon its World War II experiences. Even as the Army was being restructured to meet the needs of modern warfare, however, budgetary cutbacks were reducing the sizes of all branches of the military and making many of the improvements moot.

❑ In a reversal of World War II doctrine, military planners determined that "the medium tank is the best antitank weapon." As a result, infantry units were not widely equipped with other antitank weapons, and each infantry division was instead authorized an armored battalion. When the Korean War broke out in 1950, however, each of the four U.S. infantry divisions stationed in Japan had only a single tank company attached to it.

❑ One ostensible improvement to U.S. infantry units, from platoons right up to divisions, was the authorization for organic weapons that had previously been attached from other units. An example of this is the inclusion of an armored battalion with each infantry division, rather than the attachment of tanks from another unit; another is the inclusion of a weapons squad in each infantry platoon, rather than having just a weapons platoon to support all the platoons in a company.

Practically, however, these improvements often proved to be double-edged swords. For example, tanks were reduced to the role of antitank weapons and became tied to infantry formations, rather than being able to manuever freely and exploit enemy vulnerabilities. In addition, infantry platoons, which now had their own light machine guns and bazookas, consequently had fewer riflemen.

❑ In 1950, an infantry platoon consisted of three nine-man rifle squads and one weapons squad, armed with a bazooka and a light machinegun. Such reorganized platoons were able to fire and maneuver with greater independence than World War II platoons (which consisted of three 12-man squads and lacked a weapons squad). Once they suffered casualties, however, the smaller, nine-man squads lacked staying power.

U.N. Forces in Korea

On July 7, 1950, the United Nations passed a resolution calling for all U.N. forces in Korea to be unified under the leadership of the United States. President Harry S. Truman subsequently appointed Gen. Douglas MacArthur, America's senior military commander in the theater, as Commander in Chief of the United Nations Command, whose headquarters were established in Tokyo.

❑ With a few notable exceptions, ground forces in Korea came under the direct operational control of 8th U.S. Army, air forces under the Far East Air

Force (see Chapter II, *War in the Air*) and naval forces under the U.N.C. Naval Command Far East Blockade and Escort Force (see Chapter III, *War at Sea*).

❑ U.N. ground forces were grouped into three large U.S. Army corps, I Corps, IX Corps, and X Corps, along with two ROK Army corps. Each of these corps was further divided into U.S., ROK, and other allied divisions and regimental combat teams.

❑ U.S. ground forces included the 1st Cavalry Division, the 2nd, 3rd, 7th, 24th, 25th, 40th, and 45th Infantry Divisions, and the 1st Marine Division, as well as the 5th Regimental Combat team and the 187th Airborne Regimental Combat team.

❑ South Korean and allied ground forces from 15 other U.N. nations are discussed in the Chapter VI, *South Korean Miliary Forces*, and Chapter VII, *Allied Forces*.

❑ Not all of the allied corps, divisions, and other units were active at the same time (e.g., the 40th and 45th Infantry Divisions did not arrive in Korea until 1952). In the text below, unit organization is described under the I, IX, and X Corps headings, while the experiences of the subordinate divisions and regimental combat teams during the Korean War are described under their individual headings.

8TH U.S. ARMY

On June 10, 1944, the 8th U.S. Army (EUSA) was officially activated in the United States and sent to the Pacific Theater of World War II, where it participated in more than 60 island hopping assaults against the Japanese.

❑ When World War II ended, the 8th U.S. Army and the 6th U.S. Army were assigned to occupation duties in Japan. They landed peacefully in northern Japan on August 30, 1945, and by January 1, 1946, were established throughout the country.

❏ EUSA's occupational duties were interesting and varied compared with its wartime responsibilities. They included overseeing government operations; disarming Japanese military forces; destroying Japan's ability to make war; trying war criminals; guiding the nation toward peaceful pursuits and democracy; encouraging economic rehabilitation; education; land reform; guarding military installations; and protecting supply routes.

❏ Within days of the June 25, 1950 invasion of South Korea, it was evident that U.S. naval and air support were not adequate to prevent total conquest of the country. An understrength, lightly armed group of just over 400 infantry and artillerymen from EUSA's 24th Infantry Division was sent to Korea.

❏ Task Force Smith arrived in Korea on June 30 and established its headquarters at Taejon. On July 5, it fought the first U.S. ground engagement in Korea at Osan, and was badly beaten and driven back by the heavily armed North Korean forces.

❏ On July 6, EUSA's 25th Infantry Division was sent to Pusan and 8th U.S. Army commander Lt. Gen. Walton H. Walker took charge of U.S. forces in Korea. EUSA's temporary advance headquarters were established at Taegu the next day and a week later the 8th Army became operational in Korea.

❏ North Korean forces continued to drive steadily southward, driving U.S. and ROK forces before them. Soldiers of the 24th Infantry Division fought desperately to slow the NKPA advance, and finally relinquished Taejon on July 21 after desperate house-to-house fighting.

❏ 24th Infantry Division commander Maj. Gen. William F. Dean disappeared during the battle for Taejon and his forces were spread out as far south as Taegu. Despite this defeat, however, the unit bought 8th U.S. Army the time it needed to strengthen its shrinking front with the newly arrived 25th Infantry Division and 1st Cavalry Division.

❏ EUSA took charge of the remnants of the shattered ROK army and fell back into the southeast corner of Korea, establishing a defensive perimeter centered on the coastal city of Pusan. "The 8th Army would stay in Korea until the invader was expelled from the territory of the Republic of Korea," claimed Gen. Walker, outlining the U.S. resolution to hold Pusan rather than use it as a venue for abandoning the peninsula. EUSA desperately held the Pusan Perimeter, growing stronger every day as men and materiel arrived at the port.

❏ On September 16, EUSA launched a general attack across the Pusan Perimeter, prompted by the X Corps' landing at Inchon the day before. For five days, 8th U.S. Army battled fierce North Korean resistance, while U.N. air forces pounded the NKPA communication and supply lines.

❑ On September 21, the North Korean defense collapsed and 8th U.S. Army forces drove northward. With their lines of retreat cut by X Corps forces moving inland from Inchon toward Seoul, the North Korean retreat degenerated into a rout in the face of 8th Army's advance, and only shattered remnants of the previously formidable army were able to make it back to North Korea.

❑ A new phase of the war began on October 1, when 8th U.S. Army's 1st Cavalry Division drove across the 38th parallel into North Korea, following ROK forces that had crossed the line several days before.

❑ 8th U.S. Army moved northward along the west side of the Taebak mountain range, while X Corps, under the operational command of Gen. MacArthur through his protege Gen. Edward M. Almond, moved northward on the east side of Korea's dividing range of mountains, both commands rolling up the rapidly disintegrating North Korean resistance.

❑ American and South Korean units—the U.S. 1st Cavalry Division and the ROK 1st Infantry Division—raced each other toward the North Korean capital of Pyongyang. On October 19, 1950, the South Koreans won the race, taking the enemy capital and reaching the banks of the Yalu River just seven days later. U.S. 7th Infantry Division forces reached the Yalu a few days later.

❑ After the fall of Pyongyang, U.N. forces paused to regroup and improve their logistical situation. On November 24, they resumed operations geared toward gaining control of all North Korea.

❑ "A brand new war" started on November 25, according to MacArthur, when massive numbers of fresh, disciplined, well-equipped Chinese communist troops attacked across the Yalu and drove back the overextended U.N. forces.

❑ 8th U.S. Army soldiers were driven steadily backward, unable to establish a lasting defensive line, in what became the longest retreat in U.S. military history.

❑ More misfortune struck the 8th U.S. Army on December 23, when Gen. Walker, its commander, was killed in a jeep accident. Three days later, Lt. Gen. Matthew B. Ridgway became commander of EUSA and assumed control of U.N. ground forces in Korea.

❑ Under Ridgway's leadership, U.N. forces were able to establish a defensive line just south of Seoul and begin planning a counterattack. By

February 1951, U.N. forces had once again driven the communists out of South Korea.

❑ On April 11, Ridgway replaced MacArthur as commander-in-chief of the U.N. Command (and as supreme commander, U.S. Army Pacific, and commander-in-chief, Far East). Lt. Gen. James A. Van Fleet assumed command of the 8th U.S. Army.

❑ By May 1951, the line of contact had solidified between the U.N. and communist forces. This line roughly corresponded to the demilitarized zone established in the armistice discussions, from less than 30 miles north of Seoul in the west to just north of the 38th parallel in the east.

❑ For the next two years, a static state of warfare between entrenched armies ensued, punctuated by skirmishes between heavily armed patrols and bloody battles over hilltops and other strategic, and sometimes arbitrary, pieces of terrain.

U.S. I, IX, AND X CORPS

Each of the U.S. Corps in Korea (I, IX and X) was a major operational command incorporating several combat divisions and able to function both on its own or in concert with one or both of the other two corps.

I CORPS

During the occupation of Japan, I Corps was headquartered at Kyoto and composed of the 24th Infantry Division, 25th Infantry Division, and various support units. It was deactivated on March 28, 1950, just three months before the outbreak of the Korean War.

❑ On August 2, 1950, I Corps was reactivated at Fort Bragg, North Carolina, with elements from the former V Corps headquarters. It deployed to Korea on September 6, 1950, and became operational a week later, when it assumed command of the 1st Cavalry Division, the 24th Infantry Division, the 1st ROK Infantry Division, the 27th British Brigade, and various supporting units.

❏ In late 1950, after the Chinese communist forces entered the war and drove the U.N. forces back into South Korea, I Corps was reorganized. In this reorganization, I Corps relinquished command of the 1st Cavalry Division, the 24th Infantry Division, and the 27th British Brigade; retained command of the 1st ROK Infantry Division; and assumed command of the 3rd Infantry Division and the 25th Infantry Division.

❏ In April 1951, I Corps lost the 1st ROK Infantry Division when it was assigned to a newly-created ROK Army corps, but regained command of the 1st Cavalry Division as a replacement.

❏ In December 1951, the 1st Cavalry Division was transferred to Japan and I Corps assumed command of the 45th Infantry Division, a unit of the Oklahoma National Guard.

❏ In March 1952, I Corps lost command over the 25th Infantry Division and gained command of the 1st British Commonwealth Division, the ROK 1st infantry Division, the ROK 8th Infantry Division, and the ROK 9th Infantry Division.

❏ In January 1953, I Corps was reorganized for the last time. It gave up command of the 3rd Infantry Division, the 24th Infantry Division, the 45th Infantry Division, the 1st British Commonwealth Division, the ROK 8th Infantry Division, and the ROK 9th Infantry Division, and gained control of the 2nd Infantry Division, the 7th Infantry Division, the 25th Infantry Division, and the 1st Marine Division.

❏ I Corps remained in Korea for nearly two decades after the July 1953 armistice, until 1971.

IX CORPS

Stationed at Sendai during the occupation of Japan, IX Corps was composed of the 1st Cavalry Division and the 7th Infantry Division. It was deactivated on March 18, 1950, about the same time as I Corps, as part of the downsizing of the occupation forces. Like I Corps, IX Corps also experienced significant organizational upheaval in Korea.

❏ IX Corps was reactivated on August 10, 1950, at Fort Sheridan, Illinois, using personnel from the 5th Army Headquarters. It deployed to Korea on September 22, 1950, and became operational the next day, when it took command of the 2nd Infantry Division and the 25th Infantry Division.

❏ In late 1950, after China entered the war, the 2nd Infantry Division and the 25th Infantry Division suffered such heavy losses in men and material that they became combat ineffective, and both were transferred from I Corps to the 8th U.S. Army reserve. As replacements, IX Corps assumed command of the 1st Cavalry Division, the 24th Infantry Division, the 187th Airborne Regimental Combat Team (ARCT), the 1st Marine Division, and the ROK 6th Infantry Division.

❏ In March 1951, the corps was again reorganized, losing the 187th ARCT and the 1st Marine Division, gaining instead the 7th Infantry Division and the ROK 2nd Infantry Division.

❏ In January 1952, all of IX Corps' divisions, except for the 7th Infantry Division, were transferred to other corps, although IX Corps gained control of the 45th Infantry Division.

❏ Just two months later, in March 1952, IX Corps lost the 45th Infantry Division but was reconstituted with the 2nd Infantry Division, the 40th Infantry Division, the ROK 2nd Infantry Division, the ROK 3rd Infantry Division, and the ROK Capital Division.

❏ IX Corps was reorganized for the last time in January 1953. It retained command over the 3rd Infantry Division and the ROK Capital Division and assumed command of the ROK 9th Infantry Division; all of its other divisions were transferred to other corps.

❏ IX Corps departed Korea for Okinawa three-and-a-half years after the signing of the armistice, in November 1956.

X CORPS

X Corps deployed to Japan at the end of World War II to serve as part of the occupation forces. On January 31, 1946, however, it was deactivated as part of the postwar drawdown of U.S. forces.

❏ X Corps was reactivated on September 12, 1950, specifically for the purpose of planning and conducting the amphibious landing at Inchon. It was composed of the 7th Infantry Division, the 1st Marine Division, and various ROK and support units.

❏ While each of the corps in Korea were uniquely organized for specific missions and tended to break regular organizational rules, X Corps was atypical even by these standards and operated independently of the 8th U.S. Army, answerable directly to MacArthur in Tokyo, until December 24, 1950.

❏ After the successful landing at Inchon in September 1950 and the liberation of Seoul, X Corps reembarked and set sail for the east coast of Korea, where it made an administrative landing at the port of Wonsan in October 1950.

❏ Moving north up the east coast toward the Chinese border in a plan to capture all of Korea by Christmas, X Corps operated under MacArthur's command as a virtually independent combat force.

❏ In late November, X Corps' advance was halted when it smashed into a wall of Chinese troops. Many X Corps soldiers were killed, wounded, and captured during this encounter, especially around Chosin Reservoir.

❏ In spite of its casualties and the bitter cold of an early Korean winter, X Corps managed to regroup and retreat eastward, toward the coast. At Hungnam, more than 100,000 troops and a like number of Korean refugees boarded ships or were airlifted to ships off the coast in one of the largest and most most successful amphibious evacuations in history.

❏ Within weeks of the Hungnam evacuation, elements of X Corps reentered combat in South Korean alongside other 8th U.S. Army units.

❏ X Corps left Korea in 1955 and sent to Fort Riley, Kansas. It was deactivated once again on April 27, 1955.

U.S. ARMY DIVISIONS
AND REGIMENTAL COMBAT TEAMS

Each U.S. Army corps was divided into a number of divisions, regimental combat teams, and various support elements. During the war, eight U.S. Army divisions, one U.S. Marine Corps division, and two U.S. Army regimental combat teams served as major commands within the three corps (these assignments are listed in the corps descriptions).

Because of budget cuts and downsizing in the years following World War II, most of these combat divisions had only two regiments, rather than the three specified by the U.S. Army's Table of Organization and Equipment (TO&E). Furthermore, each of those regiments had only two battalions, rather than the requisite three. Likewise, each of those battalions was likely to have only two, rather than the regulation three, infantry companies (plus a heavy weapons company). Thus, when the Korea War broke out, most of the major commands in the U.S. Army and Marine Corps were at half strength or less.

1ST CAVALRY DIVISION (DISMOUNTED)

At the end of World War II, the 1st Cavalry Division (Dismounted) became part of the Allied occupation forces in Japan. At this time, its designation as a "cavalry" unit and of its soldiers as "troopers" was purely traditional, and it was organized and equipped like a regular infantry division.

❑ When the Korean War began, the 1st Battalion of the 7th Cavalry Regiment was the first element of the 1st Cavalry Division to be sent to Korea, and on July 9, 1950, landed at Pohang-dong, on the east coast of South Korea. While waiting for the rest of the regiment to arrive, the battalion guarded K-3, the main airfield being used by the U.N. to bring troops and materiel into Korea.

❑ On July 18, 1950, the 5th, 8th, and balance of the 7th Regiments of the 1st Cavalry Division arrived in Korea from Japan. Elements of the 1st Cavalry Division, moving west to Taegu and then north toward Taejon, engaged the North Korean army at Yongdong on July 24, 1950.

❑ Initially, the 1st Cavalry Division thought it would accomplish its mission of driving the North Korean forces out of South Korea in a mere six weeks. The division, however, engaged in heavy, difficult combat for nearly a year and a half.

❑ The 1st Cavalry Division redeployed to Japan on October 22, 1951, where it served in the Far East Command reserve until the armistice in July 1953, after which it returned to Korea. Casualties for the 1st Cavalry Division were 3,811 killed in action and 12,086 wounded in action.

❏ Elements of the 1st Cavalry Division included:

Headquarters and Headquarters Company
5th Cavalry Regiment
7th Cavalry Regiment
8th Cavalry Regiment

Division Artillery
61st Field Artillery Battalion (105mm)
77th Field Artillery Battalion (105mm)
82nd Field Artillery Battalion (155mm)
99th Field Artillery Battalion (105mm)
29th Antiaircraft Artillery Battalion

Division Troops
Company A, 71st Heavy Tank Battalion (replaced by the 70th Medium Tank
    Battalion on August 7, 1950)
8th Engineer Combat Battalion
16th Reconnaissance Company

Division Special Troops
15th Medical Battalion
13th Signal Company
27th Ordnance Maintenance Battalion
15th Quartermaster Company
15th Military Police Company
15th Replacement Company

❏ Several other units, including those sent by other allied governments, were attached to the 1st Cavalry Division during the Korean War, including:

4th Airborne Ranger Infantry Company (December 31, 1950 to August 1, 1951)
Thailand 21st Infantry Regiment
Philippine 10th Battalion Combat Team
Greek Expeditionary Force

2ND "INDIAN HEAD" INFANTRY DIVISION

When war broke out in Korea, the 2nd Infantry Division was stationed at Fort Lewis, Washington.

❑ Soon after the conflict began, the 2nd Infantry Division was ordered to deploy to Korea. Advance units of the division arrived in Korea on August 3, 1950, followed by the rest of the division near the end of the month. Once it became operational, the 2nd Infantry Division was assigned to the U.S. IX Corps.

❑ In November 1950, during the U.N. drive toward the Yalu River, the 2nd Infantry Division was cut off and ambushed by Chinese forces on a narrow road in the mountainous country around Kunu-ri, in North Korea. It was so badly mauled in this action that it became combat ineffective.

❑ After its disastrous defeat in northern Korea, the 2nd Infantry Division was quickly reconstituted and reinforced with some newly-arrived foreign units, the French Battalion, the Netherlands Battalion, and the BELUX Battalion (a unit made up of troops from Belgium and Luxembourg).

❑ In February 1951, just six weeks after it was decimated by the Chinese, the rebuilt 2nd Infantry Division broke a major Chinese offensive at the village of Chipyong-ni, in South Korea. It continued to peform well throughout the rest of the war.

❑ Casualties among the Indian Head soldiers were 7,094 killed in action, the highest of any U.S. division in Korea and about twice that suffered by the others on average, and 16,575 wounded.

❑ Units of the 2nd Infantry Division included the following:

Division Headquarters and Headquarters Company
9th Infantry Regiment
23rd Infantry Regiment
38th Infantry Regiment
Division Artillery
12th Field Artillery Battalion (155mm) (arrived in November 1951)

15th Field Artillery Battalion (105mm)
37th Field Artillery Battalion (105mm)
38th Field Artillery Battalion (105mm)
503rd Field Artillery Battalion (155mm)
82nd Antiaircraft Artillery Battalion

Division Troops
72nd Medium Tank Battalion
2nd Combat Engineer Battalion
2nd Reconnaissance Company

Division Special Troops
2nd Medical Company
2nd Signal Company
702nd Ordnance Maintenance Battalion
2nd Quartermaster Company
2nd Military Police Company
2nd Replacement Company

❏   Several units were also attached to the 2nd Infantry Division during the Korean War:

1st Airborne Ranger Infantry Company (October 23, 1950 to August
    1,951)
Netherlands Infantry Battalion
French Infantry Battalion
Belgian Infantry Battalion

3RD "MARNE" INFANTRY DIVISION

When the Korean War began, units of the 3rd Infantry Division were stationed at opposite ends of the East Coast, its headquarters and the 15th Infantry Regiment in Fort Benning, Georgia, and the 7th Infantry Regiment at Fort Devens,

Massachusetts. A third regiment, the 30th Infantry Regiment, existed only on paper and was at zero strength.

❏ Soon after the conflict started, the 3rd Infantry Division was further weakened, when four of its battalions—one from each of its regiments, plus the 73rd Tank Battalion and the 41st Field Artillery Battalion—were taken away and sent to Korea to become part of the 1st Cavalry Division.

❏ Nonetheless, in early July 1950, the Marne division was ordered to deploy to Asia. It was reinforced with the 65th Infantry Regiment from Puerto Rico, which was sent directly to Korea, and left for Japan on August 20, 1950.

❏ While in Japan, the 3rd Infantry Division was brought up to full strength, and on November 10, 1950, was sent to Korea, where it was joined by the Puerto Rican regiment and became part of the U.S. X Corps.

❏ In October 1954, the 3rd Infantry Division left Korea and returned to the United States. Its casualties were 2,160 killed in action and 7,939 wounded in action.

❏ Elements of the 3rd infantry Division included the following:

Division Headquarters and Headquarters Company
7th Infantry Regiment
15th Infantry Regiment
65th Infantry Regiment

Division Artillery
9th Field Artillery Battalion (155mm)
10th Field Artillery Battalion (105mm)
39th Field Artillery Battalion (105mm)
58th Armored Field Artillery Battalion (105mm)
3rd Antiaircraft Artillery Battalion

Division Troops
64th Medium Tank Battalion
10th Combat Engineer Battalion
3rd Reconnaissance Company

Division Special Troops

3rd Medical Battalion
3rd Signal Company
703 Ordnance Maintenance Battalion
3rd Quartermaster Company
3rd Military Police Company
3rd Replacement Company

❑   Two special units were also attached to the 3rd Infantry Division during the Korean War.

Eighth Army Raider Company, 8245th Army Unit (from November 12, 1950 to December 26, 1950)
3rd Airborne Ranger Infantry Company (April 31, 1951 to August 1, 1951)

7TH "BAYONET" INFANTRY DIVISION

At the end of World War II, the 7th Infantry Division was given occupation duty in Korea. This tour lasted until 1948, when it was withdrawn incrementally through December 31 and sent to join the Allied occupation of Japan on the northern island of Hokkaido.

❑   After war broke out in Korea, the Bayonet division was initially kept in Japan as part of the Far East Command General Reserve and its troops were parcelled out to understrength units already in Korea.

❑   Additional units were needed, however, for the planned landing at Inchon, and the 7th Infantry Division was assigned to the U.S. X Corps, a command specially formed to carry out the operation. Because it had been depleted in the preceding months, its ranks were rounded out with South Korean troops, most of them with little or no military experience.

❑ After the armistice, the 7th Infantry Division remained in Korea until 1971, when it was deactived. Casualties for the division during the Korean War were 3,905 killed in action and 10,858 wounded in action.

❑ Units of the 7th Infantry Division included the following:

Division Headquarters and Headquarters Company
17th Infantry Regiment
31st Infantry Regiment
32nd Infantry Regiment

Division Artillery
31st Field Artillery Battalion (155mm)
48th Field Artillery Battalion (105mm)
49th Field Artillery Battalion (105mm)
57th Field Artillery Battalion (105mm)
15th Antiaircraft Artillery Battalion

Division Troops
Company A, 77th Tank Battalion (replaced by the 73rd Medium Tank Battalion in August 1950)
13th Combat Engineer Battalion
7th Reconnaissance Company

Division Special Troops
7th Medical Battalion
7th Signal Battalion
707th Ordnance Maintenance Battalion
7th Quartermaster Company
7th Military Police Company
7th Replacement Company

❑ One unit was also attached to the 7th Infantry Division, the 2nd Airborne Ranger Infantry Company, from December 31, 1950 to August 1, 1951.

24TH "VICTORY" INFANTRY DIVISION

When World War II ended, the 24th Infantry Division was assigned to occupation duty in Japan, on its southernmost island of Kyushu.

❑ Less than a week after the Korean War began, soldiers from the 24th Infantry Division, the closest to the peninsula, were used to form 406-man Task Force Smith. The first of many U.S. soldiers sent to oppose the communist presence in Korea, they deployed from Itazuke Air Base on July 2, 1950.

❑ After arriving in South Korea, lightly armed and understrength Task Force Smith moved into the vicinity of Osan and dug in on a pair of hills straddling the road. In the ensuing battle, they were overrun by numerically superior and heavily armed North Korean forces.

❑ Elements of the 24th Infantry Division continued to arrive in Korea over the following weeks, and were defeated in encounter after encounter with the North Koreans. They were driven steadily southward, trading their lives for the time U.S. forces needed to establish a foothold on the peninsula.

❑ On January 23, 1952, after a long, hard tour, the 24th Infantry Division was relieved by the 40th Infantry Division. The 24th transferred to Japan and did not return to Korea again until July 16, 1953, less than two weeks before the armistice was signed.

❑ Casualties for the 24th Infantry Division were 3,735 killed in action and 7,395 wounded in action.

❑ Units assigned to the 24th Infantry Division included the following:

Division Headquarters and Headquarters Company
19th Infantry Regiment
31st Infantry Regiment
34th Infantry Regiment

Division Artillery
11th Field Artillery Battalion (155mm)

13th Field Artillery Battalion (105mm)
52nd Field Artillery Battalion (105mm)
63rd Field Artillery Battalion (105mm)
26th Antiaircraft Artillery Battalion

Division Troops
Company A, 78th Heavy Tank Battalion (replaced by the 6th Medium Tank
    Battalion on August 8, 1950)
3rd Combat Engineer Battalion
24th Reconnaissance Company

Division Special Troops
24th Medical Battalion
24th Signal Company
724th Ordnance Maintenance Battalion
24th Quartermaster Company
24th Military Police Company
24th Replacement Company

❑   A number of other units were also attached to the 24th Infantry Division
during the Korean War. These included:

5th Infantry Regiment (from September 30, 1950 through January 1952)
555th Field Artillery Battalion
8072nd Provisional Tank Battalion
Eighth Army Ranger Company (from October 10, 1950 to March 28, 1951)
8th Airborne Ranger Infantry Company (April 31, 1951 to August 1, 1951)
British 27th Commonwealth Brigade

25TH "TROPIC LIGHTNING" INFANTRY DIVISION

When World War II ended, the 25th Infantry Division was sent to Osaka, Japan, to serve in the Allied occupation forces.

❏ On July 10, 1950, the 25th Infantry Division began deploying to Korea. By July 18, all of its units had arrived on the peninsula, including two battalions of the 29th Infantry Regiment, stationed in Okinawa when the Korean War began, which became the 3rd battalions of the division's 25th and 27th Infantry Regiments.

❏ Tropic Lighting soldiers went into combat against the North Korean army almost immediately, but suffered setbacks and defeats in their first engagements. They went on, however, to become one of the U.S. military's most active units and compiled an excellent combat record.

❏ After the armistice, the 25th Infantry Division remained in Korea until October 1954, when it returned to Hawaii. Casualties for the 25th Infantry Division were 3,048 killed in action and 10,186 wounded in action.

❏ Elements of the 25th Infantry Division included:

Division Headquarters and Headquarters Company
24th Infantry Regiment (replaced August 1, 1950 by 14th Infantry Regiment)
27th Infantry Regiment
25th Infantry Regiment

Division Artillery
8th Field Artillery Battalion (105mm)
64th Field Artillery Battalion (105mm)
69th Field Artillery Battalion (105mm)
90th Field Artillery Battalion (155mm)

Division Troops
Company A, 79th Heavy Tank Battalion (replaced on August 7, 1950, by the 89th Medium Tank Battalion)
65th Combat Engineer Battalion
25th Reconnaissance Company

Division Special Troops
25th Medical Battalion
25th Signal Company
725th Ordnance Maintenance Battalion
25th Quartermaster Company
25th Military Police Company
25th Replacement Company

❏   Two special units were also attached to the 25th Infantry Division during the Korean War included:

5th Airborne Ranger Infantry Company (April 31, 1951 to August 1, 1951)
The Turkish Brigade

40TH "GRIZZLY" INFANTRY DIVISION
(CALIFORNIA NATIONAL GUARD)

Before war broke out in Korea, the 40th Infantry Division, a unit of the California National Guard, was headquartered in Los Angeles. On September 1, it was activated by the federal government and deployed to Camp Cooke, California, for training.

❏   In April 1951, after its soldiers were done with their training, the 40th Infantry Division deployed to Japan. It was not until the next year, however, after undergoing more training in Japan, that the Grizzlies were finally sent to Korea, on February 3, 1952.

❏   Once in Korea, the 40th Infantry Division relieved the 24th Infantry Division, which returned to Japan to become the Far East Command General Reserve.

❏   After the armistice, the 40th Infantry Division returned to California and reverted once again to reserve status on June 30, 1954. Casualties for the 40th Infantry Division were 376 killed in action and 1,457 wounded in action, the lowest of any U.S. division during the Korean war.

❏   Elements of the 40th Infantry Division included the following:

Division Headquarters and Headquarters Company
160th Infantry Regiment
223rd Infantry Regiment

224th Infantry Regiment
Division Artillery
143rd Field Artillery Battalion (105mm)
625th Field Artillery Battalion (155mm)
980th Field Artillery Battalion (105mm)
981st Field Artillery Battalion (105mm)
140th Antiaircraft Artillery Battalion

Division Troops
140th Medium Tank Battalion
578th Combat Engineer Battalion
40th Reconnaissance Company

Division Special Troops
115th Medical Battalion
40th Signal Company
740th Ordnance Maintenance Battalion
40th Quartermaster Company
40th Military Police Company
40th Replacement Company

❏ From July 1, 1951 until September 1, 1951, while it was stationed in Japan, the 11th Airborne Ranger Infantry Company was attached to the 40th Infantry Division.

45TH "THUNDERBIRD" INFANTRY DIVISION
(OKLAHOMA NATIONAL GUARD)

Prior to the outbreak of the Korean War, the 45th Infantry Division, a unit of the Oklahoma National Guard, was headquartered in in Oklahoma City, Oklahoma.

❏ On September 1, 1950, the federal government activated the 45th Infantry Division and sent it to Fort Polk, Louisiana, to undergo training and have its ranks rounded out.

❏ In April 1951, after its soldiers had completed their training and the division was brought up to strength, the Thunderbirds were deployed to Japan.

❏ In December 1951, after receiving advanced training, the 45th Infantry Division was sent to Korea to replace the 1st Cavalry Division.

❏ During its first exposures to combat, the 45th Infantry Division did not perform well. It improved quickly, however, and went on to redeem its reputation before leaving Korea. Casualties for the 45th Infantry Division were 834 killed in action and 3,170 wounded in action.

❏ Elements of the 45th Infantry Division included the following:

Division Headquarters and Headquarters Company
179th Infantry Regiment
180th Infantry Regiment
279th Infantry Regiment

Division Artillery
158th Field Artillery Battalion (105mm)
160th Field Artillery Battalion (105mm)
171st Field Artillery Battalion (105mm)
189th Field Artillery Battalion (155mm)
145th Antiaircraft Artillery Battalion

Division Troops
245th Medium Tank Battalion
120th Combat Engineer Battalion
45th Reconnaissance Company

Division Special Troops
120th Medical Battalion
45th Signal Company
700th Ordnance Maintenance Battalion
45th Quartermaster Company
45th Military Police Company
45th Replacement Company

❏ While it was stationed in Japan, the 10th Airborne Ranger Infantry Company was attached to the 45th Infantry Division, from July 1, 1951 to September 15, 1951.

5TH REGIMENTAL COMBAT TEAM

Deactivated after World War II, the 5th Infantry Regiment was reactivated in Korea on January 1, 1949, with soldiers and support units of the departing 7th Infantry Division, and tasked with providing security while U.S. forces withdrew from the country.

❏ On June 31, 1949, almost a year exactly before North Korea invaded the south, the 5th Infantry Regiment departed Korea for Schofield Barracks, Hawaii.

❏ On July 25, 1950, the 5th Infantry Regiment redeployed to Korea, where it was assigned to the 25th Infantry Division and redesignated a regimental combat team. Just a month later, in August 1950, it was reassigned to the 1st Cavalry Division.

❏ In September 1950, the 5th was assigned to the 24th Infantry Division, where it relieved the 34th Infantry Regiment and was treated as a regular infantry regiment, rather than a regimental combat team.

❏ In January 1952, the unit was reassigned to IX Corps, where it once again became a separate regimental combat team.

❏ Casualties for the 5th Regimental Combat Team during the Korean War were 867 killed in action and 3,188 wounded in action.

❏ Units of the 5th Regimental Combat Team included the following:

5th Infantry Regiment
555th Field Artillery Battalion (105mm)
72nd Engineer Company

187TH AIRBORNE REGIMENTAL COMBAT TEAM (RAKKASANS)

Activated during World War II as the 187th Glider Infantry Regiment, on June 30, 1949, it became the 187th Airborne Infantry Regiment and made part of the 11th Airborne Division at Fort Campbell, Kentucky.

❏ On August 1, 1950, a month after the United States entered the war in Korea, supporting units were added to the regiment and it was redesignated the 187th Airborne Regimental Combat Team (ARCT). It was deployed to Asia and arrived in Japan on September 20, 1950.

❏ On October 20, 1950, the regiment made combat parachute jumps into the towns of Sukchon and Sunchon, north of the communist capital of Pyongyang, in an attempt to cut off escaping North Korean civilian and military leaders. While the operation was a nominal success, North Korea's government had already fled northward, and most of the prisoners taken were fleeing soldiers.

❏ On June 26, 1951, the 187th ARCT was redeployed to Japan, where it became a strategic reserve for the U.N. forces. While serving in this capacity, it made a second successful airborne attack on March 23, 1952.

❏ The 187th ARCT returned to Korea on May 24, 1952, and soon thereafter, on October 18, 1952, it was again sent back to Japan. The regiment was sent to Korea one last time on June 22, 1953, right before the signing of the armistice.

❏ In July 1955, the regiment returned to the United States and, in 1956, was assigned to the reactivated 101st Airborne Division, at Fort Campbell, Kentucky.

❏ Casualties for the 187th Airborne Regimental Combat Team during the Korean War were 442 killed in action and 1,656 wounded in action.

❏ Several elements comprised the 187th Airborne Regimental Combat Team:

187th Airborne Infantry Regiment
674th Airborne Field Artillery Battalion (105mm)
Airborne Antiaircraft Artillery Battery, 187th ARCT
Airborne Engineer Company, 187th ARCT
Military Police Traffic Platoon, 187th ARCT

Quartermaster Parachute Maintenance Company, 187th ARCT
Medical Ambulance Platoon, 187th ARCT
Medical Clearing Platoon, 187th ARCT
Pathfinder Team, 187th ARCT

❑ Three units were also attached to the 187th Airborne Regimental Combat Team during the Korean War:

2nd Airborne Ranger Infantry Company (3 March 1951 - 4 April 1951)
5th Airborne Ranger Infantry Company (3 March 1951 - 4 April 1951)
FECOM Tactical Liaison Office Team, 8177th Army Tactical Intelligence
    Unit

U.S. MARINE CORPS

When war broke out in Korea July 1950, the U.S. Marine Corps was, like the U.S. military as a whole, understrength and equipped with old and insufficient equipment, much of it retrieved from the World War II battlefields of the Pacific. Nonetheless, the Marine Corps was able to rally its resources and quickly proved itself an asset in the war in Korea.

1ST PROVISIONAL MARINE BRIGADE

Initially, the Marine Corps was able to send only a single ad-hoc unit element to the battlefront in Korea. Dubbed the 1st Provisional Marine Brigade, it was formed at Camp Pendleton, California, from elements of the 1st Marine Division and the 1st Marine Aircraft Wing.

Two major elements comprised the 1st Provisional Marine Brigade, the 5th Marine Regiment and Marine Aircraft Group 33. The brigade was activated on July 7, 1950, and operated as an independent command until September 13, 1950, when it was incorporated into the 8th U.S. Army.

5TH MARINE REGIMENT

The 5th Marine Regiment was organized as a regimental combat team, reinforced with various assets to allow it to operate independently and without support from other units.

❏ It was composed of the following elements:

H&S Battalion, 1st Provisional Marine Brigade
HQ Company, 1st Provisional Marine Brigade
Detachment, Military Police Company, 1st Marine Division
Detachment, Reconnaissance Company, 1st Marine Division
Counter Intelligence Corps and Military Intelligence Special
    Detachment (USA)

5th Marine Regiment
H&S Company
1st Battalion, 5th Marines (minus Company C)
2d Battalion, 5th Marines (minus Company F)
3d Battalion, 5th Marines (minus Company I)
4.2-inch Mortar Company, 5th Marines
Antitank Company, 5th Marines
Company A, 1st Engineer Battalion (Reinforced)
Company C, 1st Medical Battalion
Company A, 1st Motor Transport Battalion
Detachment, 1st Ordnance Battalion
Detachment, 1st Service Battalion
Company A, 1st Shore Party Battalion
Detachment, 1st Signal Battalion
Company A, 1st Tank Battalion
1st Amphibian Tractor Company
Detachment, 1st Combat Service Group
1st Platoon, 1st Amphibian Truck Company, FMF

MARINE AIRCRAFT GROUP 33 (MAG-33)

Collectively, MAG-33 and the various other elements that augmented it were designated Forward Echelon, 1st Marine Aircraft Wing, Marine Aircraft Group 33. Its commander was also deputy brigade commander for the 1st Provisional Marine Brigade.

❑ This unit consisted of the following components:

HQ Squadron, Marine Aircraft Group 33
Service Squadron, Marine Aircraft Group 33
Marine Fighter Squadron 214
Marine Fighter Squadron 323
Marine Fighter Squadron (Night) 513
Marine Tactical Air Control Squadron 2
Marine Observation Squadron 6 (under operational control of the 1st Provisional Marine Brigade)

❑ Troops from other 1st Marine Division units were quickly reassigned to the 1st Provisional Marine Brigade. About 6,800 marines were pulled from the 2nd Marine Division, stationed at Camp Lejeune, North Carolina, for both immediate deployment to Korea with the provisional brigade and for the reconstitution of the depleted 1st Marine Division.

❑ Most of the brigade's arms, equipment, and vehicles came from the Marine Supply Depot in Barstow, California, where they had been refurbished and stored after being recovered from Pacific islands in Operation Roll-Up in the late 1940s.

❑ Despite the efforts to bring the brigade's elements up to full strength, many of them were still short of men and equipment when they embarked for Asia. Like their U.S. Army counterparts, each of the three battalions of the 5th Marine Regiment had only two, rather than the requisite three, rifle companies. When they deployed, each of these companies was still short by about 50 troops.

❑ Additionally, the regiment's three artillery batteries had only four of the requisite six 105mm howitzers and the regimental antitank company did not have an organic tank platoon, and thus lacked its most potent antitank weapon.

❑ Soon after the brigade was activated, its 6,534 troops departed for Japan from the nearby port of San Diego, California.

❑ A Brigade Advance Party, which included the commander, the deputy commander, and some of their staffs, left by air on July 16 and arrived in Tokyo three days later.

❑ Its air component, MAG-33, embarked upon two troop transports and an escort carrier.

❑ Its ground component, the reinforced 5th Marine Regiment, had a total of 266 officers and 4,503 enlisted men and departed between July 12 through July 14 on three troop transports, two attack cargo transports, and three LSDs.

❑ While the brigade was still en route to Japan, the situation along the Pusan Perimeter worsened, and the 5th Marine Regiment was ordered to bypass Japan and sail directly to Korea. The same day, the advance party left Japan for Korea and upon arrival established itself at Taegu, within the Pusan Perimeter.

❑ MAG-33 arrived at Kobe, Japan, on July 31. Two of its elements, Marine Tactical Air Control Squadron 2 (MTACS-2) and the ground echelon of VMO-6, headed straight for Pusan, arriving there August 1.

❑ Its fighter elements, VMF-214, VMF- 323, and VMF(N)-513, deployed from their transport to Itami, Japan, where they prepared for combat. By August 5, their 70 aircraft had landed aboard USS *Sicily* and USS *Badoeng Strait.*

❑ On August 2, the brigade's ground component arrived in Pusan and was assigned to 8th U.S. Army. The marines were sent immediately onto the line west of and along the Naktong River, where they arrived just on time to counter a heavy North Korean assault.

❑ In spite of suffering heavy casualties, the brigade continued to withstand North Korean attacks against the Pusan Perimeter for more than a month. Aircraft from MAG-33 provided close air support, resupply, and medical evacuation throughout the action.

❑ In September, it was pulled off the line and sent to join the forces preparing for the landing at Inchon, and on September 13, the 1st Provisional Marine Brigade ceased to exist as an independent unit when it became part of the 1st Marine Division.

1ST MARINE DIVISION
(REINFORCED)

From September 1945 to June 1947, the 1st Marine Division was part of the Allied occupation force in northern China, after which it returned to Camp Pendleton, California, where it was stationed when the Korean War began.

❑ Like other major commands in the U.S. military, the 1st Marine Division was markedly understrength in the summer of 1950, and reservists were used to bring it up to full strength. Between August 10 and September 3, 1950, the 1st Marine Division sailed to Korea from the port of San Diego, California.

❑ Lead elements of the division arrived in Japan in early September 1950, while the remainder of the division went straight on to Korea. Once there, the division absorbed the 1st Provisional Marine Brigade and was assigned to U.S. Army X Corps. On September 21, the division also regained the 7th Marine Regiment, which arrived in Korea from California.

❑ In mid-September, the 1st Marine Division played a major role in the amphibious assault on Inchon, first capturing sentinel Wolmi Island and then storming the seawalls of the port. Once Inchon fell, the marines moved inland and participated in the bloody, street-to-street battle to recapture Seoul.

❑ After helping take the South Korean capital, the marines reembarked at Inchon and sailed around the peninsula to the opposite coast of Korea, where they made an unopposed landing at the North Korea port of Wonsan (already captured by ROK forces), an operation completed on November 9, 1950.

❑ Along with the other U.N. forces, the 1st Marine Division began to move northward toward the Yalu River. By Thanksgiving 1950, they were strung out in a handful of villages parallel to the Chosin Reservoir, from which they would make their last thrust to the Chinese border.

❑ Chinese forces entered the war with a vengeance at the end of November 1950, halting the 1st Marine Division and cutting off its line retreat. Marine commanders had slowed their advance as much as possible, however, despite exhortations from MacArthur, allowing them to make a bloody, fighting withdrawal in sub-zero weather to the port of Hungnam, where they embarked on ships and sailed out of North Korea.

❏ During the last two years of the war, the 1st Marine Division, like its Army counterparts, adjusted its tactics to meet the needs of the static warfare that ensued.

❏ In April 1955, the 1st Marine Division was relieved by the 25th Infantry Division and returned to Camp Pendleton. Casualties for the 1st Marine Division during the Korean War were 4,004 killed (second only to the 2nd Infantry Division) and 25,864 wounded—more wounded than any other U.S. division during the Korean War.

❏ Throughout the course of the Korean War, 42 marines won the Medal of Honor, America's highest military award, for heroism above and beyond the call of duty in Korea. Twenty-seven of the awards were given posthumously. In addition, marines were awarded 221 Navy Crosses and more than 1,500 Silver Stars. Marine reservists were awarded 13 of the Medals of Honor, 50 of the Navy Crosses, and more than 400 of the Silver Stars.

❏ Elements of the 1st Marine Division included the following:

Division HQ and HQ Battalion
1st Marine Regiment
5th Marine Regiment
7th Marine Regiment
11th Marine Artillery Regiment
1st Tank Battalion
1st Amphibian Tractor Battalion
1st Armored Amphibian Battalion
1st Engineer Battalion
1st Shore Party Battalion
1st Signal Battalion
1st Amphibious Reconnaissance Company
1st Military Police Company
1st Service Support Group
1st Motor Transport Battalion
7th Motor Transport Battalion
1st Ordnance Battalion
1st Service Battalion
1st Medical Battalion
Battery C, 1st Rocket Battalion

1st Air Delivery Platoon
1st Fumigation and Bath Platoon
Carrier Platoon

❏ In addition, several units were attached to the 1st Marine Division during the Korean War:

1st Korean Marine Corps Regiment
1st Korean Marine Corps Artillery Battalion
1st Naval Construction Battalion ("Seabees")

1ST MARINE AIRCRAFT WING

Activated in September 1951, the 1st Marine Aircraft Wing provided close air support for the 1st Marine Division throughout the war in Korea. It was made up of three main components, Marine Aircraft Group 12, Marine Aircraft Group 33, and the 1st Antiaircraft Artillery Gun Battalion.

❏ In April 1955, the 1st Marine Aircraft Wing returned to Japan, at the same time as the 1st Marine Division headed home to Camp Pendleton. Its casualties during the Korean War were 258 killed and 174 wounded.

PROVISIONAL MARINE UNITS IN KOREA

From 1951 to 1952, the 1st Marine Division helped form several provisional units in order to fulfill specific needs.

❏ On March 31, 1952, the division created the Kimpo Provisional Regiment to defend the Kimpo Peninsula, west of Seoul and on the division's left flank. It was disbanded after the armistice.

❏ The Kimpo Provisional Regiment consisted of the following elements:

Headquarters and Headquarters Company
1st Armored Amphibian Tractor Battalion (as supporting artillery)

2d Battalion, 7th Marines (this battalion and its replacement were rotated
   from the 1st Marine Division's reserve regiment)
5th Korean Marine Corps Battalion
13th ROK Security Battalion
Company A, 1st Amphibian Tractor Battalion
Company B, 1st Shore Party Battalion (as engineers)
Company D, 1st Medical Battalion
Reconnaissance Company, 1st Marine Division
Detachment, Air and Naval Gunfire Liaison Company, 1st Signal Battalion
163d Military Intelligence Service Detachment
Detachment, 61st Engineer Searchlight Company
Detachment, 18 1st Counterintelligence Corps Unit

❏ Other provisional marine units formed in Korea included the 1st
Provisional Casual Company; the 1st Provisional Antiaircraft Artillery
Automatic Weapons Battery, activated in April 1953; and the 1st Provisional
Demilitarized Zone Military Police Company, activated in September 1953.

❏ In addition, a number of U.S. Navy units provided direct support for the
1st Marine Division at various times during the Korean War and there were a
handful of Marine units not affiliated with the division. These included a
detachment from Navy Underwater Demolition Team 1, a detachment from
Navy Underwater Demolition Team 3, Navy Underwater Demolition Team
5, and a Marine Security Guard Detachment on duty at the U.S. Embassy.

SPECIAL U.S. MILITARY UNITS

U.S. MILITARY ADVISORY GROUPS

*Soon after U.S. forces occupied southern Korea in September 1945,
they began to train what became the armed forces of the Republic of Korea.*

❏ On August 15, 1948, the Republic of Korea was established and the
Allied occupation forces began preparing to withdraw from the peninsula
and entrust its security to the South Korean constabulary. This constabulary
was redesignated as the Republic of Korea Army and a U.S. unit was
established to train and provide logistical support for it.

❏ This unit, called the Provisional Military Advisory Group (PMAG), initially had 100 men unit, but by December 31, 1948, was enlarged to include 241 officers and enlisted men.

❏ On July 1, 1949, exactly six months after the United States formally recognized the Republic of Korea, the last U.S. occupation troops left Korea. When they did, PMAG was redesignated the Korean Military Advisory Group (KMAG).

❏ Technically, KMAG was part of the U.S. State Department mission to South Korea rather than part of the U.S. armed forces. As a result, it was independent of the U.S. Far East Command (headquartered in Tokyo under Gen. Douglas MacArthur) and South Korea was considered to be outside of the U.S. strategic sphere of interest.

❏ Soon after war broke out in Korea, command of KMAG reverted to the 8th U.S. Army and redesignated as U.S. Military Advisory Group, Korea, 8668th Army Unit. On December 28, 1950, it was once again redesignated, as the 8202nd Army Unit.

RANGERS

In the years after World War II, the U.S. Army Ranger program fell victim to the downsizing that affected all the armed services. Once the Korean War began, however, the military once again had a need for units specialized in unconventional operations.

❏ On September 15, 1950, U.S. Army Col. John Gibson Van Houten was ordered to establish a ranger training program at Fort Benning, Georgia, and he began to look for soldiers willing to undertake "extremely hazardous" duty in Korea.

❏ Thousands of volunteers responded to the call, as many as 5,000 from the 82nd Airborne Division and many of the rest from World War II organizations like the original ranger battalions, the Canadian-U.S. Special Service Force, and the Office of Strategic Services.

❏ By October 2, 1950, the first group of volunteers had been formed into three companies and had begun the six-week training program.

❏ On October 9, a group of black paratroopers entered the ranger training program. They would eventually become the 2nd Airborne Ranger Infantry Company, the only all-black ranger unit ever created by the U.S. Army.

❏ Initially, the U.S. Army planned to train one ranger headquarters detachment and four 112-man ranger companies, each of which would be attached to an infantry division. Ultimately, however, the program produced eight ranger companies.

❏ On December 17, the 1st Airborne Ranger Infantry Company arrived in Korea, where it was attached to the 2nd Infantry Division. Two more of the companies arrived less than two weeks later; the 2nd Airborne Ranger Infantry Company was attached to the 7th Infantry Division and the 4th Airborne Ranger Infantry Company to 8th U.S. Army Headquarters initially and then to the 1st Cavalry Division. The 3rd Airborne Ranger Infantry Company stayed at Fort Benning to train the second group of ranger companies.

❏ The ranger companies participated in a wide variety of activities in Korea, from pitched battles—during which they were frequently used to counterattack against enemy breakthroughs—to raids behind the communist lines.

❏ In February 1951, for example, the 1st Airborne Ranger Infantry Company, while acting as the regimental reserve for the 23rd Infantry Regiment, fought in the Battle of Chipyong-ni. A few months later, in April 1951, a detachment of rangers slipped behind enemy lines in an abortive attempt to sabotage the equipment at Hwachon Dam.

❏ On March 23, the 2nd and 4th Airborne Ranger Infantry Companies, while attached to the 187th Airborne Regimental Combat Team, participated in Operation Tomahawk, the last combat jump of the war, parachuting into the North Korean town of Munsan-ni.

❏ On July 14, 1951, 8th Army headquarters directed the commanders of the 1st Cavalry Division and the 2nd, 3rd, 7th, 24th, and 25th Infantry Divisions to deactivate their attached ranger units. By November 5, 1951, the ranger companies were disbanded, and many of the rangers were transferred to the 187th Airborne Regimental Combat Team, where their special skills could still be utilized.

VI

SOUTH KOREAN MILITARY FORCES

"The South Koreans have the best damn army outside the United States!"

—KMAG Commander Brig. Gen. William L. Roberts
(in a 1950 interview with *Time* magazine)

Whrn war erupted in Korea, the ROK Army, the Yuk Gun, was understrength, ill-equipped, badly led, and poorly advised by the United States; U.N. intervention was the only thing that allowed it to survive its first encounters with its North Korean counterpart. In the months and years following the communist invasion, however, the ROK armed forces were rebuilt and reorganized and gradually evolved into a mature and effective fighting force.

In addition to an army, the Republic of Korea also had a small air force, navy, and marine corps, each of which was, like the army, enlarged and strengthened throughout the course of the Korean War. In addition to these services, South Korea also had a civilian police force with a strength of about 48,000, many of whom ended up in military formations after the war began.

THE ROK ARMY (ROKA)

On September 8, 1945, three weeks after the surrender of Japan ended World War II, U.S. occupation troops began arriving in the southern half of the former Japanese colony of Korea (Soviet troops simultaneously occupied the northern half of the peninsula). Replacing the Japanese police and security forces with similar Korean organizations was one of their first priorities.

ROK forces were almost wholly trained and equipped by the United States prior to and during the Korean War. This ROK soldier mans an U.S.-made M-2 .50 caliber machine gun.

❑ To facilitate this, the U.S. military government established a police academy to train a civilian police force and began to create "constabulary regiments" modelled after U.S. Army infantry regiments. On January 14, 1946, they activated the 1st Battalion of the 1st Korean Constabulary Regiment and began training its members at a former Japanese military base northeast of Seoul.

❑ By April 1946, seven more constabulary units had been established, one for each South Korean province, and were based at Chongju, Chunchon, Iri, Kwangju, Pusan, Taegu, and Taejon. At that point, the entire constabulary force consisted of about 2,000 officers and enlisted men. It grew steadily, however, and by spring of 1948 had a total strength of about 26,000.

❑ Many of the leaders in these constabulary units had served as officers and noncommissioned officers in the Imperial Japanese armed forces prior to and during World War II. Ironically, many of their counterparts in the North Korean armed forces had gained their military experience in anti-Japanese guerrilla units.

❏ On March 10, 1948, nine days after the U.S. military government in Korea announced that elections would be held south of the 38th parallel in May 1948 and a democratic government established in South Korea, the U.S. Joint Chiefs of Staff approved plans to expand the constabulary force to 50,000 men and to arm it with U.S. weapons, armored cars, M-24 tanks, and artillery pieces up to 105mm in size.

❏ In late November 1948, a little more than three months after the Republic of Korea was founded, the nation's new national assembly passed the "Republic of Korea Armed Forces Organization Act," calling for the creation of a ROK Army, Navy, and Department of National Defense.

❏ These entities were officially established on December 15, 1948, and the 1st, 2nd, 3rd, 5th, 6th, and 7th Constabulary Regiments became the 1st, 2nd, 3rd, 5th, 6th, and 7th Republic of Korea Infantry Divisions.

❏ In February 1949, the two remaining constabulary regiments were formed into the ROK 8th and 11th Infantry Divisions and the Capital Security Command was converted into the ROK Capital Infantry Division, which included the ROK 1st Cavalry Regiment, one of the only South Korean units equipped with armored vehicles, as well as horse cavalry.

❏ On July 1, 1949, the last U.S. military forces departed the peninsula and training of the South Korean armed forces became the responsibility of the Korean Military Advisory Group, part of the U.S. State Department mission to the Republic of Korea.

AMERICA'S INFLUENCE

❏ Because the South Korean army was trained, equipped, and advised by Americans, it naturally incorporated the strengths and weaknesses of the contemporary U.S. armed forces, which were themselves understrength and poorly trained and equipped.

❏ For example, in mid-1950, the ROK 1st, 2nd, 6th, and 7th Infantry Divisions had the requisite three regiments each, while the rest, like their U.S. counterparts, had only two each. Overall strength was about 95,000, but about a third of them were support, rather than combat troops.

❏ ROK units were also poorly equipped in part because of U.S. government fears that bellicose ROK President Syngman Rhee would try to unify the peninsula under his leadership by force if he were able. They responded to these concerns by refusing to give the South Korean armed forces the types of heavy weapons they would need to launch such an attack.

❑ Other reasons, even if they were given in good faith at the time, seem spurious in retrospect. For example, KMAG advisors asserted that the South Korean troops did not need tanks which, they said, would be of little use in the mountainous terrain of Korea. Experience proved, of course, the marked usefulness of tanks on both sides during the Korean War.

❑ Unfortunately, even weapons the United States deemed appropriate for the ROK forces were in short supply in June 1950. When war broke out, only about half the soldiers in the understrength ROK units were equipped with U.S. small arms, with the balance carrying Japanese weapons from World War II.

❑ Authorized heavy weapons and armored vehicles were also in short supply. None of the armored units had their allocation of M-24 "Chaffee" or M-4E8 "Sherman" tanks, and the two dozen M-8 and M-20 armored cars and one dozen M-3 halftracks of the ROK 1st Cavalry Division were some of the army's only armored vehicles. Similarly, most ROK artillery units were armed with only a quarter of their requisite 105mm artillery pieces, and infantry units were not properly equipped to engage enemy tanks.

❑ Nonetheless, KMAG commander Brig. Gen. William L. Roberts, at sea on his way back to the United States when the war began, probably believed his own words when he said, in an interview with *Time*, "The South Koreans have the best damn army outside the United States!" If the North Koreans had believed that bit of fiction, however, or been intimidated by the army of the United States, they might never have invaded their southern neighbor.

❑ When the communists did cross the 38th parallel in June 1950, it was guarded by a mere handful of ROK regiments, while the rest were either in reserve 10 or more miles south of the border or stationed elsewhere in the country.

REFORGED IN COMBAT

❑ Although some elements of the ROK armed forces tried to stand their ground against the communist forces, North Korea's army quickly defeated them and steadily drove their remnants southward.

❏ Those fragments retreated into the protective circle of the Pusan Perimeter, and in August 1950 the shattered ROK Army was reorganized, and rebuilt as much as possible. Its 2nd, 5th, and 7th Infantry Divisions were disbanded and assimilated into the ROK 1st, 3rd, 6th, 8th, and Capital Infantry Divisions.

❏ During the defense of the Pusan Perimeter in August and the first half of September 1950, the five divisions of the ROK I and II Corps held the right sector of the U.N. line, along its northern edge. Then, after U.N. forces landed at Inchon, the ROK divisions participated in the breakout from the perimeter and the subsequent advance northward.

❏ ROK units led the way across the 38th parallel, driving the now-broken North Korean People's Army before them and advancing into Wonsan, the communist capital Pyongyang, and other North Korean locations ahead of the U.S. and other U.N. forces. On October 26, the ROK 6th Division (ROK II Corps) reached the Yalu River, the peninsula's northern border with China.

❏ When the Chinese communist forces intervened in the Korean War beginning in October 1950, they hit the ROK formations especially hard, often targeting them as the units most likely to break and allow the U.N. lines to be breached. Before the end of the year the ROK forces were once again on the verge of crumbling.

❏ As with the rest of the U.N. forces, the ROK units were driven out of North Korea and back across the 38th parallel in an uncontrolled rout that did not stop until they were south of Seoul. Once there, the ROK Army was reorganized and reformed into a combat effective force.

❏ After the lines of contact solidified in mid-1951, the ROK Army continued to mature, growing in experience and confidence on patrols, ambushes, and innumerable battles to take or hold nameless hilltops. They also suffered many thousands of troops killed, wounded, or missing in action.

❏ Throughout the course of the war, South Korea continued to expand and strengthen its army. By the summer of 1953, the Yuk Gun was a battle hardened force of 590,000, led by tough, experienced officers and NCOs. It was organized into the ROK I, II, and III Corps, which incorporated 18 divisions and a number of other elements, as follows:

1st ROK Division (11th, 12th, and 15th Infantry Regiments)
2nd ROK Division (17th, 31st, and 32nd Infantry Regiments)

3rd ROK Division (22nd, 23rd, and 18th Infantry Regiments)
5th ROK Division (27th, 35th, and 36th Infantry Regiments)
6th ROK Division (2nd, 7th, and 19th Infantry Regiments)
7th ROK Division (3rd, 5th, and 8th Infantry Regiments)
8th ROK Division (10th, 16th, and 21st Infantry Regiments)
9th ROK Division (28th, 29th, and 30th Infantry Regiments)
Capitol Division (1st Cavalry and 26th Infantry Regiments)
11th ROK Division (9th, 13th, and 20th Infantry Regiments)
12th ROK Division (37th, 51st, and 52nd Infantry Regiments)
15th ROK Division (38th, 39th, and 50th Infantry Regiments)
20th ROK Division (60th, 61st, and 62nd Infantry Regiments)
21st ROK Division (63rd, 65th, and 66th Infantry Regiments)
22nd ROK Division (67th, 68th, and 69th Infantry Regiments)
25th ROK Division (70th, 71st, and 72nd Infantry Regiments)
26th ROK Division (73rd, 75th, and 76th Infantry Regiments)
27th ROK Division (77th, 78th, and 79th Infantry Regiments)
53rd, 55th, and 59th Independent Infantry Regiments
1st Anti-Guerrilla Group (1st, 3rd, 5th, 13th, and 15th Security Battalions)
3 1st, 33rd, 35th, and 36th Security Guard Battalions
1st, 3rd, 8th, and 11th Field Artillery Groups
88th, 93rd, 95th, and 99th Independent Field Artillery Battalions
51st, 53rd, 55th, and 59th Tank Companies
1st and 2nd ROK Army Replacement Centers
Ground General School

THE KOREAN MARINE CORPS (KMC)

❏ Formed in April 1949 of volunteers from the South Korean navy and coast guard, the ROK Marine Corps, widely known as the Korean Marine Corps, was advised from its start by U.S. Marine Corps personnel.

❏ By the end of 1949, the Korean Marine Corps consisted of two battalions. In August 1950, two months after the outbreak of the Korean War, a third battalion was added to the force and it was redesignated the 1st Korean Marine Corps Regiment and attached to the U.S. 1st Marine Division.

Troops of the ROK 5th Marine Regiment are loaded onto an amphibious tractor (AMTRAC) prior to moving up to positions along the Han River during the U.N. advance on Seoul, October 3, 1950.

❏   In March 1952, the U.N. Command decided that partisan infantry forces operating out of several islands off the coast of North Korea would be more effective if they did not have to provide for their own local security. Korean marines were selected as the most appropriate troops for this task, and thus the 2nd Korean Marine Corps Regiment was raised.

❏   Two battalions of the new regiment were deployed to a number of islands in the Yellow Sea, among them Paengnyong-do and Cho-do, off the west coast of North Korea, while the third battalion was stationed on the other side of the peninsula, primarily on islands near the mouth of Wonsan harbor.

THE ROK AIR FORCE

❑ When conflict erupted on the peninsula in June 1950, the ROK Air Force had a strength of about 2,000 personnel, and was equipped with a handful of L-4 and L-5 single engine, two-person liaison aircraft and a few C-47 transports. It had no combat aircraft, but had tried to obtain them from the United States.

❑ Shortly after the war began, a number of ROK Air Force volunteers were sent to the United States for training. They returned to their homeland in late 1951 as qualified F-51 "Mustang" fighter pilots, and were formed into a squadron that was stationed at Kangnung (K-18), on South Korea's east coast. Additional South Korean F-51 squadrons were established in 1952 and 1953.

THE ROK NAVY

❑ When the communists invaded in June 1950, South Korea's 6,000-man navy/coast guard was equipped only with a few U.S.-made, 105-foot patrol vessels and a number of tank landing ships (LSTs). Like the South Korean Air Force, however, it was strengthened and reinforced as the war progressed, and increasingly proved itself an asset, especially in the U.N. blockade of North Korean ports.

OTHER KOREAN MILITARY CONTRIBUTIONS

Beyond those that served in the ROK armed forces, Koreans from both sides of the 38th parallel fought against the communist forces in a number of ways, both as augmentees to various U.N. contingents and in special warfare units.

KOREAN AUGMENTATION TO THE U.S. ARMY (KATUSA)

❑ Soon after war broke out, the United States and the Republic of Korea launched the Korean Augmentation to the Army (KATUSA) program, under which 100 South Korean recruits would be assigned to each U.S. Army company and battery.

Many KATUSA troops were only teenagers when they
joined U.S. units. Private Yun Chun Gi, age 15,
nicknamed Poncho by the U.S. troops, was the first
KATUSA to be assigned to Company K, 3rd Battalion,
19th Infantry Regiment.

❑ Such soldiers were administered and paid by the ROK Army, but were
paired up with an American "buddy" and fed and equipped by the unit to
which they were assigned.

❑ On August 15, 1950, the Far East Command ordered the Eighth U.S.
Army to utilize such Korean augmentees, both in the divisions operating in
Korean and in the 7th Infantry Division, at that time training in Japan.

❑ Some 8,625 KATUSAs were assigned to the 7th Infantry Division, which
had been stripped of troops by the three divisions preceding it to Korea.
They arrived in the division's camps in Japan just three weeks before its
participation in the Inchon landing.

❑ Initially, the KATUSA program was too extreme, utilizing school boys
and young men who had been pulled off the streets and pressed into service.

A few weeks of training could not make these KATUSAs into real soldiers, and their shortcomings became apparent soon after their first exposures to combat.

❏ Problems with the program became apparent during the fighting withdrawal from North Korea in November and December 1950. KATUSAs quickly became demoralized under the extreme conditions of the campaign and when under fire, many of them to hid in foxholes and would not fire their weapons.

❏ As the war progressed, each major command dealt with the KATUSA program in different ways. In the 1st Cavalry Division and 2nd Infantry Division, for example, the buddy system was continued and American soldiers trained their Korean counterparts in U.S. weapons and tactics. In the 24th Infantry Division, however, the KATUSAs were organized into separate platoons and squads, used for specialized tasks like guard duty, patrolling, moving heavy weapons over rough terrain, and scouting, tasks at which the all-KATUSA elements proved effective. Korean soldiers were also able to teach the GIs how to camouflage using straw and other local materials.

❏ Reluctance from U.S. units prevented the KATUSA program from quickly reaching its anticipated level, and by June 1951 there only 12,718 KATUSAs.

❏ When properly trained and equipped, however, Korean troops functioned as well as U.S. soldiers, and plans were made to expand the program. By late 1952, a total of 20,000 KATUSAs were assigned to each of the eight U.S. divisions and another 7,000 to combat support units.

❏ After the armistice, the KATUSA program was reduced in scope. Today, about there are about 7,000 South Korean soldiers in the KATUSA program, a level that was reached in mid-1971, following the reduction of U.S. ground forces in Korea.

KOREANS IN OTHER U.N. UNITS

❏ During the war a number of other U.N. units, including the Belgian Battalion, the Dutch Battalion, and the Commonwealth Division, used programs similar to KATUSA to round out their ranks. Like the U.S. army's program, these efforts enjoyed mixed results.

❑ A program called Koreans Attached to the Commonwealth Forces (KATCOM) was started in October 1952, when 1,000 ROK recruits were assigned to the Commonwealth Division, two per infantry squad. As in the U.S. program, such soldiers were used mainly as drivers, mechanics, sentries, and in other support positions.

❑ KATCOMs were issued uniforms, weapons, and equipment appropriate to the Commonwealth units to which they were attached and could attain noncommissioned officer rank within those units. For pay and administrative purposes, however, they were still considered members of the ROK Army.

❑ A similar program was established by the Belgian Battalion in 1951, when up to 100 soldiers from the Korean Service Corps were assigned to it, a number that was increased to 250 in 1952. Such troops were used mainly as unskilled laborers, but could be promoted to noncommissioned officer rank within the battalion, with authority over other Korean soldiers. Some of them eventually became frontline soldiers or moved into support positions (e.g., as cooks, mechanics, or truck drivers).

UNITED NATIONS PARTISAN INFANTRY

❑ After the U.N. forces were driven back across the 38th parallel at the end of fall in 1950, thousands of North Koreans who had helped them had to flee as well, or face death at the hands of the advancing communists.

❑ Many of these people escaped to the islands off the west coast of North Korea, where they organized themselves into partisan units, more out of a need to defend themselves than from a sense of ideology.

❑ In February 1951, the U.N. Command armed and equipped these disparate guerilla bands and organized them, along with some Americans, into the U.S. 8th Army G-3 Miscellaneous Group, 8086th Army Unit, which they began to use for raids behind the communist lines.

❑ Ten months later, in December 1951, the Koreans and Americans in the 8086th were incorporated into the Far East Command's 8240th Army Unit and redesignated the United Nations Partisan Infantry Korea (UNPIK).

❑ UNPIK remained active under U.S. Army command until mid-1953, by which time it had claimed a total of 69,000 enemy casualties. At its peak in 1953, UNPIK had a strength of about 22,000.

VII

ALLIED FORCES

"All Members have undertaken to make available to the [Security] Council on its call, in accordance with special agreements to be negotiated on the initiative of the Council, the armed forces, assistance, and facilities, including rights of passage, necessary for maintaining international peace and security."

—U.N. Department of Public Information

U.S. and ROK forces did not fight the Korean War alone. Sixteen other members of the United Nations sent military contingents, the Scandinavian nations and Italy sent medical detachments, and various other countries sent limited quantities of food and money.

❏ On June 25, 1950, the same day North Korean forces crossed the 38th parallel, the United Nations passed a resolution calling for its members to "furnish such assistance to the Republic of Korea as may be necessary to repel the armed attack and to restore international peace and security in the area."

❏ Many European nations were still suffering from the effects of World War II when war in Korea broke out. Several had been or were still combating guerrilla insurgencies, either at home or in rebellious colonies. Most had military commitments to the North Atlantic Treaty Organizations (and, in the cases of Great Britain and France, to the occupation of Germany) and were concerned about the direct threat to their countries posed by the Soviet Union.

❏ As a result, many countries were reluctant and a bit slow to commit military forces in Korea. Total contributions by all the U.N. member nations participating in the war, other than South Korea, were about one-tenth of the U.S. commitment to the conflict.

❏   As various U.N. member nations began offer forces for the defense of South Korea, the Security Council recommended they be placed under a unified command. Thus, the United Nations Command was established and headquartered in Tokyo under the command of U.S. Gen. Douglas MacArthur.

❏   Most of the soldiers sent to Korea by the allied nations were elite or experienced troops, and American troops generally considered themselves inferior to those of the other allied nations. Despite this, however, captured communist documents consistently reflected the Chinese belief that the American soldiers were the best.

AUSTRALIA

❏   Australia sent ground forces consisting of three infantry battalions; naval forces consisting of one aircraft carrier, two destroyers, and one frigate; and air forces composed of one fighter squadron and one air transport squadron. It was the first country after the United States to commit forces from all three of its major services.

❏   Two of the Australian elements, the 3rd Battalion, Royal Australian Regiment (3 RAR—the "Diggers") and 77 Squadron of the Royal Australian Air Force, were stationed in Japan as part of the British Commonwealth Occupation Force when the war broke out.

❏   3 RAR arrived in Korea on September 28, 1950, and joined the British 27th Infantry Brigade, which was assigned to the U.S. 24th Infantry Division (8th U.S. Army) and redesignated the 27th Commonwealth Infantry Brigade.

❏   As part of the 8th U.S. Army, Australian troops participated in the breakout from the Pusan Perimeter and the advance north across the 38th parallel. They fought their first major action of the war near Pyongyang, the North Korean capital.

❏   Australian troops participated in two major actions in 1951. On April 22, 1951, a U.N. force that included Australian soldiers counterattacked Chinese forces in the Kapyong Valley that had driven ROK and New Zealand forces out of the area. During a night of fierce fighting in which they suffered a relatively modest 32 men killed and 53 wounded, the Australians were overrun, recaptured their position, and succeeded in stalling the Chinese advance. Their role in the battle earned them a U.S. Presidential Citation. On October 3, 1951, Australian forces attached to the Commonwealth Division took part in Operation Commando, an attack against a Chinese salient in a bend of the Imjin River. The division had two main objectives, Hills 317 and 355, which they captured after five days of heavy combat. Australian casualties consisted of 20 killed and 89 wounded.

❏ From 1951 until the end of the war, Australian troops occupied trenchworks at the eastern end of the Commonwealth Division's sector in the hills northeast of the Imjin River, separated by a 300- to 2,000-meter-wide no man's land from heavily fortified Chinese positions.

❏ Even as other U.N. countries sought to extricate themselves from Korea, Australia increased its commitment. A second infantry battalion, 1 RAR, arrived in Korea in March 1952 and joined the Commonwealth Division on June 1, 1952. It left Korea in March 1953 and was replaced a month later by 2 RAR.

❏ Casualties suffered by Australia throughout the course of the entire war consisted of about 1,200 wounded and 339 killed.

BELGIUM

❏ Belgium decided to commit forces to Korea on August 25, 1950, and raised a Korean Volunteer Corps (Corps Voluntaires Corea) consisting of a single infantry battalion. Once in Korea, this force was augmented by a platoon of volunteers from Luxembourg and the combined unit was collectively known as the BELUX Battalion.

❏ Belgium also sent several DC-4 transportation aircraft to support the U.N. efforts in Korea and two nurses to work in Japan.

❏ Commanded by Lt. Col. Albert Crahay, the 900-man 1st Belgian Battalion (1st Bataillon Belge) arrived in Korea in December 1950 and was attached the following month to the U.S. 3rd Infantry Division. A year and half later, in August 1951, this unit was replaced by the 2nd Belgian Battalion, which remained in country until June 1955.

❑ Belgium, a bilingual nation, divided its battalion into three separate French- and Flemish-speaking rifle companies. Luxembourg's soldiers were incorporated into a French-speaking company.

❑ During 1951, as many as 100 ROK soldiers from the Korean Service Corps were assigned to the Belgian Battalion, and in 1952 this number was increased to 250. Initially, such men were used mainly as unskilled labor, serving as coolies and stretcher-bearers. They could be promoted to NCO rank within the battalion, however (with authority over other Korean soldiers), and some of them eventually became frontline soldiers or moved into support positions (e.g., cooks or truck drivers).

❑ Belgian soldiers experienced their heaviest fighting in April 1951. On April 22, elements of a massive Chinese offensive surrounded and cut of the Belgian Battalion, which occupied an isolated position near the Imjin River. Part of a British Battalion and then a force of tanks tried to relieve the Belgians, but were unsuccessful. On April 23, however, the Belgians managed to slip across the Chinese lines on their right flank and withdraw.

❑ On April 24, the Belgian troops returned to the area they had abandoned the day before, as part of a multinational force attempting to rescue the British 1st Battalion, Gloucestershire Regiment. This attempt was not successful, and the Glosters were overrun and destroyed, only a handful of them managing to escape.

❑ Belgian soldiers also participated in heavy fighting in October 1951, at Haktang-ni, a village north of Chorwon.

❑ At peak strength, the battalion numbered 945, and some 3,498 Belgians served in its ranks during its four-and-a-half years in Korea. Of those, 101 were killed, 350 were wounded, five were missing, and one died in captivity. A single Belgian prisoner was repatriated in 1953.

CANADA

❑ Canada sent ground forces consisting of one army brigade of three infantry battalions, one artillery regiment, and one armored regiment; naval forces consisting of three destroyers; and air forces consisting of one air transport squadron.

❑ Asia had never been an area of strategic interest for Canada, whose armed forces had been reduced to peacetime strength and trained only for national defense in the wake of World War II. Thus, while Canada supported in principle the U.N. decision to defend South Korea, it hesitated initially to commit forces to the conflict.

❏ Canada had been involved in U.N. discussions on the Korean issue since 1947, however, and had served on the U.N. Temporary Commission on Korea (but not its successor, the U.N Commission on Korea). This involvement, along with a desire to close ranks with the United States against communist aggression, contributed to Canada's eventual decision to send forces to Korea.

❏ On July 12, 1950, the Royal Canadian Navy destroyers HMCS *Cayuga*, *Athabaskan*, and *Sioux* were dispatched to Korean waters. On August 15, *Cayuga* bombarded communist positions in Yosu in defense of the Pusan Perimeter. In the following months all three of the Canadian warships served as escort vessels during the landings at Inchon and Wonsan.

❏ In December 1950, after China entered the war and began to drive the allied forces out of northern Korea, the three destroyers, along with an Australian and an American destroyer, moved up the mouth of the Taedong River to rescue a large number of U.N. troops trapped near Chinnampo. This action constituted the Canadian naval force's largest and most significant operation during the war.

❏ Royal Canadian Air Force No. 426 Transport Squadron was also deployed to Asia in July 1950. U.N. forces were falling back into the Pusan Perimeter when the squadron arrived, and it was immediately tasked with flying supplies from Japan to the defending forces.

❏ By early 1951, the 426th was performing routine transportation duties, including regularly scheduled flights between Hameda Airfield, near Tokyo, and McChord Air Force Base, Washington.

❏ In addition to the transportation squadron, 22 Royal Canadian Air Force pilots served in U.S. aircraft formations. None of the men or aircraft of the 426 Transport Squadron were lost during the war; one of the pilots flying with the U.S. units was shot down and captured, but was repatriated at the end of the war.

❏ On August 7, 1950, Canada authorized the formation of the Canadian Army Special Force, which included Lord Strathcona's Horse and Princess Patricia's Light Infantry. These units arrived in Korea in December 1950.

❏ Just a few months later, the Canadian ground forces became engaged in heavy combat during the Chinese spring offensives of 1951, and formed part of the force that battled the communists at Kapyong and along the Imjin River.

❑ Canada sent additional units to Korea in May 1951, and consolidated them and its forces already on the ground into the 25th Infantry Brigade Group.

❑ In July 1951, after some hesitation, Canada allowed the 25th Infantry Brigade Group to become part of the 1st Commonwealth Division, a conglomerate of British, Canadian, Australian, Indian, and New Zealand forces.

❑ In May 1952, Canadian troops were among those sent to quell rioting at the U.N. prisoner of war compound on Koje Island. Canada had not agreed to let its contingent be used for this sort of duty, however, and was displeased its troops were utilized in this manner.

❑ Canadian forces in Korea peaked in January 1952 at about 8,000, although by the armistice a year and half later they still exceeded 7,000. Altogether, a total of 21,900 Canadians served in the ground forces during the Korean War. Of these, more than 300 were killed, more than 1,200 were wounded, and 32 were captured by the communists.

❑ Canada started to withdraw its forces after the armistice, and the last combat troops departed in April 1955. A medical detachment stayed on another two years, and then left in June 1957.

COLOMBIA

❑ Colombia sent ground forces consisting of four 1,000-man infantry battalions, one at a time, and naval forces consisting of a single frigate, the *Almirante Padilla*. It was the only Latin American nation to send forces to Korea.

❑ In June 1951, the 1st Colombian Battalion (1st Batallon Colombia) arrived in Korea. In July 1952, it was replaced by the 2nd Colombian Battalion, which remained in country until November 1952, when it was replaced by the 3rd Colombian Battalion. In June 1953, the 3rd Colombian Battalion was replaced by the 4th Colombian Battalion, which remained in Korea until October 1954.

❑ The Colombian battalions were attached to various U.S. infantry divisions during the war and fought in such actions as the Battle of Old Baldy and the Kumsan offensive. Many Colombian soldiers were awarded bronze and silver stars for their actions, and the battalions suffered about 600 casualties during the Korean War.

❑ Colombia was torn by civil strife in the early 1950s, and right-wing dictator Laureano Gomez may have sent troops in order curry U.S. favor, draw attention away from domestic repression, and temporarily exile military opponents.

ETHIOPIA

❑ Ethiopia agreed to send an infantry battalion to Korea, which included volunteers from Emperor Haile Selassie's Imperial Security Guard, a unit of elite six-foot-tall soldiers. Dubbed the Kagnew, or Conquerors Battalion, the unit was relieved by fresh battalions twice during the Korean War. (Kagnew, according to some sources, was an imperial warhorse and the namesake of the unit.)

Ethiopian soldiers, like those of the other U.N. contingents, were among the best their country could send. These members of the Kagnew Battalion are admiring a U.S.-made semiautomatic carbine.

❏ Ethiopia's 1st Kagnew Battalion, a 931-man unit, arrived in Korea in May 1951 and was attached to the 32nd Regiment of the U.S. 7th Infantry Division in June 1951. In April 1952, the 1st Kagnew Battalion was replaced by the 2nd Kagnew Battalion. In April 1953, it was relieved in its turn by the 3rd Kagnew Battalion, which remained in Korea until April 1954.

❏ Ethiopian soldiers fought in many battles during the war, and were highly regarded for their skill in hand-to-hand and bayonet fighting, patrolling, and night fighting. Altogether, 3,158 Ethiopians served in the Kagnew battalions. Of those, 121 were killed, 536 were wounded, and none were taken prisoner.

❏ A number of Ethiopian nurses also worked with the Red Cross in Japan.

FRANCE

❏ France sent ground forces consisting of one infantry battalion and naval forces consisting of one warship, the frigate *La Grandiere*, which it committed on July 22, 1950.

❏ On August 24, 1950, France set about raising a volunteer battalion of both reservists and active duty soldiers. Many of those selected for the unit were combat veterans with experience fighting in France's overseas colonies, including Algeria.

❏ Departing the port of Marseille on September 25, 1950, the French Battalion arrived in Korea on November 30 and was completely debarked by December 5. Under the command of Lt. Col. Ralph Monclar, it consisted of 39 officers, 172 noncommissioned officers, and more than 800 enlisted men, many of them Algerian colonial troops.

❏ Equipped with U.S. weapons and vehicles, and reinforced with a company of ROK soldiers, the French Battalion was attached for the duration of the war to the 23rd Infantry Regiment (U.S. 2nd Infantry Division).

❏ French soldiers fought in a number of intense battles during the Korean War, engaging in everything from firefights to bayonet charges. In 1951 alone, they fought at Wonju, the Twin Tunnels, and Chipyong-ni during the U.N. advance on Seoul; against the Chinese spring offensives; and at Heartbreak Ridge and the Punchbowl.

❏ In October 1952, in a sideline to the Battle of White Horse Hill, the French Battalion successfully defended Arrowhead Hill against a determined Chinese offensive, holding their ground against the communists for nearly a week until the attack was broken. They took part in other actions in the Iron Triangle and at the Hook throughout the winter of 1952-1953.

❏ At peak strength, the French contingent numbered 1,185 men, and a total of 3,421 French soldiers served in Korea during the conflict. Of these, 287 were killed, 1,350 were wounded, seven were missing in action, and 12 became prisoners of war. Many citations were awarded to the unit and its members.

❏ On October 22, 1953, the French Battalion left Korea for Vietnam. After it arrived the following month, it was renamed the Korea Regiment and reinforced with additional troops to form the *Groupement Mobile Nr. 100*. This unit was wiped out the following July in a series of Viet Minh attacks.

❏ France's 4th Frigate Squadron also served as part of U.S. Navy Task Group 90.04 during this period. Viet Minh guerrillas blew up one of these French ships as it departed Saigon for Korea, killing 143 of its sailors.

GREAT BRITAIN

❏ Great Britain sent ground forces totalling three army brigades (only two of which served at a time), two field artillery regiments, and one armored regiment. It also sent naval forces consisting of one aircraft carrier, two cruisers, eight destroyers, and attached marine and other support units.

❏ Elements of the 27th Infantry Brigade—the 1st Battalion of the Middlesex Regiment, the 1st Battalion of the Argyll Regiment, and the Sutherland Highlanders—and the Royal Irish Hussars arrived in Korea on August 28, 1950.

❏ These forces were initially assigned to the U.S. 24th Infantry Division and were immediately sent into the line to help defend the Pusan Perimeter, participating in heavy fighting along the banks of the Naktong River.

❏ At the end of September 1950, the British contingent was reinforced with the Australian and New Zealand forces present in Korea and redesignated the 27th Commonwealth Infantry Brigade; it was further

British forces began arriving in Korea in summer 1950 to help defend the collapsing Pusan Perimeter. Pictured are soldiers of the Middlesex Regiment, arriving at Pusan Airport on August 27, 1950.

expanded in February 1951, when a Canadian contingent arrived in Korea. This reinforced brigade was reassigned to the U.S. 1st Cavalry Division.

❑ In September 1950, the 29th Infantry Brigade Group arrived in Korea.

❑ In April 1951, the commander and staff of the 28th Infantry Brigade arrived in Korea and took control of the 27th Commonwealth Infantry Brigade, after which it was once again redesignated, as the 28th Commonwealth Infantry Brigade.

❑ In July 1951, the British, Australian, Canadian, New Zealand, and Indian contingents were organized into the Commonwealth Division. This division was under the operational control of the U.N. Command, but was administered by the Commander-in-Chief of the Commonwealth Forces, headquartered in Japan.

❑ Many of the British units were of an illustrious lineage. For example, components of the 29th Infantry Brigade included the 1st Battalion, Royal Northumberland Fusiliers, formed in 1674, and the 1st Battalion, Gloucestershire Regiment, "Glosters," which was formed in 1694 and had earned in its 256 years 44 battle streamers, more than any other regiment in the British Army.

❏ By the time the armistice was signed in July 1953, 14,000 British soldiers had served in Korea. About 700 of them were killed, and about 4,000 of them were wounded or taken prisoner, 977 of whom were repatriated at the end of the war.

❏ *A Hill in Korea* (a 1956 film featuring Korean War veteran Michael Caine in his first movie role), depicts a patrol of British soldiers trapped in a Korean village and forced to fight their way back to friendly lines.

GREECE

❏ Greece sent ground forces consisting of one volunteer infantry battalion of soldiers drawn from the regular Greek army, many of whom were veterans of the 1946 Greek Civil War, fought between the government and communist insurgents. Greece also sent air forces consisting of one air transport squadron.

❏ On December 9, 1950, the 840-man battalion, known as the Royal Hellenic Expeditionary Force, arrived in Korea. After undergoing additional training and receiving equipment, it was assigned to the 7th Cavalry Regiment (1st Cavalry Division), which it served with during much of the Korean War.

❏ In December 1950, the Greek forces (as part of the 7th Cavalry) moved southward from a position north of Seoul, then northward once again toward the Imjin River area, then to positions near the 38th parallel, in the middle of the Korean Peninsula. During this period, they regularly battled the Chinese forces pouring into the area, sometimes engaging them in hand-to-hand and bayonet combat.

❏ In May 1952, a company of the Hellenic battalion was sent to help quell riots provoked by communist agitators in the U.N. prisoner of war camp on Koje Island.

❏ A second infantry battalion arrived in Korea shortly after fighting ended in 1953, bringing the Hellenic forces up to regimental strength. This reinforced unit was reduced once again to battalion strength in March 1955 and was deactivated later that year; by December 1955, the Greek forces had returned home to Greece.

❏ Greek soldiers were respected for their fighting prowess in Korea and received many citations for their actions. From 1950 to 1955, 10,184 Greek soldiers served in Korea, 184 of whom were killed, 543 of whom were wounded, and two of whom were captured.

❏ Greece's air contribution, the 13th Hellenic Air Force Squadron, comprised eight C-47 cargo planes and was assigned to the U.S. 21st Troop Carrier Squadron. It flew its first mission in December 1950, immediately after arriving in Korea, helping to evacuate 1,000 wounded members of the U.S. 1st Marine Division from their positions near the Chosin Reservoir.

❏ Some 397 men served in the Greek transportation squadron, 12 of whom were killed during the war.

❏ A multinational combat engineer unit under the command of a Greek officer is depicted in the 1953 film *The Glory Brigade*, one of the few films to examine the international nature of the U.N. involvement in the Korean War.

INDIA

❏ India sent a unit of the Indian Army Medical Corps to support the U.N. forces in Korea. Although India emphasized its neutrality by sending only medical personnel and not combat troops, the 60th Parachute Field Ambulance Unit, under the command of Lt. Col. A.G. Rangaraj, was a uniformed contingent that served alongside other Commonwealth units.

❏ In December 1950, the 346-member Indian contingent, which included a number of Sikhs, advanced northward with the British 27th Infantry Brigade to the North Korean capital of Pyongyang. On December 5, however, U.N. forces began a general retreat in the face of overwhelming opposition from the newly-arrived Chinese forces.

❏ Ordered to destroy their medical supplies, the stalwart Indians instead loaded them onto a commandeered train and managed to escape the enemy capital minutes before the last railroad bridge was destroyed.

❏ For the remainder of the war, the 60th Parachute Field Ambulance Unit supported the 1st Commonwealth Division in the central sector of Korea, operating a helicopter medical evacuation service and parachuting into the combat zone to provide medical assistance.

❏ A smaller Indian detachment, under Maj. N.B. Banerjee, was stationed in Taegu, in South Korea, where it provided medical and surgical support for various Korean military and civilian hospitals.

Indian medical personnel of the 60th Parachute Field Ambulance Unit served alongside other Commonwealth troops during the war, jumping into the front lines on several occasions to support British, Canadian, Australian, and New Zealand combat forces.

❏ In August 1953, the Indian parachute unit left the Commonwealth Division to provide support for the Indian Custodial Force, which oversaw the screening of North Korean and Chinese prisoners unwilling to return to their home countries.

❏ In February 1954, after the Indian Custodial Force's mission was complete, the 60th Parachute Field Ambulance Unit returned home to India.

LUXEMBOURG

❏ Luxembourg sent a single, 44-man, all-volunteer infantry platoon to Korea in November 1950. This platoon was attached to a French-speaking company of the Belgian Battalion and the augmented force became known collectively as the BELUX Battalion.

❏ Along with the Belgian forces, which were themselves assigned to the U.S. 3rd Infantry Division, Luxembourg's platoon experienced its heaviest fighting in April 1951 at the Battle of the Imjin River. Six months later, in October 1951, the Luxembourgers again engaged in heavy combat at Haktang-ni.

❑ The Luxembourg platoon returned home in late 1953. A total of 89 soldiers from the tiny duchy served in the Korean war and two of them were killed during the conflict.

THE NETHERLANDS

❑ The Netherlands sent one understrength infantry battalion and a Dutch navy destroyer. The Netherlands was fighting a guerilla insurgency in Indonesia in 1950, and its forces were deployed directly from combat in Southeast Asia.

❑ An advance party of the Netherlands Battalion arrived in Korea on October 24, 1950, and the balance of the unit arrived on November 23, 1950. This battalion—636 men and a few nurses organized into two infantry companies and one heavy weapons company—was assigned to the U.S. 2nd Infantry Division as part of its 38th Infantry Regiment in December 1950.

❑ In January 1951, Dutch soldiers battled communist forces around Wonju during Operation Thunderbolt.

❑ In February 1951, the Netherlands Battalion fought at Hoengsong during Operation Roundup, an abortive offensive east of Seoul that was smashed by a communist counteroffensive. During this action, Chinese soldiers killed more than 100 Dutch troops, including the battalion commander, when they infiltrated the Dutch positions disguised as ROK troops.

❑ A few months later, in April 1951, the Netherlands Battalion fought around Kumhwa during the Chinese spring offensive, during which they made a 24-hour forced march without rations.

❑ In 1952, Dutch forces fought along the 38th parallel in the Iron Triangle. During the same year, they helped suppress the communist-backed riot at the U.N. prisoner of war compunds on Koje Island.

❑ The Netherlands Battalion served in Korea until October 1, 1954. Despite the fact that the Dutch soldiers had deployed from a tropical climate to one subject to near-arctic extremes, the Netherlands Battalion fought well and was regarded as an excellent combat unit.

❏ A total of 3,148 Dutch infantrymen served in Korea during the war (3,972 by the time the Netherlands Battalion left in 1954). Of these, 120 were killed, 645 were wounded, and three were repatriated. A great number of Dutch soldiers were awarded for their actions by the Netherlands, the United States, and South Korea.

❏ A Dutch navy destroyer, HNLMS *Evertsen*, was deployed from the waters off Indonesia immediately after the Netherlands agreed to commit forces to the conflict and arrived in Korea on July 19, 1950. It was eventually relieved by another Dutch ship, and by January 24, 1955, two other destroyers and three frigates had served in Korean waters.

❏ HNLMS *Evertsen* was part of the screening force of destroyers that provided covering fire for U.N. forces during the Inchon landing. It served until April 1951, and was replaced by a succession of Dutch warships: the destroyers HNLMS *Van Galen* (April 1951 to January 1952), and HNLMS *Piet Hem* (January 1952 to January 1953); the frigates HNLMS *Johan Maurits van Nassau* (January 1953 to May 1953) HNLMS *Dubois* (May 1953 to October 1954), and HNLMS *van Zijll* (October 1954 to January 1955).

❏ Dutch warships, operating in the waters off both the east and west coasts of the Korean peninsula, participated in patrols, blockades, shore bombardments against communist coastal guns, transportation, and fortifications, in support of ground forces, and as carrier escorts. Altogether, 1,360 Dutch personnel served in the Netherlands naval contingent, two of whom were killed.

❏ HNLMS *Piet Hem* was distinguished for destroying an enemy train with its guns, and the four vessels that served prior to the armistice were awarded ROK presidential unit citations for their actions as part of the U.S. 7th Fleet (HNLMS *Evertsen* and HNLMS *Van Galen* also served with Task Force 95 and received the award twice).

❏ *Field of Honour*, a 1986 film, depicts the experiences of a Dutch soldier who is left for dead and must work his way back to U.N. lines.

NEW ZEALAND

❏ New Zealand sent ground forces consisting of one artillery regiment and naval forces consisting of six frigates. New Zealand was one of the first nations to respond to the U.N. appeal for assistance in South Korea and sent more troops in proportion to its population than any allied country except the United States.

❑ On June 29, 1950, New Zealand offered to support the U.N. forces with a naval contingent and on July 3, HMNZS *Pukaki* and HMNZS *Tutira*, a pair of two Royal New Zealand Navy Loch-class frigates, sailed for Korea. These ships were succeeded later in the war by four other frigates HMNZS *Rotoiti*, HMNZS *Hawea*, HMNZS *Taupo*, and HMNZS Kaniere.

❑ HMNZS *Pukaki* and HMNZS *Tutira* were assigned to the U.S. Navy's Far Eastern Command and served with the screening force during the Inchon landing. For the remainder of the war, the various New Zealand ships participated in coastal raids, shore bombardment, and blockading, mostly off the western coast of North Korea. About half of New Zealand's sailors, more than 1,300 of them, served in Korea.

❑ On July 26, New Zealand responded to further U.N. appeals by deciding to recruit, train, and equip 1,000 men for a transportation platoon and an artillery unit, the 16th Field Artillery Regiment. Because the island nation had an army of only 3,000 men at the time, it had to initiate a special recruiting program, which yielded 6,000 volunteers.

❑ New Zealand's Korea force, or "Kayforce," left for Korea on December 11, arrived in Pusan on December 31, and was fighting as part of the 27th Commonwealth Brigade by January 23. In April 1951, Kayforce fought in the Battle of Kapyong, during the 5th Chinese Phase Offensive.

❑ Later in 1951, New Zealand sent a transportation company to Korea to augment its contingent, and on July 28, 1951, the New Zealanders were incorporated into the 1st Commonwealth Division. They stayed busy during the last two years of the war, as artillery duels began to play an increasingly prominent role in combat between the entrenched armies.

❑ During Kayforce's six years in Korea, 46 New Zealanders died from all causes (including one sailor killed during a shore raid), at least 79 were wounded, and one was captured by the communists.

❑ New Zealand's reasons for actively supporting the U.N. mission in Korea included an opposition to Soviet-backed aggression, a commitment to the U.N. principles of collective security, a desire to follow the example of Great Britain, and a wish to foster good relations with the United States (as demonstrated by their push for the ANZUS Treaty).

THE PHILIPPINES

❑ The Philippines was one of the first U.N. nations to send forces to Korea, and provided four motorized battalion combat teams (BCTs), one at a time, during the conflict (and a fifth one after the armistice was signed).

❑ Each of the reinforced Filipino units had about 1,500 men and was composed of three infantry companies, one M-4A3E8 "Sherman" tank company, one reconnaissance company, and one 105mm howitzer battery. As motorized units, they were equipped with trucks and other vehicles for transportation.

❑ The 10th BCT arrived in Korea in September 1950, and remained in country until September 1951; the 20th BCT arrived in September 1951, and remained until June 1952; the 14th BCT arrived in June 1952 and remained until April 1953; and the 2nd BCT arrived in April 1953 and remained until April 1954. A fifth battalion combat team relieved it and remained in Korea until May 1955.

❑ During the Korean War, the Filipino units were attached to various U.S. divisions and, for a short time, to British and Canadian Brigades. In 1950 and early 1951, the 10th BCT supported counterinsurgency efforts in South Korea.

❑ In spring 1951, the Filipinos were sent northward, where they helped combat the 5th Chinese Phase Offensive in April. During the Battle of Gloster Hill, they made an unsuccessful attempt to relieve a surrounded British unit, the 1st Battalion of the Gloucestershire Regiment, with a force of tanks.

❑ For the balance of the war, the Filipino battalion combat teams were active along the line of contact in the central sector of Korea.

❑ From 1950 to 1955, 7,420 Filipinos served in the battalion combat teams. Of those, 112 were killed, 299 were wounded, 16 were missing in action, and 41 were taken prisoner, all of whom were repatriated. Various citations were awarded to the units and their members.

SOUTH AFRICA

❑ South Africa sent the 2nd Squadron of the South African Air Force (SAAF), the "Flying Cheetahs," a fighter aircraft unit of 49 officers and 157 enlisted men equipped with F-51D Mustangs.

❑ Deployed on September 26, 1950 from South Africa to Johnson Base in Tokyo, 2nd Squadron was assigned to the U.S. Air Force's 18th Fighter Bomber Wing and arrived at U.N.-held Pyongyang East Air Field (K-24) in North Korea on November.

❑ Three days after arriving in Korea, 2nd Squadron flew its first sorties, first in support of U.N. forces moving north toward the Yalu River, and then against the communist forces driving U.N. troops out of northern Korea. Despite freezing cold and inclement weather, its crews had to refuel and rearm their planes in the open.

❑ As the communist forces moved southward and recaptured Pyongyang, 2nd Squadron's base of operations was moved progressively southward to Suwon Airbase (K-13) and then Chinhae Airbase (K-10).

❑ After the lines of battle solidified in 1951, the Flying Cheetahs made both reconnaissance flights and bombing raids over North Korean airfields, communication lines, hydroelectric plants, supply dumps, and weapons depots.

❑ In January 1953, the South African squadron relocated to Osan Airbase (K-55) and began to convert over from its Mustangs to F-86 Sabre jets. On March 11, 1953, 2nd Squadron flew its first sortie with the new aircraft.

❑ The Flying Cheetahs left Korea in July 1953. Throughout the course of the war, they flew 12,067 sorties and lost 34 pilots, two other men killed or missing, 74 of their 97 Mustangs, and four of their 22 Sabres. Nine prisoners of war were repatriated after the armistice.

❑ 2nd Squadron was awarded both U.S. and ROK Presidential Unit Citations, and some of its members were awarded both U.S. and South African decorations for bravery.

THAILAND

❑ Thailand sent a Royal Thai Expeditionary Force to Korea that included a regimental combat team, four frigates and a cargo ship, one air transportation squadron, and three medical service detachments.

❑ On November 7, 1950, the 2,100 men of the 21st Royal Thailand Regimental Combat Team arrived in Korea, one of the first non-American units to do so. Over the course of the war, it was assigned to several U.S. Army commands, starting with the 1st Cavalry Division.

❏ In late November 1950, the 21st Regimental Combat Team advanced to the North Korean capital of Pyongyang. By January 1951, however, it had to withdraw southward, and was part of the force that covered the U.N. retreat from Seoul.

❏ In spring 1951, Thai forces engaged in heavy combat during both of the Chinese offensives launched that season.

❏ In October and November 1952, the Thais helped capture Pork Chop Hill and subsequently occupied it for a time. When they turned it over to the U.S. 7th Division, they left written on their bunker walls the words "Take good care of our Pork Chop."

❏ Thailand's soldiers saw hard fighting during the Korean War, earning the nickname "Little Tigers" and a number of citations for their valor. About 4,000 men served in the Royal Thai Expeditionary Force during the conflict, and of them 125 were killed, 959 were wounded, and five were missing.

❏ Thailand's naval detachment, operating out of Sasebo, Japan, from November 9, 1950, to January 21, 1955, served with the U.N. Naval Command's Far East Blockade and Escort Force. It operated mainly in the waters off the east coast cities of Songjin and Wonsan, where it took part in escort duties, patrols, and shore bombardments.

❏ One of its frigates was damaged and had to be replaced, bringing up to five the number of vessels that saw action during the war. Some 2,485 Thais served with the naval contingent during the war, four of whom were killed.

❏ From June 23, 1951 to November 6, 1964, three C-47 cargo planes of the Royal Thai Air Force were based at Tachikawa, Japan, as part of the U.N. air command. From there they flew missions both within Japan and between Japan and Korea.

❏ Thailand's medical service detachments served both in Japan and Korea during the war and included a Red Cross medical unit of 66 doctors and nurses stationed at Pusan, a mobile surgical hospital group that served in various U.N. hospitals, and an air medical team used for evacuating wounded personnel and nursing at U.N. hospitals.

TURKEY

❏ Turkey sent one 5,200-man army brigade to Korea, relieving it with fresh units twice during the conflict and with an additional brigade after the

Turkish troops, shown here preparing to assault a hill, proved themselves some of the most savage fighters of the Korean War. They were largely equipped with U.S. Weapons, uniforms, and equipment.

armistice was signed in 1953. During the war, the Turks suffered high casualties and became known as fierce, highly-disciplined fighters willing and able to engage in hand-to-hand and bayonet combat.

❑   On October 19, the Turkish Army Command Force—consisting of three infantry battalions and an artillery regiment—arrived in Korea and was attached to the U.S. 25th Infantry Division (U.S. IX Corps). Just a month later, on November 26, the Turks were sent to guard the east flank of the U.S. 2nd Division against an expected Chinese attack. Unfortunately, U.S. officers failed to brief the Turks as to what to expect, and they marched east toward Wawon, near Kunu-ri in North Korea, with no idea of what was going on around them.

Outside of Wawon, they mistakenly engaged a fleeing force of soldiers from the ROK II Corps, defeated them, and captured a large number of prisoners. Shortly thereafter, the main body of the Chinese offensive slammed into the Turkish Brigade. Many Turks fought to the death or launched bayonet counterattacks against the Chinese. When the brigade finally fell back and rendezvoused with the U.S. 38th Infantry, it had been all but destroyed. About 1,000 of the Turks were dead or missing and only a few of its companies were still combat effective, and the survivors retreated southward with the rest of the U.N. forces.

❑ On January 3, 1951, the Turkish brigade was reassigned to the U.S. I Corps and a few months later fought in the central sector of the line of contact against the two Chinese spring offensives of that year.

❑ During most of 1952, the Turkish soldiers were tasked with patrolling the area around Heartbreak Ridge. In May 1953, they engaged in heavy fighting from their positions north of Munsan.

❑ At peak strength, the Turkish contingent had 5,455 men, and a total of 14,396 Turks served in the three brigades active during the war. Of those, 741 were killed, 2,068 were wounded, 163 were missing, and 244 were taken prisoner. The killed included four commanding officers or company commanders.

❑ Turkish soldiers held up in captivity better than any other U.N. personnel, maintaining their discipline and refusing to cooperate with the communists. Reasons for this may have included a language barrier with their captors, an innate stoicism, and a high level of unit cohesion.

❑ The fourth Turkish brigade arrived in Korea on July 6, 1953, and remained in country until May 1954.

❑ Turkey supported the U.N. efforts in Korea both because of its anti-communist stance and as a matter of national pride. After South Korea, the United States, and the Commonwealth nations, Turkey provided the largest contingent of troops to the Korean War.

1ST COMMONWEALTH DIVISION

On July 28, 1951, a collection of British, Australian, Canadian, Indian, and New Zealand units that had been operating in Korea under the control of various U.S. divisions was consolidated and activated as the 1st Commonwealth Division. It came to be regarded as one of the best U.N. formations operating in Korea and bore much of the combat in the center of the line of contact.

❑ During the first year of the war, the Canadian 25th Infantry Brigade, the British 29th Infantry Brigade, and the Commonwealth 28th Infantry Brigade (composed of British, Australian, New Zealand, and Indian units) all earned impressive military reputations.

❑ One of the main reasons the Commonwealth Division was formed was to resolve some of the administrative, logistical, and operational conflicts caused by being attached to American divisions, and after its formation it maintained separate lines of supply and communication between Korea and Japan.

❑ In October 1951, the new division took part in its first major action, Operation Commando, moving into the area northeast and west of the Imjin River to create the Jamestown Line. After establishing the improved line of contact, the Commonwealth Division remained on it until the armistice, except for February and March 1953, when the U.S. 2nd Infantry Division relieved them.

❑ While on the Jamestown Line, Commonwealth troops withstood a number of heavy Chinese attacks against their positions, especially ones against Little Gibraltar and during the Battles of the Hook. They also made several company-sized or larger raids into the Chinese lines.

❑ When the war ended in July 1953, 14,200 Commonwealth troops were serving in Korea. Total Commonwealth Division casualties (including the period before it was formed), were 93 officers and 1,170 enlisted men killed; 301 officers and 4,516 enlisted men wounded; and 60 officers and 1,128 enlisted men missing, 1,036 of whom were taken prisoner and eventually repatriated.

U.N. MEDICAL DETACHMENTS

Denmark, Norway, Sweden and Italy professed neutrality when the Korean War erupted and declined to send combat contingents to the peninsula. They did, however, agree to support the U.N. by sending and funding the efforts of medical detachments, most of which established hospitals in South Korea. India also sent a medical detachment, but because it was a military unit that directly supported Commonwealth units in the field, it is described with the military contributions to the U.N. cause.

DENMARK

❑ Denmark sent a 100-member medical detachment and the Red Cross hospital ship *Jutlandia* to Korea in March 1953. It remained active in and around Korea until after the armistice, returning home in August 1953.

❑ Initially, the Danish medical team treated mostly U.N. military casualties, working both on the *Jutlandia* and in field hospitals near the front and using the ship's ambulance helicopter to evacuate casualties. Eventually, however, the Danes extended their services to civilians as well.

❑ *Jutlandia* was based mainly out of Pusan, but frequently moved to other areas and periodically transported casualties from Korea to Japan.

ITALY

❑ Italy sent 77 Italian Red Cross medical personnel to Korea in November 1951. They ran a hospital in Seoul, providing outpatient services mainly to civilians, until January 1955. In February 1953, the Italian contingent had to rebuild their hospital after it burned down. In doing so, they nearly tripled its capacity, expanding it from 50 to 145 beds.

NORWAY

❑ Norway sent a 105-member mobile surgical hospital to Korea, a detachment that became known as NorMASH. It arrived in Korea in June 1951 and remained until November 1954. During its time in Korea, NorMASH operated its 200-bed field hospital primarily near Tongduchon, north of Seoul. It provided inpatient and outpatient services to both military personnel and civilians.

NorMASH was administered by the Norwegian Red Cross during its first half year in Korea. From November 1951 onward, however, while it was still staffed by Norwegians, it received logistical support directly from the U.S. Army medical services.

SWEDEN

❏ Sweden sent a 154-member medical team to Korea in September 1951. This team established a field hospital in Pusan, using both existing buildings and tents, which was eventually expanded to 450 beds.

❏ During the heavy fighting of the first year of the war, the Swedes were kept busy mainly with military casualties. From mid-1951 until they left Korea in April 1957, however, they provided medical services to civilians as well.

VIII

NORTH KOREAN AND CHINESE FORCES

"This army is powerful because all its members have a conscious discipline; they have come together and they fight not for the private interests of a few individuals or a narrow clique, but for the interests of the broad masses and of the whole nation."

—Mao Tse-Tung, *Quotations from Chairman Mao Tse-Tung* ("Little Red Book")

Both the North Korean and Chinese armies were tough, doctrinaire, professional military organizations whose manpower and discipline made them a match for the technologically superior armies that opposed their attempts to unify Korea under communist rule. (Many different types of weapons are referred to in this chapter; more complete descriptions are found in Chapter IX, Weapons, Vehicles, and Equipment.)

NORTH KOREAN FORCES

❏ U.S. claims in 1950 that the South Korean armed forces were among the best in the world proved to be painfully untrue. However, the North Korean People's Army (NKPA), or Inmingun, was one of the most heavily armed, disciplined, and effective forces in the world, and certainly in Asia, in 1950. This communist army's roots can be traced to the anti-Japanese guerrilla groups that operated in Korea and Manchuria in the years prior to and during World War II.

❏ When the Soviet Union occupied the northern half of Korea in 1945, it began to organize these partisan groups into a Soviet-style modern army. Most of the Soviet efforts were toward the creation of ground forces, mostly infantry formations, while fewer resources were devoted to air and naval forces.

❏ Many of the officers and troops of the North Korean People's Army were combat veterans who had served with the communist forces during the Chinese Civil War or with the Soviet forces during World War II. Indeed, according to some accounts, Kim Il Sung, premier of North Korea and the commander-in-chief of the Inmingun, fought in a Soviet unit against the Germans at the Battle of Stalingrad.

❏ The Inmingun was formally founded in February 1948. By the time the Democratic People's Republic of Korea was proclaimed in September 1948, the army was a formidable fighting force. Soviet influence continued even after Russian occupation troops withdrew from North Korea, and in December 1948 the Soviet ambassador (former head of the occupation forces) took charge of a military advisory group.

❏ By mid-1950, the Inmingun had a strength of about 135,000 military personnel, most of them ground combat forces. On June 25, 1950, two-thirds of this force, about 90,000 men, massed on the 38th parallel and then crossed over it into the Republic of Korea, igniting the Korean War.

Just three days after they crossed the 38th parallel and invaded the Republic of Korea, the disciplined, heavily armed soldiers of the North Korean People's Army captured the South Korean capital of Seoul.

THE NORTH KOREAN PEOPLE'S ARMY (NKPA)

❑ At the start of the war, the North Korean ground forces were organized into two corps, which incorporated eight full infantry divisions (11,000 men at full strength), two half-strength infantry divisions, two independent special forces regiments, an armored brigade, and five brigades of border constabulary troops.

❑ Armored vehicles were one advantage the North Korean forces had over their South Korean opponents. North Korean armor, the 105th Armored Brigade, was equipped with about 120 Soviet-made T-34 tanks. About 30 more of these battlefield monsters were attached to other units, for a total of about 150. In addition, it also had a number of self-propelled artillery pieces and armored cars.

❑ Another advantage possessed by the North Korean People's Army was a strong artillery arm, which included a large number of heavy artillery pieces. These weapons were brought to bear before any others in the conflict, laying down a salvo of fire ahead of the advance into South Korea.

❑ North Korea's fanatical border constabulary, the Bo An Dae, was an especially ideologically committed force trained directly by the Soviet military advisors. One of the five brigades of the these troops participated in the invasion of South Korea.

❑ When the North Korean People's Army rolled across the 38th parallel in June 1950, it quickly overran the surprised, lightly armed, and understrength South Korean army. Within hours, the communists captured major border towns like Kaesong and Uijongbu.

❑ Along the west coast of the peninsula, the NKPA's 4th Division captured the South Korean capital of Seoul on the third day of the offensive. After a brief pause, it and other units continued southward, chasing the ROK government and its shattered army. On the eastern half of the peninsula, other elements of the Inmingun, reinforced with special forces units that had landed along the coast behind the South Korean forces, drove southward as well, enjoying similar success against the shattered ROK armed forces.

❑ In early July, the Inmingun battled units of the U.S. Army for the first time—Task Force Smith followed by other elements of the 25th Infantry Division to start with—and quickly defeated them. Indeed, despite their air, sea, and technological superiority, the Americans were able to do little more than slow the communist advance southward toward Pusan and ultimate victory. The steady drive south provided a great boost to North Korean and communist morale in general, and led people on both sides to believe that the Inmingun was unbeatable.

PUSAN: ANVIL OF THE U.N. FORCES

❏ In early August 1950, the North Korean People's Army began to mass along the Pusan Perimeter, the final redoubt of the disorganized ROK and U.N. forces. Although it had suffered heavy losses over the preceding five weeks, it more than made up for them through recruitment among its own people and by impressing South Korean citizens into service; indeed, some of its brigades were swollen to division strength.

❏ While a concentrated assault against one or a few points along the Pusan Perimeter would probably have fatally breached it, the North Korean forces instead launched a succession of limited attacks all along the line, and were unable to decisively penetrate it. In two assaults in August and September, North Korean units crossed over the Naktong River, which formed one edge of the Pusan Perimeter. In the First and Second Battles of the Naktong Bulge, however, U.N. forces were able to halt the communist assaults and, after heavy fighting, reduce the North Korean bridgeheads.

❏ Every day that the communist forces battered away at the perimeter, they depleted more of their resources and grew weaker, a situation exacerbated by the fact that their supply lines were stretched to breaking point and being constantly battered by the uncontested U.N. air and naval forces. While the North Korean forces continued trying to force the perimeter, desperate U.N. defenders grew progressively stronger, as supplies and troops continued to flow into the port of Pusan.

INCHON: HAMMER OF THE U.N. FORCES

❏ In mid-September 1950, U.N. forces landed at Inchon, the port of Seoul, on the western coast of South Korea. They quickly defeated the North Korean forces holding the city, captured nearby Kimpo Airfield, and then began to advance both on the occupied city of Seoul and south, toward the besiegers of Pusan. Within days of the landing at Inchon, U.N. forces around

Although the war ended essentially in a stalemate, North Korean forces celebrated the conclusion of the armistice as a victory.

Pusan began to break out of the perimeter, even as the North Korean forces continued attempting to break in.

❑ By this time the communist supply lines had been cut by U.N. forces heading south, and other forces were driving north and west out of the perimeter against them. Caught between the hammer and the anvil of the of U.N. forces, the North Korean People's Army began to break apart. By late September 1950, a mere 38,000 men of the Inmingun were attempting to straggle back across the 38th parallel into North Korea. Thousands of North Korean troops remained behind in South Korea, some of them simply because they were cut off and others to conduct guerrilla operations against the U.N. and ROK forces.

❑ North Korean army units, including the 10th Division, seized control of the southwestern corner of the peninsula, occupying the towns of Pohang, Andong, Masan, and Sondong. It was January 1951 before the U.S. 1st Infantry Division was able to break their hold on the area, and even then not all of the communist troops were eliminated.

Remnants other units fled into the Taebak, Sobaek, and the heavily wooded Chirri mountain ranges, where they remained a thorn in the rear of the ROK and U.N. forces. Despite attempts to clear guerrillas out of this range, it remained a base of activity well into 1955—two years after the end of the war.

Many North Korean officers and NCOs, like this artillery officer captured along the Naktong River in August 1950, were tough veterans of World War II who formed a hard core for the communist forces.

CHINESE REINFORCEMENTS

❏ In October 1950, elements of the Chinese People's Volunteers began to move into northern Korea from Manchuria. This move was made in order to prevent ROK and U.N. forces from completely overrunning North Korea.

❏ Chinese intervention gave the North Korean People's Army the time and protection it needed to regroup, and by spring of 1951 it was able to take to the field in strength once more, although in a subordinate role to the now much stronger Chinese forces.

❏ By July 1951, just over a year since the war had begun, the Inmingun reached a new strength of 211,000 men and was organized into seven corps and three independent divisions. Two years later, when the armistice was signed in July 1953, the strength of the North Korean People's Army was 260,000—twice what it had been when the war began.

THE NORTH KOREAN AIR FORCE

❏ When the Korean War began, North Korea's air force had as many as 180 World War II-era piston driven attack aircraft, including Soviet-made Yak fighters. This force was far superior to anything South Korea could field (South Korea did not have any combat aircraft at this time) and provided formidable support to the North Korean offensive at the start of the conflict.

❏ North Korea's air arm was no match for a modernized air force equipped with jet aircraft, however, and the U.S. air forces were more than a match for it. Once the U.S. Far East Air Force was able to start operating out of bases on Korean soil, it was quickly able to neutralize the North Korean air force, destroying its planes both in the air and on the ground and bombing its airfields. Not until China entered the war, providing both aircraft and bases in Manchuria for them to base out of, could the communists once again contest the U.N. air supremacy.

THE NORTH KOREAN NAVY

❏ At the start of the Korean War, North Korea's navy had only a handful of patrol craft, torpedo boats, and transport vessels, and was thus not equipped to participate in much more than coastal operations. Nonetheless, it did have a command structure that went as high as admiral.

❏ On June 25, a North Korean navy transport ship, formerly a Japanese Imperial Navy vessel, was poised to enter Pusan harbor and land the 3rd Battalion, 766th Independent Regiment of the North Korean People's Army, a unit tasked with securing the port of Pusan. Had this operation succeeded, and the basis of the U.N. resistance in Korea fallen into enemy hands, the war may have ended in an early communist victory. However, a ROK patrol vessel, the N-703, attacked and sank the North Korean ship a few hours before the ground forces crossed the 38th parallel. Once the United Nations entered the war, its naval forces quickly eliminated the tiny North Korean navy.

❏ On July 2, 1950, four North Korean torpedo boats attacked targets in the waters off the east coast town of Chumunjin. U.N. forces counterattacked in what was to become the only naval battle of the war, destroying three of the communist vessels.

❏ By September 1950, North Korea's small coastal navy had been eliminated and the U.N. Command had achieved naval supremacy.

CHINESE FORCES

❏ In early 1950, leaders of the People's Republic of China desired peace in Asia in order to consolidate their victory in the Chinese Civil War and rebuild their economy. Nonetheless, they recognized the value of Korea as a buffer state and gave their blessings to the North Korean plan to consolidate the peninsula under communism.

❑ Mao Tse-Tung and his advisors also knew that there was a chance that their country might be drawn into a war in Korea, as it had in the past. Thus, during May and June 1950, they deployed the 4th Field Army (equivalent to a U.S. division) from southern China to Manchuria, along the border with North Korea.

❑ When the United States ordered the U.S. 7th Fleet to the Straits of Taiwan on June 27, in order to contain the conflict in Korea and prevent a Chinese invasion of Taiwan, China condemned the action as intervention in Chinese affairs.

❑ From that point onward, China operated under the assumption that conflict with the United States was unavoidable. The United States, on the other hand, remained largely oblivious to the Chinese threat—even after U.S. forces in northern Korea began encountering Chinese troops in October 1950.

❑ In the middle of July 1950, Chinese military leadership began organizing a Northeast Border Force around the Manchurian towns of Andong (across the Yalu River from North Korea) and Shenyang. This organization formed the core of the Chinese People's Volunteers.

Chinese forces began crossing the Yalu River at several points in October 1950 and massing to oppose the U.N. advance northward, perceived as a threat to Chinese sovereignty.

❏ Throughout August and the first half of September, the Chinese remained uninvolved at what would have been the most opportune time for them to intervene and tip the scale in the favor of the communists—when the North Korean army was desperately trying to breach the Pusan Perimeter and destroy the remnants of the ROK army and the ever-increasing forces of the U.N. allies.

❏ After U.N. forces landed at Inchon in mid-September 1950, however, China began to hint through its diplomatic contacts in India that it would intervene if foreign troops crossed the 38th parallel into North Korea; it did not object to such an action by ROK forces, however.

❏ When U.N. forces penetrated into North Korea and drove north toward the Yalu River with the stated intent of eradicating the North Korean regime, China continued to insinuate that it would intervene. U.N. Command-in-Chief Douglas MacArthur, however, who had almost complete control over the U.S. policy in Korea, ignored these hints and intelligence reports describing a Chinese military buildup in Manchuria.

THE CHINESE PEOPLE'S VOLUNTEERS (CPV)

❏ In October 1950, as U.N. forces closed in on the frontier with Manchuria, the Chinese People's Volunteers crossed the Yalu River and entered Korea, where they were officially welcomed as fellow communists and saviors of the crumbling North Korean regime.

❏ While the Chinese ranks did include some volunteers, especially from ethnic Korean communities in northeastern China, most of its troops were regulars from the Chinese People's Liberation Army (early in the war, many of them did not even know they were in Korea or why).

❏ For both psychological and political reasons, however, it was important for the Chinese to maintain the pretext that their troops were volunteers drawn to defend communism in Korea. By calling its soldiers "volunteers," the People's Republic of China was able to deny formal involvement in Korea and avoid the appearance of directly confronting the United States.

❏ By the last week of October 1950, some 180,000 of those volunteers had entered Korea under the leadership of veteran commander Gen. Peng Dehuai. This force was organized into three army groups, each roughly equivalent to a U.S. corps. Each of these army groups contained six 10,000-man field armies.

❏ These Chinese units were supported by only a handful of trucks, no armored vehicles, and only limited amounts of artillery, and the vast majority of their troops were foot soldiers armed with rifles. Indeed, in many ways the Chinese People's Volunteers army was similar to a European army of the previous century.

❏ Contemporary Chinese units normally had a great many artillery weapons. The CPV formations, however, were unable to bring their heavy artillery with them during the initial movement into Korea, and the largest weapons they had for support were 120mm mortars and a few Russian-made rockets.

❏ On October 26, the Chinese communist forces began to engage ROK army units along and south of the Yalu River, and over the following weeks inflicted heavy casualties on both South Korean and American units.

❏ On November 7, however, the Chinese forces withdrew into the North Korean wilderness once again in order to determine how the invaders would respond to their strong warning. On the same day, North Korea publicly announced that the Chinese People's Volunteers had been active in Korea on its behalf since October 25.

❏ Four days later, on November 11, the Chinese Ministry of Foreign Affairs made a similar announcement. At about the same time, it began to rally domestic support for intervention with its "Resist America, Aid Korea" campaign, which was also used to increase control over its population and to suppress internal opposition to the communist government.

❏ Chinese leaders believed that they had been sending clear warnings to the United States in response to a threat to their frontiers. Nonetheless, MacArthur and the U.S. leadership remained largely, and deliberately, oblivious to these warnings, dismissing the Chinese People's Volunteers as an insignificant force—despite increasingly desperate messages from U.S. commanders on the ground.

CHINA'S FIRST PHASE OFFENSIVE

❏ China realized its warnings were being ignored by November 24, when Gen. MacArthur launched the all-out "Home for Christmas" offensive, intended to end the war before the end of the year. Two days later, the Chinese People's Volunteers launched their First Phase Offensive, a general attack along the U.N. line of advance.

❑ Dismissed as "Chinese laundrymen" by one U.S. general, the Chinese People's Volunteers smashed into U.N. forces, breaking their advance, overrunning their dispersed and surprised units, and forcing them to retreat in disarray. Communist Chinese surrounded and completely destroyed a number of ROK and U.N. units.

❑ In the east, for example, the U.S. 1st Marine Division and the 7th Infantry Division were driven away from the Chosin Reservoir and forced to withdraw to the coast, suffering heavy casualties from both gunfire and frostbite as they retreated.

❑ In the west, Chinese forces attacked the U.S. 2nd Infantry Division near Kunu-ri and almost completely eliminated it as a fighting force. Many South Korean units were also overwhelmed and destroyed.

❑ Just six weeks after they had landed at Inchon, outflanked the North Korean army, and advanced toward the 38th parallel, U.N. forces were in full rout, unable to slow their own southward movement, much less that of the communists. This humiliating, chaotic withdrawal became the longest uncontrolled retreat in U.S. military history.

SUCCESSIVE CHINESE OPERATIONS

❑ In mid-December 1950, U.N. forces were able to establish the Imjin River defensive line north of Seoul, near the 38th parallel. During the first two weeks of January 1951, however, the Chinese launched what they called their Third Phase Offensive, which succeeded in dislodging U.N. forces.

❑ By the middle of January 1951, the Chinese People's Volunteers had driven U.N. forces another 50 miles south, past the city of Seoul, before U.N. forces were able to dig in once again. For the second time during the war, communist troops captured the South Korean capital.

❑ Beginning in late January 1951, U.N. forces began to advance northward once again, tentatively at first and then in force. After hard fighting that included a strong Chinese counterattack in mid-February 1951, the U.N. army managed to drive the communists back across the 38th parallel by early April and establish what came to be called the "Kansas Line."

❑ In the spring of 1951, Chinese communist forces, reinforced by the reformed North Korean army, launched two successive general offensives against the U.N. lines. In the First Spring Offensive, from April 22 to 29,

1951, a quarter-million Chinese troops in 27 field armies (divisions) were again able to dislodge U.N. forces from their defensive positions and drive them south. The communist forces suffered heavy casualties in this operation; however, and were unable to immediately press their advantage.

❑ When they launched the Second Spring Offensive a month later in May 1951, Chinese forces smashed into U.N. forces' "No Name Line." This time U.N. troops held their ground and repulsed the Chinese offensive, forcing communist forces back in disarray.

❑ With the failure of the 1951 spring offensives, the Chinese realized that they were not going to be able to decisively defeat U.N. forces on the battlefield, and thus responded to American overtures for peace negotiations.

❑ For two more years the Chinese launched limited offensives to harass the Americans or inflict demoralizing casualties on the South Koreans, and engaged in countless patrols, raids, and skirmishes along the line of contact. By this phase of the war the Chinese were able to bring their heavy artillery forward, using it to support their troops and batter the U.N. lines.

❑ Leaders of the Chinese People's Volunteers participated in the armistice negotiations from start to finish. On July 27, 1953, CPV commander Peng Dehuai signed the agreement ending the conflict in Korea.

CHINESE TACTICS

❑ Early in the war, Chinese tactics were especially well suited to dealing heavy blows to the spread out and disorganized U.N. forces. Once U.N. troops were able to establish and hold defensive lines and consistently make use of close air and heavy artillery support, however, Chinese methods did not fare so well.

❑ Early in the war, a specialty of the Chinese forces was to make fast attacks, inflict as many casualties as they could, and then withdraw before the technological superiority of U.N. forces could be turned against them. As the war progressed, Chinese forces were more inclined to go toe-to-toe with enemy units, leading to heavy casualties in their ranks.

❑ Throughout the war, Chinese soldiers demonstrated an ability to maneuver and fight at night. In addition and unlike their road-bound U.N. opponents, Chinese units could move rapidly over rough, mountainous terrain without being detected by U.N. air reconnaissance, and disappear into the mountainous regions of North Korea whenever necessary.

❑ Chinese troops used both grenades and submachine guns more extensively, and perhaps more effectively, than soldiers of the other allied or communist forces.

❑ When conducting company-sized assaults against enemy positions, the Chinese would frequently arm one platoon entirely with concussion grenades (as opposed to fragmentation grenades, which were much more dangerous for attacking troops to use) and the rest of the platoons entirely with submachine guns.

❑ Grenade platoon members would lead the attack, saturating the target positions with grenades and attempting to stun and injure as many of the enemy soldiers as possible so that they could be overrun by the next wave of attacking platoons. When they ran out of grenades, these soldiers would pick up weapons either from fallen enemy soldiers of members or the submachine gun platoons.

❑ Units of the Chinese People's Volunteers also employed infiltration platoons, elite groups of veteran infantrymen who would slip into U.N. lines prior to an offensive, sometimes disguised as ROK soldiers. They would then attack enemy units from within, even as they were being assaulted from without, throwing demolition packs into vehicles, weapons emplacements, and command bunkers and gunning down stunned defenders.

❑ "Human wave" tactics attributed to Chinese forces in contemporary accounts of the war were largely mythical. In actuality, Chinese infantrymen attacked in relatively open formations and their commanders were not significantly more inclined to squander the lives of their soldiers than were their U.N. counterparts.

CHINESE AIR FORCES

❑ Communist China's air force was equipped with Soviet-made MiG-15 jet aircraft, and Chinese pilots flew these planes against the U.N. air force. Perhaps more importantly, Chinese airfields just across the North Korean border in Manchuria were used as safe havens for Chinese, North Korea, and Russian pilots alike. The role of the Chinese air force and its pilots are described more fully in Chapter II, *War in the Air.*

CHINESE NAVAL FORCES

❑   Whereas China had a fairly formidably navy, which it had been preparing
when the Korean War broke out to support an invasion of Nationalist-held
Taiwan, it knew this force would be no match for the U.S. 7th Fleet, one of
the most powerful naval forces in the world at that time. Consequently, it
held its navy in reserve and did not use it to support the conflict on the
Korean peninsula.

IX

WEAPONS, VEHICLES, AND EQUIPMENT

"There is one tactical principle which is not subject to change. It is: use the means at hand to inflict the maximum amount of wounds, death, and destruction on the enemy in the minimum of time."

—George S. Patton, *War As I Knew It.*

G round forces on both sides employed a wide variety of weapons, equipment, and vehicles during the Korean War. Throughout the course of the war, both the United Nations and the communist forces used predominantly World War II-vintage equipment, and very little new or cutting-edge materiel was used. Marked exceptions to this were the introduction of jet aircraft by both sides and the use of helicopters by the allies for the transportation of troops and the evacuation of casualties (see Chapter II, War in the Air, for information about jet aircraft and their role in the war).

NOMENCLATURES

Military organizations traditionally use a nomenclature—a series of numbers and letters—to designate their military equipment. Such characters might indicate the year the equipment was developed, its place in a series of similar equipment, or how it differs from other equipment of the same type.

❑ During the Korean War, the U.S. Army Ordnance Department used a typical nomenclature system. Under this system, "T" indicated an experimental item (e.g., the T-26 heavy tank).

❑ When an experimental item underwent a major change that affected its operational characteristics, it was given the suffix "E1," "E2," etc. (e.g., the T-26E1 heavy tank, which was given a torquematic transmission in place of the original electric drive).

❑ When an item went beyond the experimental stage and was adopted as a standard, it was given the designation "M" (e.g., the M-26 "Pershing" heavy tank).

❑ When a major change is made to such a standard item, its designation is given the suffix A1, A2, etc. (e.g., the M-3A1 half-tracked personnel carrier, which had a ring mount for a .50 caliber machinegun mounted over the assistant driver's seat that the M-3 lacked).

❑ When shortages of a component used in the production of an item required major substitutions, B1 or B2 were added to the nomenclature of a piece of equipment (e.g., the M-7B1 self-propelled 105mm howitzer).

❑ When a standard item was modified by the development of an experimental process or procedure, it was given the designation E1, E2, etc. (e.g., the T-26E1 heavy tank). When such a modified item was subsequently accepted as standard, rather than experimental, it was given a place in the regular "M" series of items (e.g., the M-5 light tank was a modified version of the M-3A1 light tank).

U.N. MATERIEL

U.N. forces, representing nearly a score of nations, were armed with a staggering variety of weapons and equipment. Most of what was used during the Korean War, however, was of U.S. manufacture.

SMALL ARMS

The vast majority of weapons employed during the Korean War were arms that could be carried and utilized optimally by a single soldier. Although some foreign allied troops used their own weaponry, most

American and South Korean soldiers were equipped with U.S.-made small arms. Commonwealth troops, for example, were armed with British-made No. 4 Mark 1 rifles, Sterling submachine guns, and Bren light machineguns.

❏ *M-1 "Garand" .30 Caliber Rifle.* This gas operated semi-automatic weapon had an 8-round internal clip, a weight of 9.5 pounds (10.5 with bayonet), an effective range of about 550 meters, and a rate of fire of about 30 rounds per minute. The M-1 Garand was the primary rifle used by most U.S. and ROK and many U.N. infantry regiments.

❏ *M-1903A4 .30-06 Caliber Sniper Rifle.* A modified version of the M-1903 rifle, the basic U.S. weapon during World War I, the bolt-action M-1903A4 weighed about 11 pounds, held five rounds in a non-detachable magazine, was equipped with a telescopic site, and had an effective range of about 900 meters. Such weapons were provided to infantry units, mainly in the U.S. Marine Corps, where they were issued to platoon sergeants.

❏ *M-1 .30 Caliber Carbine.* This gas-operated weapon had both semi-automatic and fully automatic versions, accepted a 15- or 30-round detachable box magazine, weighed 6.5 pounds, and had an effective range of about 300 meters and a cyclical rate of fire of 750 rounds per minute. The M-1 carbine was designed to fire a round intermediary in weight and velocity between rifle and pistol ammunition.

Because of this lighter ammunition and shorter barrel, it had less range, accuracy, and velocity than the M-1 rifle, and was considered under powered and unreliable by many troops. M-1 carbines were carried primarily by company grade officers, noncommissioned officers, and support troops and were largely intended as a replacement for the .45 caliber pistol.

❏ *M-1918A2 Browning Automatic Rifle (BAR).* This weapon utilized the same .30 caliber ammunition as the M-1 Garand, could fire either semi- or fully automatically, accepted a 20-round detachable box magazine, weighed 19.4 pounds loaded, and had a rate of fire of 300 to 600 rounds per minute and an effective range of about 800 meters. The BAR was the basic automatic support weapon of the U.S. infantrymen in Korea and one or more of them was issued to each rifle squad. It could be fired either from the shoulder or supported by an integral bipod.

❏ *M-1911A1 Caliber .45 Caliber Pistol.* This semi-automatic weapon carried seven rounds in a detachable box magazine, weighed 3 pounds loaded, and had a maximum effective range of about 30 yards. A classic American weapon, it was the standard U.S. sidearm during the Korean War and was highly regarded for both its power and reliability.

❏ *Bayonets.* Bayonets were knives that could either be used as hand weapons or, ideally, mounted on the end of a rifle that could then be used like a spear. A bayonet was secured to a rifle by means of a ring that slipped over the barrel of the rifle and by a lug, or metal device, on the rifle that snapped onto the bayonet. While the usefulness of such weapons has been questioned in every conflict since World War I, there are many accounts from the Korean War of bayonet charges and hand-to-hand engagements.

GRENADES AND EXPLOSIVE DEVICES

U.N. forces in Korea used three basic types of hand grenades against enemy personnel: concussion, fragmentation, and chemical. Many of these grenades—small explosive or chemical weapons that could be thrown by a single soldier—could also be modified and fired from the end of a rifle.

❏ Regardless of type, grenades consisted of a hollow body filled with explosives or other agents and an opening for a fuze. In form, they included canister-shaped grenades; round, "baseball" grenades; and cast-iron, serrated "pineapple" grenades.

❏ A grenade's fuze assembly typically included a pin that could be pulled to activate the grenade and a spring-loaded safety lever, or "spoon," that could be held in place by the user until he was ready to throw or otherwise release the weapon. After the safety lever was released, the grenade would explode, typically after a 4- to 5-second delay.

❏ In addition to the three basic types of grenade used in combat, U.N. forces also used practice grenades, which contained a small explosive charge and were safer than regular grenades for use on the practice range; and training grenades, which contained no explosive at all, were used in instruction or for throwing practice.

❏ Concussion, or "offensive" grenades, were designed for an explosive effect and to stun enemy soldiers, especially in enclosed areas, so that they would be more vulnerable to follow-up attacks, like charges or small arms fire.

❏ Offensive grenades were typically used by attacking troops who, being in the open, were relatively safe from the limited, concussive effect of such weapons. Victims of such weapons, especially disciplined troops, were sometimes able to recover enough to continue fighting effectively before succumbing to more lethal attacks.

❑ Early in the war, concussion grenades used by U.N. forces included the M-1 and M-3A1, explosive-filled metal canisters with fuzes inserted into them, weighing about 14 ounces overall. By 1953, a typical concussion grenade consisted of a cardboard casing packed with a half-pound block of plastic explosive and equipped with a standard grenade fuze.

❑ Fragmentation, or defensive grenades, were designed to break apart upon explosion. Such weapons had a kill radius of 5 to 10 yards and could inflict wounds in a blast radius of up to 50 yards.

❑ Because they were usually thrown less than 50 yards in combat, defensive grenades were typically used by soldiers in fortified positions, such as bunkers or foxholes, who would be protected from their lethal fragmentation.

❑ M-2A1 fragmentation grenades were among those most commonly used. Made of cast iron and weighing about 21 ounces, these pineapple-style grenades broke into about 1,000 fragments upon detonation.

❑ Chemical grenades came in many varieties, including smoke, used for signalling or screening movement; chemical agents, such as tear gas, used to irritate, incapacitate, or kill; and incendiary, used to start fires or destroy equipment.

❑ M-15 white phosphorous grenades were among the most common chemical grenades and were originally intended for illumination. Such weapons weighed about two pounds, had a fuze with a 4- to 4.8-second delay, a blast radius of about 25 yards, and burned for up to 60 seconds. Targets within the area of effect would both be illuminated for riflemen and machine gunners and suffer horrible burns that could not be extinguished with water.

❑ TH M-14 thermite grenades were used to destroy durable metal items, such as gun tubes or vehicle engines, by burning through them. They were equipped with 2-second fuzes and designed not to roll, so that they could be placed on surfaces like vehicle hoods.

❑ Bangalore torpedoes were explosives used for blowing holes through obstacles, such as barbed wire. They generally consisted of a length of pipe, about three feet long, packed with explosives that could be shoved into position, sometimes with other torpedoes, and then detonated.

HEAVY WEAPONS

Unlike small arms, heavy weapons required two or more soldiers in order to function at their full potential. These weapons, which included heavy machine guns, recoilless rifles, and mortars, could sometimes be used by a single soldier at reduced efficiency. For example, a single soldier could load and fire a bazooka without an assistant gunner, but at the price of a slower rate of fire. Heavy weapons were often mounted on bipods, tripods, or vehicles.

❑ *M-1917A1 Caliber .30 Machine gun.* Developed during World War I, this medium machine gun fired the same round as the M-1 rifle and BAR, fed through in belts at a rate of 400 to 600 rounds per minute.

❑ The heavy, water-cooled M-1917A1 was mounted on a tripod and issued to the weapons companies of U.S. infantry battalions; each division had about 500 of them. During the frigid Korean winters, anti-freeze was frequently used as coolant in these weapons.

❑ *M-1919A3 Caliber .30 Machinegun.* This was essentially the same weapon as the M-1917, except that it was air cooled, rather than water cooled. As a result, it was much lighter but had reduced range, accuracy, and rate of fire. One or more were issued to each infantry platoon.

❑ *M-2 Caliber .50 Machinegun.* This heavy weapon was mounted on trucks, tanks, and other tracked vehicles and used as an infantry support weapon. Each infantry division had about 350 of them. Although air-cooled, the M-2 had a very heavy barrel and could fire about 575 rounds per minute out to a range of about 2,000 yards.

❑ *M-1 2.35-inch Rocket Launcher.* Commonly known as a bazooka, this World War II antitank weapon was largely inadequate against a powerful tank, like the T-34s being used by the North Koreans. However, it is also likely that U.S. soldiers using the 2.35 inch bazooka suffered from lack of training or familiarity with the weapon and that old, "dud" ammunition contributed to its inefficacy in combat.

❑ *M-20 3.5-inch Rocket Launcher.* A vast improvement upon the M-1 rocket launcher, the "super-bazooka" consisted of a 15-pound aluminum tube that fired an 8.5-pound hollow shaped charge that had a range of about 65 meters and was capable of penetrating up to 280mm of tank armor. 3.5-inch bazookas were gradually introduced to allied units in the weeks following the start of the war, replacing the obsolete 2.36-inch bazookas.

Each allied infantry division in Korea was eventually equipped with about 600 of these weapons.

❏ *Mortars, 60mm, 81mm, and 4.2 inch.* These weapons were used primarily by infantrymen as anti-personnel weapons. Their sealed-breech tubes, mounted on heavy baseplates and supported by bipods, were used to fire explosive projectiles toward targets in a high arc. As indirect fire weapons, mortars could be used to attack unseen targets hidden in "dead space" like trenches, valleys, and defiladed positions.

❏ *Recoilless rifles, 57mm, 75mm, and 106mm.* These were infantry heavy weapons that fired conventional artillery shells along a flat trajectory. Such weapons, which developed high blast from escaping gases on discharge but had no recoil, were very effective against both troops and fortifications. A single soldier, typically with an assistant gunner, could shoulder fire the smallest (57mm) recoilless rifle, while the larger varieties were crew-served and mounted on tripods. Oldest of these weapons was the 57mm weapon variety, while the much more effective 106mm recoilless rifle was developed during the Korean War.

❏ *M-40 106mm Recoilless Rifle.* Designed largely as an anti-tank weapon, the M-40 was developed during the Korean War as the T-170E1 and standardized in 1953. It required a two-man crew and had a range of up to 1,100 yards and a rate of fire of about 5 rounds per minute. It was about 11 feet long and weighed about 250 pounds, exclusive of tripod. A highly accurate, single-shot .50 caliber spotting rifle was mounted on top of the rear part of the M-40 barrel.

ARMORED VEHICLES

Korea was largely an infantry war, and weapons developed for other roles—such as tanks and anti-aircraft systems—were largely used as infantry support weapons, much as any other crew-served weapons. Tanks were used like giant bazookas, and anti-aircraft systems like mobile machine gun nests.

❏ As with small arms, a number of the foreign contingents, especially the Commonwealth forces, were armed with non-U.S.-made armored vehicles. For example, British armored troops used British-made Centurion and Meteor tanks, while some of the other Commonwealth forces were supported by Bren gun carriers.

❏ Despite the fact that World War II had demonstrated the value of armored divisions—major units organized around tanks and supported by infantry, rather than organized around infantrymen—the Western powers persisted in relegating tanks to the role of infantry support weapons.

❏ At the outbreak of the Korean War the United States had only a single armored division, in Europe, out of its 13 combat divisions (as compared with 16 armored divisions out of 89 total during World War II). In contrast, the Soviet Union had at least 50 armored divisions, about a third of its total ground forces.

TANKS

❏ During the first few months of the war, U.N. forces had no armored support. Tanks were the U.S. Army's primary anti-tank weapons, and a lack of support made infantrymen vulnerable to being overrun by enemy armor, as they were in the opening engagements of the war.

❏ Eventually, U.N. forces deployed tanks to the conflict, among them the most advanced in the U.S. arsenal, the M-26 Pershing. Ultimately, however, it was an older World War II tank, the M-4 Sherman, that proved most effective and reliable in Korea. Its underpowered 75mm main gun was replaced with a high velocity 76mm cannon.

❏ Three new tanks, conceived around 1947, were being developed during the Korean War, but did not see service in the conflict. These were the 20-ton T-41 light tank, armed with a 76mm gun; the 30-ton T-42 medium tank, armed with a 90mm gun; and the T-43 heavy tank, armed with a huge 120mm gun.

❏ In 1948, pending the release of the new tank types, an interim tank was introduced, the M-46 "Patton." Some 2,000 M-26 tanks, in storage since the end of World War II, were given newly developed engines and transmissions and were dubbed M-46s, a large tank operated with a crew of five.

❏ When the Korean War broke out, development of the T-42 was still incomplete. Its turret and range finder, however, were mounted on the M-46 chassis, and in 1951 the four-man M-47 was created.

❏ In 1952, the M-48 was released, similar in most respects to the M-47 but with a one-piece cast ellipsoidal hull and rounded turret, which increased its resistance to anti-tank weapons. It was this tank, and not the T-42 as originally planned, that became the standard U.S. Army medium tank.

❏ *M-24 "Chaffee" Light Tank.* This vehicle, first introduced in 1943, had a squat hull and turret, was protected with relatively thin armor, and was armed with a 75mm medium-velocity cannon and coaxial machine gun. It weighed about 18 tons, had a crew of four, and was capable of speeds of up to 35 miles per hour on level ground.

❏ *M-26 "Pershing" Heavy Tank.* This 46-ton tank was introduced in its final form in 1945 (having served as the T-26E3 since 1944). It was operated by a crew of five and was capable of speeds of up to 25 miles per hours on level ground. Weapons on the heavily armed Pershing included a 90mm main gun, a .50 caliber machine gun on the turret, and a .30 caliber machine gun mounted in the hull.

❏ *M-4A3E8 "Sherman" Medium Tank.* This 35-ton World War II-era armored vehicle became the U.S. force's primary battle tank during the conflict. Introduced in late 1944, the M-4A3E8 was an improvement upon the basic M-4 tank, standardized in 1941. Armaments for the M-4A3E8 included a high velocity 76mm main gun, an M-2 .50 caliber heavy machine gun mounted on top of the turret, and a .30 caliber medium machine gun mounted in the hull. Its hull was protected by 63mm armor in front and 38mm armor on the sides, and its turret by 76mm armor in front and 51mm armor on the sides. This improved version of the Sherman had wide tracks and a mechanical system that suited it well for the combat and terrain of Korea and made it more reliable than the newer M-24 and M-26 tanks. It could move at speeds of up to 24 miles per hour on open ground.

Ammunition for the Sherman included the 22.6 pound M-42A1 HE round; the M-62 APC-T round (25-pound projectile); the T4 HVAP-T, 19-pound armor-piercing round (9.4 pound projectile), and a tungsten-cored "hyper-shot" anti-tank round. APC ammunition could penetrate 90mm of armor at 1,000 meters, while HVAP rounds could penetrate 132mm of armor at the same range.

ANTI-AIRCRAFT ARMORED VEHICLES

Because the U.N. forces ruled the skies over most of Korea (with the notable exception of MiG Alley), new anti-aircraft systems were not developed for the war. Existing World War II anti-aircraft systems were shipped to Korea, but were used primarily against enemy ground forces.

Armed with a 76mm high-velocity gun and a pair of .50 caliber machineguns, the M-4A3E8 "Sherman" became the U.N. forces' primary battle tank during the Korean War. A World War II armored vehicle, it proved itself superior to many newer tanks for dealing with the climate and terrain of Korea.

❏ *M-16 Multiple Gun Motor Carriage ("Quad .50").* This 10-ton half-tracked vehicle was armed with a cluster of four .50 caliber machine guns that could be fired simultaneously. Built upon the M-3 Infantry Halftrack chassis and first produced in 1941, some 2,877 Quad .50s were manufactured during World War II as antiaircraft weapons.

Halftracks were armored vehicles equipped with a pair of wheels in front and tracks in back. A handful of other halftrack variations were used during the conflict, particularly by U.S. and ROK forces. Antiaircraft battalions were among the units equipped with the Quad .50s.

Introduction of jet aircraft made the Quad .50 largely ineffective as an anti-aircraft weapon, but it found a niche as a valuable anti-personnel weapon, and was routinely used to fire up to 100,000 rounds per day for a variety of purposes (e.g., direct fire against enemy infantry, covering routes of nighttime movement, or systematically stitching hillsides with deadly fire). Because of their powerful anti-personnel capabilities, Chinese troops made destruction of Quad .50s a priority, even over tanks, which were much less of a threat to infantrymen.

❑ *M-19 40mm Multiple Gun Motor Carriage ("Dual 40")*. This fully-tracked vehicle consisted of an M-26 tank chassis armed with a pair of Bofors 40mm automatic anti-aircraft cannon. Like the Quad .50, the Dual 40 served largely as an infantry support weapon during the Korean War. This weapon system saw action before the end of World War II and was based on Swedish designs from the late 1930s.

❑ *M-42 40mm Multiple Gun Motor Carriage ("Duster")*. Developed in the early 1950s, this mobile weapon system was very similar to the M-19 in that it was a fully tracked vehicle armed with a pair of 40mm automatic guns. It did not see extended service until the Vietnam War.

Armored Personnel Carriers

Armored personnel carriers, tracked vehicles often similar in appearance to tanks but usually without armament heavier than machine guns, were developed in the years following World War II for transporting infantrymen quickly and with some degree of protection.

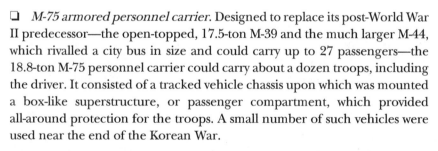

❑ *M-75 armored personnel carrier*. Designed to replace its post-World War II predecessor—the open-topped, 17.5-ton M-39 and the much larger M-44, which rivalled a city bus in size and could carry up to 27 passengers—the 18.8-ton M-75 personnel carrier could carry about a dozen troops, including the driver. It consisted of a tracked vehicle chassis upon which was mounted a box-like superstructure, or passenger compartment, which provided all-around protection for the troops. A small number of such vehicles were used near the end of the Korean War.

❑ *M-59 armored personnel carrier*. Very similar to the M-75, the 18.7-ton M-59 was introduced near the end of the Korean War and utilized civilian components in order to keep costs down. Its design took advantage of its relative bulk to give it limited amphibious capabilities, allowing it to operate in fairly calm water without any preparation.

❑ Mechanically, both the M-75 and the M-59 were similar to the M-41 light tank, and as a result were capable of accompanying tanks over any terrain they could traverse. Such capabilities helped facilitate the development of joint armor-infantry tactics.

TRACKED LANDING VEHICLES

Landing vehicles, tracked (LVTs), fully-tracked personnel carriers that could be used for ship-to-shore amphibious assaults, were used extensively by the U.S. Marine Corps, and to a lesser extent the U.S. Army, during World War II. Such vehicles, known as "amphibian tractors" or simply "amphibians," also proved their utility during operations in Korea.

❏ In the early 1930s, Donald Roebling began developing such vehicles for rescue work in the Florida Everglades. A working model existed by 1937, and within a few years the Marine Corps became interested in it. Roebling's model was redesigned for military use, and in 1940 the Marines placed an order for 100 units of the 7.8-ton, unarmored, open-topped LVT1 "Alligator," receiving the vehicles in 1941.

❏ To a large extent, LVTs resurrected the idea that amphibious operations could be successful, largely quashed by the abortive British landing at Gallipoli, Turkey, during World War I. Such vehicles proved invaluable in World War II for both initial coastal assaults and further movement inland of troops and equipment, especially during the island-hopping campaign in the Pacific.

❏ Several successors of the original LVT1—the LVT3, LVTA4, and LVTA5—remained in the U.S. arsenal when war broke out in Korea. A modified form of the LVT3C was used in the Inchon Landing and as an armored personnel carrier in the subsequent drive on Seoul and crossing of the Han River.

❏ Characteristics varied by model. For example, the LVT3 and LVTA4 both had ramps at the rear that could be lowered to load vehicles or other equipment, while the LVTA5 had a ramp in front; LVT4 was open-topped, while LVTA4 was enclosed, topped with a turret, and armed with a short-barreled 75mm howitzer.

❏ After the start of the conflict in Korea, a demonstrated need for such vehicles prompted their continued development and the production of the LVPTP5, which was larger and heavier than its predecessors and improved upon their design.

U.S. Marine Corps amphibious tractors (AMTRACs) fire on an enemy held town from positions along the Han River beach on September 25, 1950. Such versatile, mobile vehicles were used for transporting troops, fire support, and a wide variety of other roles.

ARTILLERY

While Task Force Smith was equipped with only a handful of 105mm howitzers, in its final phase the Korean War became, for the most part, an artillery conflict. By this time, the allied forces had large numbers of American-made 105mm, 155mm, and big 8-inch guns, from which they fired immense quantities of ammunition. Some of the most common types appear below. All of the weapons listed below were also used by South Korean forces in very limited numbers if at all before the North Korean invasion, but increasingly during and after the war.

❑ *M1 8-inch (203.2mm) Howitzer.* Developed during World War II, this huge weapon was mounted on a four-wheeled carriage, was about 36 feet long (from end of barrel to end of carriage trails), and weighed about 15 tons. It had a range of about 18,000 yards (10 miles) and a rate of fire of 30 rounds an hour. Such weapons were towed by either a 10-ton truck or special tracked utility vehicle, had a full crew of 14, and required at least 20 minutes to set up for firing.

❑ *M-1A1 155mm Gun ("Long Tom")*. Developed in the late 1930s from the French 155mm gun, this weapon used the same carriage as the M-1 8-inch howitzer, was transported much the same way, and was comparable in size. It had a range of about 25,000 yards (14 miles), a rate of fire of up to 60 rounds per hour, and a full crew of 14. This gun was also known in the post-World War II military as the M-59, and, when mounted on a self-propelled tracked chassis, as the M-40.

❑ *M-114 155mm Howitzer*. This medium howitzer was distinguished by small shields on either side of the barrel, was mounted on a two-wheeled split-trail carriage, was about 24 feet long, and weighed about six-and-a-half tons. It had a range of about 18,000 yards (10 miles) and a rate of fire of about 100 rounds per hour. It had a crew of 11, took about 5 minutes to set up and start firing, and was towed by either a 5-ton truck or a tracked utility vehicle.

❑ *M-101A1 105mm Howitzer*. Development of the M-101 howitzer began in the late 1920s and production of the M-101A1 howitzer began in 1939 and ended in 1953, by which time 10,202 of the weapons had been manufactured. It had a range of about 12,000 yards (nearly 7 miles), and a rate of fire of about 100 rounds per hour. It required a crew of eight, who needed only about three minutes to set up and start firing the weapon. Up to 20,000 rounds could be fired through the barrel, after which it had to be replaced. In addition to being mounted on a two-wheeled carriage, the M-101A was also used on a tracked chassis as a self-propelled artillery piece; e.g., the M-7 "Priest."

❑ In addition to U.S. weapons, some of the U.N. contingents utilized their own artillery pieces. For example, the New Zealand 16th Artillery Regiment was armed with British-made 25-pounders.

❑ Proximity fuzes, first developed during World War II, increased the effectiveness of high explosive bombs and artillery shells. Such bombs and shells used radio waves to detect aircraft, the ground, or other targets and then explode at a certain distance from them, rather than on impact.

COMMUNIST MATERIEL

Initially, the North Korean People's Army (NKPA) was better armed and equipped than any of the allied or communist forces involved in the conflict, and had far more heavy weapons and communications equipment than the Chinese People's Volunteers (CPV). Much of their heavy equipment was destroyed early in the war, however, in large part because of allied air superiority, and by 1951 the decimated NKPA and the CPV were similarly armed and equipped.

❑ Most of the weapons and equipment used by the North Korean People's Army were supplied to it by the Soviet Union. Nonetheless, while the USSR had developed weapons systems to replace those used during World War II, those that they provided the North Koreans were old and relatively obsolete.

❑ Russian-made equipment tended to be extremely rugged, of simple design, and very easy to maintain, making it ideal for the illiterate peasant armies of North Korea and China.

❑ Because U.S. forces were so prone to abandon weapons and equipment, especially early in the war or when under duress, the North Koreans also utilized a significant amount of captured American materiel.

SMALL ARMS

❑ While the communist forces did use a hodgepodge of Soviet and Japanese rifles, these were almost exclusively bolt-action, rather than semi-automatic weapons. A desire for high rates of fire led them to use submachine guns as their primary infantry weapons.

❑ Small arms carried by North Korean troops tended to be manufactured in, and provided by, the Soviet Union. Chinese small arms, on the other hand, tended to be based on Soviet designs but manufactured in China. For example, North Korean troops carried the Soviet-made PPSh-41, while Chinese troops carried a near identical copy that they referred to as a "Type 50" submachine gun.

❑ *Submachine Gun, 7.62mm, PPSh-41.* This weapon could be fired fully or semi-automatically, accepted a 35-round box or 72-round drum magazine, weighed about 8.5 pounds, had a maximum effective range of about 150 meters, and a cyclic rate of fire of 700-900 rounds per minute. It fired the Soviet 7.62mm pistol round. Cheap, simple, and dependable under extreme battlefield conditions, the Russian-made PPSh-41 was one of the best submachine guns of World War II. Its design was based on the Soviet principle that ground troops required a high rate of fire rather than accuracy from their weapons.

This was the most widespread submachine gun in the communist ranks, and was called a "burp gun" by U.N. troops because of its characteristic sound. In the final phase of the war, the Chinese carried such weapons and grenades almost exclusively when attacking.

❏ *Tokarev 7.62mm Semi-automatic Rifle.* This Soviet-made semi-automatic rifle accepted a detachable 10-round box magazine, weighed 8.7 pounds (10.8 with magazine and bayonet), and had a rate of fire of 25 rounds per minute. This weapon filled the same role as the allied BAR.

❏ *Carbine, 7.62mm, M-1944.* This Soviet-made bolt-action weapon could hold 5 rounds in a non-detachable box magazine and weighed 8.9 pounds. One of its characteristics was a permanently fixed bayonet that folded down along the right side of the stock when not in use.

❏ *Type 99 Long Rifle.* An Imperial Japanese weapon, this bolt-action rifle held 5 rounds in an internal clip and weighed 9.1 pounds. Variants included a short version (44 rather than 50 inches in length) and a sniper rifle with a four-power scope.

❏ *PTRD-1941 14.5mm Anti-tank Rifle.* Also used as a sniper rifle, this powerful weapon was even more effective against soft-bodied vehicles like trucks and jeeps than it was against armored vehicles. It chambered a single round, the largest used in any conventional firearm during the war, weighed more than 38 pounds unloaded and, at more than six-and-a-half feet long, was supported by a bipod.

❏ *Tokarev 7.62mm Pistol, TT-33.* This Soviet-made pistol, and a near-identical Chinese copy, the Type 51, were used extensively by the communist forces during the Korean War. It held eight rounds in a detachable box magazine and weighed about 1.8 pounds.

❏ *Bayonets.* Bayonets were used, when available, by communist troops on their rifles. Such weapons were not suitable for use on submachine guns, however, which were too short to be effective with a mounted bayonet (and which were not equipped with bayonet lugs, in any case).

GRENADES AND EXPLOSIVE DEVICES

This Russian-made antitank rifle fired heavy slugs that could severely damage many armored vehicles by penetrating their engine compartments. During the September 1950 breakout from the Pusan Perimeter, for example, North Korean troops used such weapons to disable a number of U.S. tanks.

Like their U.N. counterparts, communist forces in Korea used three basic sorts of hand grenades: concussion, fragmentation, and chemical.

❏ Stick grenades, one of the most common forms of grenade used by the communist forces, consisted of conventional explosive-filled metal heads mounted on wooden sticks. These were considerably bulkier than conventional grenades but could be thrown further and more accurately.

❏ Concussion grenades, for example, generally consisted of thin, explosive-filled metal canisters mounted on wooden sticks.

❏ Fragmentation grenades came in several varieties. These included pineapple grenades very similar to the U.S.-manufactured M-2A1 and stick grenades with smooth iron heads that were modeled after the Soviet-made RGD-33 hand grenade.

❏ Chemical grenades, like those used by the allied forces, included smoke, chemical agent, and incendiary varieties and were generally canister-shaped.

❏ Satchel charges were another type of small explosive used by communist forces, especially the Chinese. Unlike grenades, if used properly they could be used to disable or destroy armored vehicles, including tanks. They consisted of canvas bags filled with explosives that could be thrown short distances, typically into bunkers or against the tracks of armored vehicles.

HEAVY WEAPONS

Communist forces in Korea used several sorts of fully automatic machine guns as infantry support weapons, most of them 7.62mm weapons of Soviet design. North Korean forces tended to be armed with weapons of Soviet manufacture, while the Chinese used domestic models based on Russian designs.

❏ *Goryunov SG-43 Medium Machine Gun.* This machine gun accepted a 250-round metallic link ammunition belt, weighed 30.42 pounds, had a maximum effective range of about 1,500 meters, and had a cyclic rate of fire of 600-700 rounds per minute. It was typically mounted on a wheeled carriage that weighed 59.3 pounds.

❏ *Mortars, 120mm, 82mm, and 61mm.* Because these weapons could be cheaply manufactured and transported by foot soldiers more easily than artillery pieces, mortars were very popular in both the North Korean and Chinese armies. While a hodgepodge of mortars could be found in the communist ranks (e.g., U.S. or Imperial Japanese), most such weapons were of Soviet design or manufacture. Each NKPA division had six 120mm mortars, each of its three battalions had nine 82mm mortars, and each of its companies was likely to have some 61mm mortars.

The 82mm and 61mm mortars had the advantage of being able to fire ammunition for the U.S.-made 81mm and 60mm mortars, respectively. American-made mortars, however, were not able to fire the Soviet munitions.

❏ Rocket launchers like bazookas, recoilless rifles, and similar weapons intrinsic to the U.N. armies were not integral to the communist forces and were utilized only when captured from allied forces.

ARMORED VEHICLES

By 1950, five years into the age of atomic weaponry, conventional wisdom in the West was that armored vehicles were obsolete. This sentiment was not shared by the Soviet Union, however, the mentors and arms suppliers for North Korea.

❏ When North Korea invaded the south in June 1950, it spearheaded its assault with a mere four battalions of tanks consisting of some 150 T-34s. Faced with nothing but light anti-tank weapons, the Russian-made tanks were nearly unstoppable.

❏ *T-34/85 Medium Tank.* This 35-ton vehicle was armed with a high velocity 85mm gun and capable of speeds up to 34 miles per hour. First produced in 1941, it became the Soviet Union's main battle tank during World War II. Its hull was protected by 47mm armor in front and 45mm armor on the rear and sides, and its turret by 65mm armor in front and sides, and 47mm armor in the rear.

❏ North Korean forces were equipped with T-34s at the beginning of the war, but within several months most of them had been destroyed, largely by U.N. air forces. What few tanks remained thereafter were kept hidden and used sparingly. Ammunition for the T-34 included the BR-350A armor piercing/HE round; the OF-350 HE/fragmentation round; and the SH-350 shrapnel round.

❏ *SU-76 Self-Propelled Gun.* This Soviet-made, tracked vehicle weighed about 12 tons and was armed with a ZIS-3 76mm gun and crewed by four soldiers. It had a maximum speed of 28 miles per hour and a range of 166 miles and was nominally protected by 10mm to 35mm of armor. Such weapons could be brought into action quickly and were designed to provide mobile light artillery support for a wide variety of operations (e.g., infantry assaults).

ARTILLERY

Artillery support for both the North Korean and Chinese forces was closely based on the Soviet model (although, initially, the Chinese forces did not bring most of their heavy artillery into northern Korea). Most of the

Perfected for use against the Nazis during World War II, the T-34 was armed with a high-velocity 85mm gun and superior armor protection. It spearheaded the North Korean drive into South Korea in summer 1950, enjoying great success against the lightly armed ROK and U.S. troops.

---

artillery pieces used by the communist forces, with the exception of some Imperial Japanese guns, were provided by the Soviet Union.

❑ Communist divisions generally contained a dozen 122mm howitzers, a dozen SU-76 self-propelled guns, a dozen 45mm anti-tank guns, and three dozen 76mm howitzers (12 of which were organic to the division's three regiments, four to each).

❑ Some more powerful, long-range weapons were also used by the communist forces, such as the Soviet-made 122mm rifled cannon and 152mm howitzer. They were much more rare, however, and ammunition for them was often in short supply.

❏ In the latter part of the war, the communist forces massed artillery in great quantities and unleased massive barrages on U.N. positions. In contrast to the profligate American gunners, however, communist artillerymen were reluctant to fire at targets that they could not see, a tendency based on the more limited quantities of ammunition at their disposal.

ATOMIC WEAPONS

Lack of American battlefield preparedness at the start of the Korean War could be traced, in part, to an overdependence on atomic weapons. The United States and the Soviet Union continued to develop such weapons during and after the conflict, however, and American policy makers were forced to address the issue of using them in Korea.

❏ When war broke out in Korea, the United States immediately began to plan how nuclear weapons could be employed on the peninsula. At that time, however, America controlled only a few atomic weapons, and these were not ready to be deployed.

❏ In June 1951, Army Chief of Staff J. Lawton Collins submitted a plan to the Joint Chiefs of Staff calling for the use of atomic weapons against concentrations of communist troops, and for FEAF to begin training fighter-bomber crews to deliver such weapons. An Army Operations Division memo supported Collins' proposal, and stated that use of atomic weapons might become necessary if armistice talks failed. "In the event of a stalemate in Korea in which the communist forces pit manpower against our technological advantages, use of the atomic bomb to increase our efficiency of killing is desirable," the memo said. The Joint Chiefs endorsed this plan, but agreed to implement it only if U.S. ground forces in Korea faced annihilation.

❏ In September and October 1951, the Far East Air Force conducted Operation Hudson Harbor, which involved secretly dropping dummy atomic weapons on North Korea. In practice, those attacks would be used against enemy formations to support an attack into North Korea by U.N. ground forces.

❏ Operation Hudson Harbor demonstrated that the Truman administration was willing to use atomic intimidation to induce the communists to return to the armistice table (suspended since August 23,

1951), that they wanted U.S. atomic capabilities to be taken seriously, and that they were committed to ending the war without incurring massive ground casualties or irreparable attrition to the Air Force.

❏ Analysis of the operation revealed that the effects of tactical nuclear weapons delivered by aircraft against concentrations of enemy troops would be limited, in part because of the difficulty of ascertaining the location of enemy units in a timely manner.

❏ Nonetheless, U.S. military planners clung to the idea that delivery of atomic weapons using fighter-bombers was feasible and continued to develop them. In November 1952, the United States exploded a hydrogen bomb for the first time, and within 10 months the Soviet Union detonated a similar weapon.

❏ Development of weapons, such as tactical nuclear weapons that were smaller than the original atomic bombs and weapons systems that could be used to deliver them, also continued during the war. Such weapons included a 280mm "atomic cannon" that could fire shells on the battlefield powerful enough to vaporize entire hills, along with their fortifications and garrisons. Such a weapon was deployed to Korea near the end of the war and may have been a factor in moving along the armistice negotiations.

❏ In April 1953, President Dwight D. Eisenhower approved "NSC-147: Analysis of Possible Courses of Action in Korea," a contingency plan that allowed for atomic attacks against communist air bases and lines of communication and transportation, another measure intended to help force an acceptable armistice agreement.

X

Uniforms, Insignia, and Personal Equipment

"The Army fatigue uniform, in World War II a work and combat uniform, utilitarian and unadorned, became a wonder to behold . . . Starched, pressed with creases, complete with sewn unit patches and colored name tags, it became more colorful than the OD semidress. Soon, even in the combat zone, the old, sloppy fatigue cap was taboo—now caps had to have stiffeners to make them look like that of Gen. Ridgway."

—T. R. Fehrenbach, *This Kind of War*

A *great variety of uniforms, rank and unit insignia, and personal equipment were worn by the troops struggling for control of the Korean Peninsula. Climatic extremes in Korea—long, cold winters, and hot, wet summers—made properly clothing the combatant armies a constant logistical chore.*

A broad cross-section of the many types of uniforms, insignia, and individual equipment used during the Korean War is described below. It is intended to be representative rather than exhaustive.

U.S. AND ROK UNIFORMS

During the Korean War, the U.S. government clothed its military personnel, and those of South Korea and many of the other allied nations as well, with a wide array of summer, winter, and specialized uniform components.

❏ Conditions in Korea complicated the task of clothing and equipping U.S. military personnel, especially during the first year of the war. The distance of the United States from the theater of battle, about 6,000 miles, and the size of the U.S. military presence, second only to South Korea's among the allied nations, further exacerbated the problem.

❏ When war broke out the U.S. armed services had very limited supplies of uniforms and personal equipment, especially winter clothing. Part of this problem was based on a policy of planning for military operations in primarily temperate climates. Thus, while the military had supply depots as close to Korea as Japan, they were not stocked with enough of the right kind of clothing.

❏ America's economy had regeared itself for peacetime and the production of consumer goods in the years following World War II, and the clothing needs of the military caused nationwide shortages and price hikes of all kinds of cloth. For example, the cost of 18-ounce wool serge more than doubled in an eight month period, from $3.74 a yard in May 1950 to $8.67 a yard in February 1951.

❏ Shortages of synthetic cloths like rayon hampered production of new wet- and cold-weather gear such as field jackets, parkas, ponchos, and raincoats. Shortages of regulation cotton cloths like oxford, sateen, and twill were somewhat offset by permitting substitutions of other cloth or variations in finish or weave.

❏ U.S. military planners undertook a number of measures to help meet the clothing and equipment needs of the troops, including reducing the amount of excess clothing issued to troops (from 44.4 pounds in fall 1950 to 18.8 pounds in fall 1952).

❏ Another step was to issue certain items of equipment such as backpacks, entrenching tools, helmets, insulated rubber combat boots, and parkas only to troops headed for frontline assignments.

U.S. UNIFORM COMPONENTS

❏ Most of the uniform components worn in combat by U.S. ground forces, as well as those equipped by the United States, had been worn or designed during World War II and were olive drab in color, made of various tough cotton fabrics (such as poplin or herringbone twill), and intended for practicality rather than appearance. Many items came in more than one version.

❏ An unfortunate trend that began in Korea (and persists to this day in the U.S. Army) was an increasing insistence by commanders that the elegant functionality of U.S. fatigue uniforms be sacrificed by starching, pressing, and creasing them, and that fatigue caps be stiffened and blocked, even in the zone of combat.

❏ A great variety of dress and semi-dress uniform components were also worn by soldiers in Japan and in rear areas, but were worn by most combat troops only when on leave or R&R.

Summer Field Clothing

❏ Summer field and work uniforms included matching sets of shirts and trousers, and one-piece overall suits, intended mainly for tank crewmen, mechanics and similar personnel. Many varieties of fatigue component were issued to troops during the Korean War, most of them replete with several large cargo pockets.

❏ Headgear included herringbone twill fatigue caps, intended for work details under temperate conditions. Footwear included black leather and suede combat boots.

Winter and Wet-Weather Field Clothing

❏ When properly clothed and equipped for the cold and wet Korean winters, soldiers were literally cocooned in multiple layers of cotton and wool clothing. During the first winter in Korea, however, most U.N. troops had not been issued such equipment by the time cold weather set in, and critical shortages of items persisted throughout the war.

❏ Winter clothing included wind-resistant, cotton-shell field jackets that were intended to be worn over several other layers of clothing; cotton poplin, artificial-fur-lined pile field jackets designed to be worn under the field jacket; cotton sateen field jacket liners, designed to be worn under the field jacket; wool sweaters; wool shirts and trousers; and several varieties of heavy parka, meant to be worn in lieu of the field jacket in very cold weather.

❏ Winter headgear included pile field caps, designed for damp, snowy cold weather environments, like Korea; cotton field caps, designed for dry cold weather environments, but used out of necessity in Korea; and detachable hoods for field jackets and parkas, both with and without fur trim.

❏ Other winter clothing accessories included hooded white parkas and trousers, intended to be worn over other clothing and provide camouflage under snowy conditions; wool scarves; leather gloves with wool inserts;

This experimental cold-weather suit was developed by the Army Quartermaster Corps during the last year of the war, too late to be issued to troops in the field.

cotton-wool blend undergarments; wool socks; and trigger-finger mittens, which had a place for a forefinger so that soldiers could fire their weapons while wearing them.

❏ Wet-weather gear included resin-coated, nylon ponchos and rubber-coated cotton parkas and trousers. Such items were especially important during the damp Korean springs and falls.

❏ Cold- and wet-weather footwear included rubber overshoes; strap-on crampons called "ice creepers"; arctic felt boots; insulated rubber combat boots called "Mickey Mouse boots"; and rubber-covered combat boots called "shoepacs" or "swampers," which caused feet to sweat and become damp during movement but did not keep them from freezing when immobile.

U.S. Rank Insignia

❏ U.S. enlisted rank was based on point-up yellow chevrons worn on the uniform sleeve. Officer rank was based on silver and gold bars, oak leaves, eagles, and stars, worn on the uniform collar. Patches signifying unit affiliation were worn on the left shoulder.

Enlisted Men

Private: no insignia
Private First Class: one chevron
Corporal: two chevrons
Sergeant: three chevrons on top of one rocker
Sergeant First Class: three chevrons on top of two rockers
Master Sergeant: three chevrons on top of three rockers
First Sergeant: three chevrons on top of three rockers, with a diamond in the middle

Company Grade Officers

Second Lieutenant: one gold bar
First Lieutenant: one silver bar
Captain: two silver bars

FIELD GRADE OFFICERS

Major: a gold oak leaf
Lieutenant colonel: a silver oak leaf
Colonel: a silver eagle

GENERALS

Brigadier General: one five-pointed silver star
Major General: two five-pointed silver stars
Lieutenant General: three five-pointed silver stars
General: four five-pointed silver stars
General of the Army: five five-pointed silver stars

INDIVIDUAL EQUIPMENT

❑ When in combat, U.S. infantrymen carried a basic load of equipment that included their weapon, ammunition, steel canteen, entrenching tool, and first aid kit. When conditions permitted, field packs, bedrolls, and rations were brought forward for the troops.

❑ Each soldier was issued a cotton-duck belt appropriate to his assigned function. For example, riflemen armed with the M-1 .30 caliber rifle were given a belt with 10 pockets, each of which could hold a single, eight-round clip of rifle ammunition. Soldiers armed with the Browning Automatic Rifle were given a belt with six pockets, each of which could hold one 24-round magazine. Troops armed with pistols or carbines were issued another sort of belt and pouches for their ammunition magazines. Various pieces of gear, such as canteen, entrenching tool, and ammunition cases and bayonet scabbards, could be attached to these various belts with built-in metal fasteners.

❑ Specialized bags, cases, and other containers were designed to hold ammunition clips, magazines, and belts; mortar rounds; bazooka rockets; grenades; and other types of weapons and equipment.

❑ Several sorts of entrenching tool were used by troops in Korea for digging foxholes and other tasks. One of the most common had a wooden haft and a folding steel pick and shovel blade, and could be carried in a canvas case.

❑ Other equipment included field packs; packboards, designed to carry bulky or heavy materials, such as crates of ammunition; canvas shelter halves, which could be snapped together to form two-man tents; and sleeping bags in a number of weights, along with various liners and cases.

HELMETS

❑ U.S., ROK, and other allied soldiers and marines fighting in Korea wore the standard G.I. steel helmet made famous by American troops in World War II. These helmets provided protection from shell fragments and other flying debris. Helmets also saw service as wash basins, urinals, or cooking pots, as necessity dictated.

❑ This helmet was actually an assembly consisting of an olive drab steel helmet; a resin-impregnated, cotton duck helmet liner that looked like a small helmet and was worn inside the steel pot; two helmet band liners; and a chin strap. Overall, the helmet assembly weighed 2 pounds, 7 5/8 ounces. Keeping this assembly together was a constant problem for troops, especially because so many of them preferred to keep their chin straps unfastened. Methods included pulling the chin strap over the visor of the steel pot, and holding the helmet on with one hand when running, which also helped keep it from falling off. Needless to say, such solutions were far from satisfactory, and many commanders bristled at formations of troops with unfastened chin straps.

❑ Part of the problem was a persistent and largely unfounded fear among U.S. troops since World War II was that a nearby explosion could cause the helmet to break the neck of, or even decapitate, a man who kept his chin strap tightly fastened. In all likelihood, however, any blast powerful enough to kill a man in this manner would kill him anyway.

❑ Nonetheless, the Army Quartermaster Corps responded to these fears, or bought into them, by developing near the end of World War II the T-1 chin strap release, a ball-and-socket device that would disengage under 14 pounds of pressure.

❑ Because the round, steel helmets did not provide good concealment and made noise if they fell off or objects brushed against them, soldiers covered them with sandbags and scraps of cloth. They also used elastic bands and pieces of net to hold bits of foliage or twigs, in order to break up their profiles and muffle noise. During the first year of the war, many soldier discarded the bulky helmets, especially when conducting patrols or raids, and wore some sort of soft headgear instead, such as knit wool watch caps.

This practice resulted in an increased number of head wounds, however, as a 1951 Army Surgeon General's report points out.

❏ Troops resumed using their helmets more frequently during the last two years of the war, when the opposing forces settled down into fortified positions. Head injuries were a much greater threat under such conditions, when more artillery was used and when the head and upper body were the only exposed parts of soldiers in entrenchments.

BODY ARMOR

❏ Personal body armor was widely used by U.N. troops during the Korean War. It is believed that "flak jackets" saved many lives and contributed to a 60

percent reduction of abdominal and chest wounds. Such armor was constructed of multiple layers of fiberglass laminated with resin, a material known as Doron II, and was effective against mortar, grenade, and artillery fragmentation. It was not effective, however, against small arms fire.

❏ Several types of armor were used increasingly as the Korean War progressed, from leftover World War II flak jackets to newer versions

Fragmentation vests vastly reduced the numbers of deaths and injuries suffered by U.N. troops. Here, Sgt. Bob W. Dobie of the 40th Infantry Division shows where shrapnel pierced his armored vest, leaving him unharmed.

developed during the conflict. In 1950, some marines used Doron-augmented "Webster prototype" flak jackets. From June through October 1951, the M-1951 "Marine vest" being developed by the Naval Medical Research Laboratory was evaluated in Joint Army-Navy Mission tests. It was well-received by ground troops, and in March 1952, each division was given 350 armored vests, mostly of the M-1951 type.

❑   The M-1951 vest fastened on the side and protected the abdomen, lower chest, back, and shoulders. It consisted of curved, overlapping Doron plates and weighed 7.75 pounds. Downsides to the vest were that its cloth coverings for the plates wore out quickly and its snug fit sometimes hampered quick movement.

❑   Another type of armor, developed by the Army Quartermaster Corps, was the M-12, a two-piece, semirigid vest consisting of 39 duralumin plates held in individual pockets and covered by eight layers of nylon. However, it was considered restrictive and uncomfortable and weighed more than 12 pounds.

❑   Eventually, the Army produced the best type of armor used during the war, the M-1952, tested extensively in the T-1952 test program (vest models T-1952-1 through T-1952-3A). The M-1952 vest had two front panels and one back panel, was made of 12-ply basket-weave ballistic nylon spot-bonded with resin and encased in a heat-sealed vinyl film, and was contained in an outer shell of nylon cloth. It weighed 8.5 pounds.

SOUTH KOREA UNIFORMS

❑   South Korean uniforms and individual equipment, both winter and summer, were provided almost entirely by the U.S. government or were based on U.S. patterns.

ROK RANK INSIGNIA

❑   South Korean enlisted rank was based on point-down yellow chevrons worn on the uniform sleeve. Officer and warrant officer rank was based on silver diamonds, flowers, and stars worn on shoulder straps. ROK ranks were similar in appearance to those worn by U.S. military personnel and ROTC cadets.

ENLISTED MEN
Private: no insignia
Lance Corporal: one chevron
Corporal: two chevrons
Sergeant: three chevrons
Staff Sergeant: three chevrons and one horizontal bar
Sergeant First Class: three chevrons and two horizontal bars
Master Sergeant: three chevrons and three horizontal bars
First Sergeant: three chevrons and three horizontal bars, all under a star

QUASI-OFFICERS
Warrant Officers: one gold diamond

JUNIOR OFFICERS
Second Lieutenant: one silver diamond
First Lieutenant: two silver diamonds
Captain: three silver diamonds

SENIOR OFFICERS
Major: one nine-petalled silver flower
Lieutenant Colonel: two nine-petalled silver flowers
Colonel: three nine-petalled silver flowers

GENERALS
Brigadier General: one five-pointed silver star
Major General: two five-pointed silver stars
Lieutenant General: three five-pointed silver stars
General: four five-pointed silver stars

ROK BRANCH INSIGNIA

❏   Branch insignia for the ROK ground forces was based on that used by the U.S. Army:

Armor: front profile of a tank over crossed sabers (brass)

Artillery: crossed gun barrels (brass)

Bands: a lyre (brass)

Engineer Corps: a silver castle gate around a gold star

Infantry: a crossed rifle and saber

Medical Corps: a caduceus (brass)

Military Police: a star over crossed pistols (silver)

NBC Corps: a shield emblazoned with crossed retorts (brass)

Ordnance Corps: a gold grenade imposed upon three interlocking silver rings

Quartermaster Corps: a laurel wreath around a key and wings (silver)

Signal Corps: a silver torch beneath a pair of crossed signal flags

Transportation Corps: a wing inside a ship's wheel (brass)

Women's Army Corps: a female head (brass)

U.N. Uniforms, Equipment, and Insignia

❏ A preponderance of the uniforms and insignia worn by U.N. forces in Korea was of American manufacture or design. Indeed, even troops of many of the allied nations wore uniforms and equipment provided by the United States (e.g., Turkey, South Korea, etc.).

❏ Some of the uniforms worn by allied troops reflected a colorful international character. For example, summer uniforms for Australian infantrymen consisted of a distinctive brown bush hat, khaki shirt and trousers, and black leather boots with canvas gaiters.

❏ Other international troops had a similarly unique appearance. Foremost among these were the neutral Indian troops of the 60th Parachute Field Ambulance Regiment, many of whom were Sikhs. While their rank insignia and uniforms were essentially British in style (e.g., olive trousers and shirt, wool sweater, black leather boots), they were easily distinguished by their crimson turbans and the steel bracelets worn on their right wrists.

Commonwealth Troops

❏ British, Australian, Canadian, Indian, and New Zealand troops were organized during the Korean War into a Commonwealth Division. Soldiers of this division wore the uniforms and equipment of their armed forces and carried their own weapons, but were distinguished by a Commonwealth

Division patch worn on the sleeve of the upper arm (above the rank badge of an enlisted man).

TURKISH TROOPS

❏ Uniforms and equipment for the troops from Turkey serving in Korea were provided entirely by the United States, and these soldiers were distinguished only by their own rank insignia and by arm and helmet badges displaying the Turkish star and crescent on a red field.

TURKISH RANK INSIGNIA

❏ Turkish enlisted men's rank was denoted by point-down chevrons worn on the upper arms. Turkish officers had a rank system based on five-pointed gold stars worn on their shoulder straps.

ENLISTED MEN
Private Second Class: one red chevron
Private First Class: two red chevrons
Lance Corporal: one yellow chevron, with a yellow star and crescent inside a
    circle in its center
Staff Sergeant: four red chevrons
Sergeant Major: Five red chevrons

OFFICERS
Second Lieutenant: one star
First Lieutenant: two stars
Captain: three stars
Major: a gold wreath closed with the Turkish star and crescent at the base of
    the strap surmounted by one five-pointed gold star
Lieutenant Colonel: the wreath and two stars
Colonel: the wreath and three stars;
General: generals of increasing rank wore the wreath over a pair of silver
    crossed sabers on a red field, and one, two, or three stars

COMMUNIST UNIFORMS AND EQUIPMENT

Field uniforms worn by the communist forces tended to be just as functional as those worn by U.S. troops, but were somewhat more austere. Communist troops also had far fewer uniform and equipment components, and tended to be poorly equipped with winter and wet-weather gear.

NORTH KOREA

❏ Just as South Korean uniforms and insignia were based upon those of the United States, the uniforms and equipment of North Korea bore a striking resemblance to those of the Soviet Union. This is not surprising, however, when it is considered that the USSR trained and equipped the NKPA from 1945 to 1952.

❏ The summer field uniform, worn by the North Korean troops who stormed across the South Korean border in June 1950, consisted of mustard-colored trousers and Russian-style *gymnastjerka* tunic, worn over the pants and cinched with a broad leather belt and large brass buckle; calf-high, brown boots; and a cloth cap or Soviet-style steel helmet.

❏ Rank, insignia, and uniform accessories were nearly identical to those of contemporary Soviet troops during the Korean War.

CHINA

❏ Chinese uniforms, unlike those of North Korea, were not based on those of the Soviet Union and had much more of a unique national character in the early 1950s.

❏ Summer uniform was similar in appearance to the traditional Chinese peasant shirt and trousers.

❏ Winter field uniform consisted of quilted cloth trousers, a quilted jacket worn outside of the trousers, winter boots, and a padded cloth cap with ear flaps. Not all Chinese troops had such uniforms in early winter 1950, and thousands of troops suffered from exposure and cold-weather injuries like frostbite.

CHINESE RANK INSIGNIA

❑ Chinese rank and branch insignia at the time of the Korean War was very similar to that used by the Soviet Union, and included a red star cap badge, displaying the communist national identity.

❑ Chinese insignia was minimalist in nature, and Chinese uniforms looked quite austere when compared to those of the United States. Furthermore, Chinese troops operating in Korea frequently wore no insignia at all, in part to obscure their identity.

❑ Patches bearing rank insignia to the front and branch insignia to the rear were worn on the collars of field and work uniforms by soldiers of all ranks. Such collar patches were light blue for airborne and air force personnel, black for navy and public security personnel, and red for all other troops.

❑ Warrant officers and officers also wore rank and branch insignia on the shoulder boards of their parade uniforms.

❑ Chinese rank insignia was based on silver, five-pointed stars.

ENLISTED MEN

Private: one star on a plain red patch
Lance corporal: two stars on a plain red patch
Corporal: one star on a red patch bisected by a yellow stripe
Sergeant: two stars on a red patch bisected by a yellow stripe
Senior Sergeant: three stars on a red patch bisected by a yellow stripe

QUASI-OFFICERS
Warrant Officer: a plain yellow patch (no stars)
Officer Cadet: red patch edged with yellow (no stars)

JUNIOR OFFICERS
Second Lieutenant: one star on a red patch bisected by a yellow stripe
First Lieutenant: two stars on a red patch bisected by a yellow stripe
Captain: three stars on a red patch bisected by a yellow stripe
Senior Captain: four stars on a red patch bisected by a yellow stripe

SENIOR OFFICERS

Major: one large star on a red patch bisected by two yellow stripes

Lieutenant Colonel: two large stars on a red patch bisected by two yellow stripes

Junior Colonel: three large stars on a red patch bisected by two yellow stripes

Senior Colonel: four large stars on a red patch bisected by two yellow stripes

Generals

Major General: one larger star on a red patch edged with gold

Lieutenant General: two larger stars on a red patch edged with gold

Colonel General: three larger stars on a red patch edged with gold

Senior General: four larger stars on a red patch edged with gold

Marshal: One larger silver star beneath the Chinese crest

Senior Marshal: one larger silver star inside a pine frond wreath beneath the Chinese crest

CHINESE BRANCH INSIGNIA

❏ Chinese branch insignia was worn to the rear of the collar, behind the rank insignia. It was very similar to that used by the Soviet and Western armies.

Administration: a disk emblazoned with a five-pointed star

Airborne: a winged parachute

Armor: side profile of a tank

Artillery: crossed gun barrels

Cavalry: crossed sabers

Infantry: no badge

Maintenance: crossed pliers and spanner

Medical: a disk emblazoned with an upright cross

Pioneers: crossed pickaxe and shovel

Railroad construction: a stylized railroad crossing

Signal: a disk emblazoned with an aerial mast, lightning bolt, and telephone

Transportation: side profile of a truck

AWARDS

❏ Participation in the war was recognized by both sides with a wide variety of formal, and sometimes informal, awards and commendations. Allied military forces, particularly those of the United States, were far more lavish in granting awards and honors than were the communist forces.

❏ During the Korean War, the highest collective award for bravery that could be bestowed by the United States was the Presidential Unit Citation. This award was granted to several U.S. and foreign units during the war. Among these were the 3rd Battalion of the Royal Australian Infantry Regiment and the 2nd Battalion of Princess Patricia's Canadian Light Infantry, both of which distinguished themselves in the April 1951 Battle of Kapyong, when they helped break the advance of an entire division during the Fifth Chinese phase offensive.

❏ To this day, the highest honor that can be bestowed upon an individual by the United States is the Medal of Honor. During the Korean War, this award was bestowed upon some 300 individuals, many of them posthumously.

❏ Many countries, as well as the United Nations, issued a Korea campaign ribbon or medal for their troops. Some of these medals were also granted to the soldiers of other nations when appropriate. For example, non-British soldiers of the Commonwealth Division were authorized to wear Great Britain's medal for Korean service.

❏ Some awards were less tangible but no less meaningful. For example, one of the Chinese infiltration platoons that took part in actions against the U.S. 1st Cavalry Division was dubbed the "Sharp Swords" for its actions against the Nationalist Chinese during the Chinese Civil War.

XI

WARLORDS
AND STATESMEN

"The commander's purpose . . . is to deliver victory by the by the quickest and cheapest means he can find, leaving it to statesmen to decide what 'cheapness' means in that context and how victory is to be used once it has been won."

—John Keegan, *The Mask of Command*

Military and political leaders on both sides played large roles in the beginning, continuation, and end of the Korean War. In the months leading up to its outbreak, the statements, beliefs, and actions of key individuals on both sides set the stage for the start of the Korean War. Three years after it began, changes in the leadership of the superpowers, through both death and the political process, helped bring about the conclusion of hostilities.

Many of South Korea's highest ranking military leaders had received their initial military training in the army of Imperial Japan, and some of them had made careers as officers in its forces. Ironically, many of North Korea's leaders had fought against the Japanese occupation of the Korean Peninsula or had served in the communist armies of China or the Soviet Union. Thus, the leaders on both sides were enemies even before the establishment of the opposing states.

U.S. AND SOUTH KOREAN LEADERS

In 1950, men like President Harry S. Truman and his cabinet saw communist expansion in any quarter of the globe as an ultimate threat to the

United States, a belief that led to intervention when North Korea invaded its southern neighbor.

❑ *Dean Acheson* (1890-1971) served as secretary of state from 1949 to 1953. In this role, he spearheaded the Cold War policy of containment of communism and reflected the vigor of President Truman in the prosecution of the Korean War.

❑ On January 12, 1950, Acheson gave a speech at the National Press Club in Washington, D.C., in which he stated that South Korea was outside of the U.S. strategic sphere of interest. Critics often blame this speech for giving the communists a green light to invade South Korea. It is unlikely, however, that Acheson realized that South Korea faced an immediate armed threat. After the North Korean invasion of June 25, 1950, Acheson authorized Gen. Douglas MacArthur to supply South Korea with weapons and equipment above and beyond the amounts allocated under the terms of the U.S. military assistance program.

❑ Acheson had a well-known disdain for the United Nations. He also believed that Asia was secondary to Europe as a U.S. sphere of interest.

❑ *Maj. Gen. Edward Mallory Almond* (1892-1971) was serving as chief of staff to General of the Army Douglas MacArthur when war broke out in Korea. In September 1950, MacArthur selected him to take command of X Corps, a unit created for the amphibious Inchon Landing.

❑ *Gen. Omar Nelson Bradley* (1893-1981) was commander of the 12th Army in the European Theater during World War II and became Army Chief of Staff on February 7, 1948. Less than a year later, on January 16, 1949, he became the first chairman of the Joint Chiefs of Staff. In September 1950, a few months after war broke out in Korea, Bradley was promoted to General of the Army. He served actively as the head of the Joint Chiefs of Staff throughout the Korean War, relinquishing this position in 1953.

❑ *Adm. Robert Pearce Briscoe* became commander of the U.S. Seventh Fleet in January 1952. In June 1952, he succeeded Adm. C. Turner Joy as commander of Naval Forces Far East, a position he held for the rest of the war.

❑ *Gen. Clifton Bledsoe Cates* was the four-star commandant of the U.S. Marine Corps when war broke out in Korea, and in this capacity oversaw the massive expansion of the corps for the conflict. In January 1952, he stepped down from this position (reverting to the three-star rank of lieutenant general) and became head of the Marine Corps Schools until he retired in 1954.

❏ *Chae Byung Dok* (1917-1950), a major in the Japanese Imperial army during World War II, was chief of staff of South Korea's armed forces when the Korean War began. He joined the Korean National Guard in 1945, became an officer in the Korean Constabulary army in 1946, and was commander of its 4th Brigade when the regular ROK army was established in 1948. Dok became chief of staff in May 1949 but was forced to retire in October 1949 as the result of a feud with Brig. Gen. Kim Suk Won, commander at the 38th parallel. He regained his post in April 1950, however, just before the outbreak of war.

During the two months prior to the start of the war, he made several questionable personnel changes and ignored reports warning of the imminent North Korean invasion. As a result, he was held responsible for the failure of the ROK army to defend the country's borders. Five days after the invasion, he was sacked and replaced with Gen. Chung Il-Kwon. Chae was made commander of the Interim Armed Forces and was killed at the Battle of Hadong on July 26, 1950.

❏ *Chung Il-kwon* (1917-), a brigadier general and the vice chief of staff for the ROK Army, arrived in South Korea on June 30, returning from military training in the United States. He was immediately promoted to major general and made overall commander of the ROK armed forces, replacing disgraced Gen. Chae Byung Dok.

His primary responsibilities during the first year of the war involved coordinating relations between the disparate forces operating under the U.N. command and regrouping, reorganizing, and sending back into combat routed South Korean soldiers. And, like other ROK generals, Chung often found himself trying to reconcile the conflicting orders of the U.N. command and Syngman Rhee's government.

Chung was once again sent to the United States for training in July 1951. When he returned in July 1952, Rhee demoted him to a divisional command, possibly to give him front line combat experience. Three months later, however, he was made deputy commanding officer of the U.S. IX Corps. Three months after that, Chung was made commander of the ROK II Corps, a post he held until the end of the war.

❏ *Gen. Mark Wayne Clark* (1896-1984), a prominent European Theater commander during World War II, succeeded Gen. Matthew B. Ridgway as both commander in chief of the Far East Command and commander in chief of the United Nations Command on May 12, 1952.

As the overall commander of operations in Korea, Clark inherited a stalemate along the lines of contact with the enemy, stalled armistice talks at Panmunjom, and violent uprisings among communist prisoners held in the Koje-do prisoner of war camps. Believing that the communist powers understood only force, he intensified military pressure in the theater of war in hopes of reinvigorating the armistice talks.

On July 27, 1953, Clark signed the Military Armistice Agreement on behalf of the U.N. Command, with the North Korean Army and the Chinese People's Volunteers at Panmunjom. He retained command of the U.N. forces until October 7, 1953. Ever afterwards, Clark regretted being the first American commander to end a war short of complete victory.

❏ *Gen. Joseph Lawton "Lightning Joe" Collins* (1896-1987) was U.S. Army chief of staff throughout the Korean War. His most important role was providing adequate men and materiel to Korea without weakening the U.S. military presence elsewhere.

❏ *Maj. Gen. William F. Dean* (1899-1981) was commanding general of the 24th Infantry Division when it was sent from occupation duties in Japan to Korea in the first weeks of the war. From October 1947 to October 1949, he had served as military governor of South Korea.

During the Battle of Taejon, on July 20-21, 1950, Dean repeatedly risked his life by leading troops in attacks against North Korean armor, at one point attacking a tank with a hand grenade. He also directed the fire of friendly armor from an open position exposed to artillery and small arms fire. When Taejon was finally overrun, Dean refused to leave with the departing elements, and instead stayed behind to organize his retreating forces and direct stragglers.

Dean became separated from his men following the fall of Taejon on July 20, and was last seen helping wounded soldiers to a place of safety. He managed to evade the enemy until August 25 when, weak with hunger, he was captured. Dean, North Korea's highest ranking POW, was credited with setting an example and slowing the North Korean drive south, and for his actions at Taejon, Truman awarded him the Medal of Honor in January 1951, while he was still listed as missing in action.

Dean survived 33 difficult months as a prisoner of war, during which he resisted pressure to participate in enemy propaganda schemes, including repeated attempts to force him to make false confessions. North Korea released Dean on September 3, 1953. After his return to the United States, he served as deputy commander of the 6th Army in San Francisco, until he retired in 1955.

❏ *John Foster Dulles* (1888-1959) was a Truman-appointed advisor to the State Department when the Korean War began and Eisenhower's secretary of state during the final months of the conflict. Dulles initially supported the Truman administration's policies toward Korea, but became increasingly critical of them. By 1952, he was staunchly pro-Eisenhower and wrote "With foresight, the Korean War would never have happened." During the last year of the conflict, Dulles resolutely supported the Eisenhower's strategy for ending the war.

In May 1953, Dulles visited Indian Prime Minister Jawaharlal Nehru in New Delhi. Assuming their conversation would be relayed to the communist Chinese leadership, he made it clear that the United States would "make a stronger rather than a lesser military exertion" if the armistice talks collapsed.

❏ *Dwight David Eisenhower* (1890-1969), overall commander of U.S. forces in the European theater of World War II, retired from the Army in 1948 but returned to active duty in 1951 to serve as supreme commander of the North Atlantic Treaty Organization (NATO).

After just a year, however, Eisenhower resigned his post as head of NATO to run for president. He was elected 34th President of the United States in November 1952, after having run on a platform of ending the Korean War. After the election, he did in fact travel to Korea and tour frontline positions.

Eisenhower and his cabinet, notably John Foster Dulles, were resolute that the war should be ended quickly, either through the successful completion of an armistice or through an intensification of the war, including, if necessary, the use of atomic weapons. Eisenhower and his staff credited this strategy with the finalization soon afterward of an armistice in Korea. It is more likely, however, that it was one of several factors that led to the finalization of the armistice negotiations.

❏ *Adm. William Morrow Fechtler* (1896-1967) was commander of the Atlantic Fleet when the Korean War began. In August 1951, he was chosen to replace Adm. Forrest P. Sherman, who had died unexpectedly the previous month, as the U.S. Navy chief of operations. Fechtler served in this post until the end of the war.

❏ *W. Averell Harriman* (1891-1986) was President Truman's special assistant for security affairs when the Korean War began. He served in this role until 1952, when he made an unsuccessful bid to become the Democratic presidential nominee. In August 1950, Harriman flew to Tokyo to convince MacArthur to cooperate with the Truman administration's policy toward China.

During his tenure, Harriman also played a critical role in the formulation of U.S. Cold War policies, in protecting Dean Acheson from the administration's Republican opponents, and in mediating between MacArthur and the Joint Chiefs of Staff over the plans for the Inchon landing.

❏ *Adm. C. Turner Joy* (1895-1956) was commander, U.S. Naval Force, Far East when the Korean War began. A seasoned veteran of the 1941 to 1945 island-hopping war against Japan, Joy helped MacArthur plan and execute the Inchon and Wonsan landings.

From July 1951 to May 1952, Joy was senior U.N. delegate to the Korean Armistice Conference, proving himself both a grim, determined negotiator and an incisive analyst of the communist mind. Joy was displeased with what he perceived as vacillation from the U.N. delegation and insincerity from the communists, publicly criticizing North Korea and China but curbing his opinions about U.S. Policy.

In May 1952, Joy asked to be relieved of command and was made superintendent of the U.S. Naval Academy. After he retired in 1955, he began criticizing the policies of the Eisenhower administration and wrote *How Communists Negotiate,* an indictment of the way both sides had participated in the armistice talks. In 1978, his full assessment of the armistice talks was revealed in a posthumously published work.

❏ *Kim Suk Won* (1893-1978), a tough, capable officer, was a retired brigadier general when the Korean War began. He had become a full colonel in the Japanese Imperial army during World War II and was personally decorated for bravery by Emperor Hirohito. Kim took control of the ROK 3rd Division in 1948 and assumed command at the 38th parallel soon afterwards. As the result of conflicts with ROK Chief of Staff Chae Byong Dok, however, he relinquished this post in 1949 and retired from the military.

Kim strongly favored invasion of North Korea and had predicted a swift victory over the communists, "with breakfast in Wonsan, lunch in Pyongyang, and dinner in Sinuiju." This comment was publicly repeated by several other ROK proponents of unification and was exploited by North Korea after its invasion as evidence of South Korean aggression.

In August 1950, Kim was once again made commander of the ROK 3rd Division and in September was made head of the Taegu Defense Command. Later in the war, he commanded the ROK Capital Division.

❑ *Gen. Douglas MacArthur* (1880-1964) was America's highest ranking general and one of its most popular, influential, and outspoken citizens during the first 10 months of the Korean War.

In December 1944, MacArthur was promoted to general of the army, and in April 1945 was made commanding general of all U.S. Army forces in the Pacific. He was subsequently made supreme commander for the Allied powers and entrusted with accepting the Japanese surrender and overseeing the occupation of Japan.

A year before Dean Acheson excluded South Korea from the U.S. sphere of interest, MacArthur had dismissed Korea as unimportant to the United States. When North Korea invaded, however, he recommended that Truman commit ground forces.

After being appointed commander of the U.N. forces being sent to defend South Korea, MacArthur consistently pushed for a full commitment of U.S. power and a broadening of the war beyond the Korean Peninsula. He made his sentiments known through press conferences, news releases, and letters to political allies in the United States.

In September 1950, MacArthur convinced the Joint Chiefs of Staff—against their better judgment—to accept his plan for an amphibious landing at Inchon, on the southwest coast of Korea. The subsequent assault was one of the most brilliant and successful amphibious operations in history.

"If the Chinese Communists cross the Yalu [River], I shall make of them the greatest slaughter in the history of mankind," MacArthur is said to have told Truman. Nonetheless, when the Chinese did finally enter Korea, it was several weeks before MacArthur accepted that they had even done so in large number. When he realized the size of the invasion, his immediate reaction was to predict doom for the U.N. forces and to beg Washington for reinforcements.

In March 1951, MacArthur undermined Truman's ceasefire initiative by releasing one of his own a few days before the president's. That, along with public statements critical of the administration's policy and threats to carry the war into China, led Truman to sack him for insubordination on April 11, 1951.

❑ Gen. *George C. Marshall* (1880-1959), a World War II hero and one of the most revered figures in postwar American society, served as secretary of state from 1947 to 1949, giving his name to the Marshall Plan for European economic rehabilitation. In September 1950, he replaced Secretary of State Louis A. Johnson, who resigned under a cloud. His first priority was restoration of good relations between the State and Defense departments, which had been damaged by Johnson.

Marshall tried to support MacArthur's war aims and made it plain that he preferred a clear victory to an armistice. Nonetheless, he concurred with Truman's decision to relieve MacArthur of command and saw no benefit in an expansion of the conflict. Marshall stepped down in the fall of 1951 and was replaced by under secretary of defense Robert A. Lovett.

❏ *John Joseph Muccio* (1900-1989) was the first U.S. ambassador to the Republic of Korea and served in that capacity during the first 26 months of the Korean conflict. Before the war, he had actively called for expansion of U.S. economic and military aid for South Korea.

On June 25, 1950, Muccio informed the leadership in Washington, D.C., that North Korea had invaded the south. In the days that followed, he oversaw the U.S. evacuation of Seoul and then followed the government of Syngman Rhee to its emergency capital in Taejon.

During the first desperate weeks of the war, Muccio and his embassy bolstered the flagging morale of Syngman Rhee and his cabinet and convinced them that victory was still possible. They also acted as a crucial liaison between the South Korean government and the U.S. Army. Muccio and his staff were also instrumental in convincing the U.S. Army to use South Korean paramilitary police battalions in U.S. divisional areas as light infantry and for routing out infiltrators, and to begin rounding out understrength U.S. formations with Korean soldiers.

In October 1950, after his embassy was able to return to Seoul, Muccio accompanied MacArthur to the Wake Island meeting with President Truman, and the following month flew to Washington to discuss U.S. policy in Korea following occupation of the entire peninsula.

After Chinese soldiers occupied Seoul, Muccio's embassy moved to Pusan. He remained in Korea until August 1952, dedicating most of his time to trying to convince the Rhee government that the United States would not abandon South Korea and that a negotiated end to the conflict was in its best interests.

❏ *Frank J. Pace* (1912-1988) served as U.S. secretary of the army for most of the Korean War, from April 1950 until January 1953. As head of the Bureau of the Budget since 1949, he had impressed Truman with his administrative ability and fiscal conservatism, and the president appointed him to the top Army post in hopes keeping a lid on defense spending.

Pace was, admittedly, not a military expert, and as a result had minimal influence on U.S. policy during the war. He backed most of Truman's decisions during the conflict and accompanied the president to the Wake Island conference with MacArthur in October 1950.

Pace's main challenges during the war centered on manpower problems caused by remobilization, inequities in the selective service system, and the need to keep forces in reserve in case of a crisis outside of Korea. In 1951, Pace instituted the point-based troop rotation system that allowed National Guardsmen and reservists to rotate back to the United States after accumulating 36 points.

In 1953, facing imminent replacement by an Eisenhower appointee, Pace resigned his post as secretary of the army and subsequently became director of major defense contractor General Dynamics.

❑ *Paik Sun-yup* (1920-), a junior officer in the Japanese Manchurian army during World War II, was commander of the ROK 1st Division when the Korean War began. He proved himself one of South Korea's ablest battlefield commanders and was well regarded by many American leaders.

When North Korea invaded the south in June 1950, Paik was away at a military staff college and half of his troops were absent on weekend leave. Nonetheless, he managed to rally his command and fought against the superior NKPA forces for four days; only after Seoul fell and his men ran out ammunition did the 1st Division retreat south of the Han River.

In the battle to hold the Pusan Perimeter, Paik personally led an infantry battalion in a charge against a North Korean-held position, ordering his own men to shoot him if he retreated. After the breakout from the perimeter, Paik led the 1st ROK Division in a race against the 1st U.S. Cavalry Division to capture the North Korean capital of Pyongyang. His command won the race, entering the enemy city on October 19, 1950.

Paik subsequently served as chief of staff of the South Korean armed forces from 1952 to 1954, and was made the first ROK general of the army in 1953, at the age of 33. He also served as the South Korean representative to the armistice talks.

❑ *Adm. Forrest P. Sherman* (1896-1951) was chief of naval operations when the Korean War began and successfully worked to expand and strengthen the Navy during the first year of the conflict. On July 22, 1951, he suffered a series of heart attacks and died.

❑ *Syngman Rhee* (1875-1965), president of the Republic of Korea from 1948 to 1960, was a vehemently anti-Japanese, anti-communist, nationalistic leader who wanted to unify Korea forcibly through an invasion of North Korea. Rhee fled the Japanese occupation of Korea and spent several years in the United States. He studied at George Washington, Harvard, and Princeton universities, and was the first Korean to earn a doctorate.

Despite his American education and role as the first elected leader of the Republic of Korea, Rhee had a very paternalistic attitude toward his nation and was not particularly interested in democracy. He used violence and political manipulation more than consensus building to achieve and hold on to his presidency.

Rhee opposed an armistice that would leave Korea divided and went out of his way to both turn the Korean people against such an agreement and to sabotage it. His other conditions included complete removal of Chinese forces from the peninsula, total disarmament of North Korea, full South Korean participation in any postwar political conferences, and a unilateral U.S. agreement to protect his country from future communist aggression.

Many of Rhee's policies angered U.S. leaders, who considered removing him from power in a U.N.-sponsored *coup d'etat*. Throughout the war, he engaged in heavy-handed repression of his opponents, and in June 1953 tried to derail the armistice process by freeing thousands of North Korean POWs.

❏ *Gen. Matthew B. Ridgway* (1895-1993) was serving as deputy to Army chief of staff Gen. J. Lawton Collins when the Korean War broke out. He was subsequently chosen to replace Gen. Walton Walker as 8th U.S. Army commander in December 1950 and MacArthur as U.N. commander in April 1951. He proved himself tough and relentless in both these roles.

On January 2, 1951, Ridgway determined that his shattered U.N. and ROK forces could not hold their line of defense along the 38th parallel and ordered a withdrawal south of the Han River, once again abandoning Seoul to the communists.

Ridgway was able to reconstitute his forces within a few weeks and to launch a counterattack, utilizing what he referred to as a "meat grinder" strategy. By March 14, the 8th U.S. Army had recaptured Seoul and continued northward to the Kansas Line, on and somewhat north of the 38th parallel.

Ridgway opposed MacArthur's plan to try to drive the Chinese forces back to the Yalu, believing it had no chance of success and that it risked starting World War III in the process. Ridgway replaced MacArthur when he was relieved in April 1951, and passed his own command on to Lt. Gen. James A. Van Fleet.

As commander of the U.N. forces in Japan, Ridgway advocated stalemate in Korea rather than an expansion of the conflict, and in July 1951 opened the armistice talks with the North Koreans and Chinese. In May 1952, Ridgway left Tokyo to succeed Eisenhower as supreme allied commander in Europe. He was replaced by Gen. Mark W. Clark.

❑ *Harry S. Truman* (1884-1973) was president of the United States and commander in chief of its armed forces during most of the Korean War. "By God, I'm going to let them have it!" he declared after learning of the North Korean invasion, and successively ordered air, sea, and ground forces to the theater of battle.

Truman decided not to ask Congress for a declaration of war and dismissed the increasingly bloody conflict as a "police action." He also refused to ask for rationing or other economic controls that the public might have associated with full-scale war. In September 1950, Truman approved MacArthur's decision to cross the 38th parallel and expunge the government of North Korea, an action that led to Chinese intervention and escalation of the war.

After China entered the war, Truman blustered in a press conference that the United States would use any weapons at its disposal, including the atomic bomb, to prevail in Korea. British Prime Minister Clement Atlee immediately flew to the United States to meet with Truman, desperately hoping to avoid atomic war and to convince Truman to negotiate with the Chinese.

In April 1951, Truman was forced to relieve MacArthur for insubordination, an act that resulted in public outcry. Truman suffered public criticism for his conduct of the war in Korea for the remainder of his second term in office, largely because of the protracted armistice talks at Panmunjom. In 1952, Truman decided not to run for reelection, certain that he would be defeated if he did.

❑ Gen. *Hoyt S. Vandenberg* (1899-1954) served as the U.S. Air Force chief of staff during the Korean War. He was promoted to full general in 1948, becoming the youngest four-star officer in the U.S. armed forces.

When war broke out in Korea, Vandenberg set out to strengthen what he referred to as "a shoestring air force." He realized the limitations of the service in 1950 and opposed MacArthur's plans to extend strategic bombing to communist China, saying that attrition from such a campaign would cripple its capabilities for many years.

After Soviet MiGs threatened to take control of the skies over Korea, Vandenberg began to send quantities of the Air Force's most advanced fighter, the F-86 Sabre, to the theater of battle. Vandenberg fell ill in May 1952, and Gen. Nathan F. Twining served as acting chief of staff for four months. When Vandenberg retired in May 1953, Twining replaced him.

Gen. James VanFleet (left), who replaced Gen. Matthew Ridgway as commander of the U.S. 8th Army, is greeted by ROKA Chief of Staff Gen. Lee Chong Chan and KMAG Commander Brig. Gen. C. E. Ryan on January 27, 1952.

❑ Gen. *James A. Van Fleet* (1892-1992), a corps commander during World War II, succeeded Ridgway as commander of the 8th U.S. Army when Ridgway was selected to replace MacArthur as U.N. Commander.

When he took command in April 1951, Van Fleet's first task was to strengthen the line of contact inherited from Ridgway. After convincing South Korean President Syngman Rhee of the need to reform and reorganize the ROK military, Van Fleet employed an intensive training program to turn it into an effective combat force. By late 1952, nearly three out of every four of his front-line soldiers were Korean.

Van Fleet became frustrated with the static nature of combat in Korea during the second and third years of the war, and in the spring of 1953 he left Korea and resigned from the Army.

❏ *Lt. Gen. Walton H. "Johnnie" Walker* (1899-1950) was commander of the U.S. 8th Army, the main troop command in MacArthur's occupation forces in Japan, from September 1948 to December 1950. Like his World War II mentor, Gen. George S. Patton, he was tough, aggressive, and a bit flamboyant.

During World War II, Walker earned the high esteem of both Patton, whom he had served as a corps commander, and Eisenhower, which probably led to his assuming command of 8th Army in September 1948. He disliked MacArthur, however, and did not get along well the supreme commander's chief of staff, Edward M. Almond.

When the Korean War began, Walker assumed command of all U.S. and ROK forces in Korea. These forces—understrength, poorly equipped, and ill-trained—were steadily driven southward until Walker was able to establish a defensive perimeter around the port city of Pusan. After the breakout from the perimeter and the subsequent advance into North Korea, Walker's

Tough, aggressive Gen. Walton Walker commanded the U.S. 8th Army until his death in late December 1950. He was killed when a truckload of South Korean soldiers ran into his jeep on a road outside of Seoul.

troops were once again forced to retreat south, this time by the Chinese, in what was essentially the worst rout ever suffered by an American army.

Walker faced many difficult circumstances during the first six months of the Korean War, not the least of which was MacArthur, who was always ready to take credit for successes and to blame his subordinates for failures. Nonetheless, although a competent battlefield commander, Walker made mistakes that led to U.S. troops being killed and to enemy troops escaping destruction, and both MacArthur and the leadership in Washington considered sacking him on several occasions.

On December 23, 1950, Walker was in the process of establishing a defensive line along the 38th parallel when he was killed in a jeep accident near Seoul. His untimely death, uncannily like that of Patton just a few years earlier, probably saved him from being relieved of his command.

COMMUNIST LEADERS

Most of North Korea's top leadership had received military or political training from the communist Chinese or the Soviet Union in the years leading up to the Korean War. Indeed, North Korea's inner circle of leaders were members of the Kapsan, or Soviet exile faction, and had been forced to seek refuge in the USSR during World War II. Consequently, the leaders of the two large communist states bordering North Korea ended up playing a role in the desire of DPRK leader Kim Il Sung to unify Korea by force.

❏ **Choi Yong-kon** (1900-1976), North Korea's defense minister and commander of the NKPA, played a prominent role in the planning and execution of his country's June 25 invasion of South Korea.

Choi received military training in China in the 1920s and subsequently served in the communist anti-Japanese guerilla movement. He became a close comrade of Kim Il Sung while a member of the Chinese-led Northeastern Anti-Japanese Allied Army, and fled with him to exile in the Soviet Union around 1940. When World War II ended, Choi returned to Korea with Kim and played a major role in the establishment of the communist regime in North Korea.

After the Korean War began, Kim promoted Choi to the post of deputy prime minister, making him the number-two person in North Korea's communist hierarchy, and named him commander for the defense of Seoul against the U.N. Forces.

In 1955, he presided over the court that sentenced to death political rival Pak Hon-yong. He served in various posts in the two decades after the war, including ceremonial head of state, a role Kim forced him to relinquish in 1972.

❑ *Chou En-lai* (1898-1976) was premier and foreign minister of the People's Republic of China during the Korean War. Throughout the summer of 1950, Chou strove to avert warfare between China and the United States. He announced that the approach of South Korean troops to the Yalu River would not be considered a threat, but that the approach of U.S. troops would be. Chou's warnings went unheeded in the West, and when U.N. troops crossed the 38th parallel into North Korea, Chinese military intervention became a certainty.

On December 22, 1950, Chou announced that a ceasefire in Korea had to be based on withdrawal of U.S. forces from both Korea and Taiwan, and the granting of a seat in the United Nations to communist China. In August 1952, Chou led a delegation to Moscow to seek Soviet assistance in Korea, but was unable to secure their cooperation.

Chou served as his country's minister of foreign affairs until 1958 and as its premier until his death in 1976.

❑ *Kim Il Sung* (1912-1994) was premier of North Korea, chairman of the Korean communist party, and supreme commander of the NKPA when the Korean War began. A Korean nationalist, he was also the driving force behind his country's decision to invade the south.

Born Kim Song-ju into a peasant family, he joined an anti-Japanese communist youth organization in 1929. Adopting the *nomme de guerre* Kim Il Sung soon afterwards, he became well known as an anti-Japanese guerrilla fighter in the 1930s. Around 1940, increasing Japanese military pressure forced Kim and a number of his comrades to flee to the Soviet Union. He undoubtedly received military training in the USSR and, for the balance of World War II, probably served as an officer in the Soviet armed forces.

In 1945, Kim and a cadre of communist Korean soldiers returned to Soviet-occupied North Korea. Supported by the Soviet Union and drawing upon their wartime reputation as guerrilla fighters, Kim and the members of his Kapsan faction politically outmaneuvered the communist leadership that had remained in Korea. By 1949, they had gained control of both the ruling party and the government of North Korea.

Kim's decision to invade South Korea when he did may have been influenced both by Syngman Rhee's threats to invade the north and by pressure for military action from political rival Pak Hon-yong. After the U.N.

counterattack smashed the North Korean army in the fall of 1950 and China assumed responsibility for carrying on the communist effort, Kim largely lost control over the military conduct of the war.

Kim blamed his political rivals for North Korea's failure to unify the peninsula and, after the armistice, consolidated his personal power by having them purged. He remained in power for more than four decades after the war until his death in 1994, when power passed to his son, Kim Jong Il.

❑ *Jacob A. Malik* (1906-1980), a career Soviet diplomat, was a deputy foreign minister and his country's permanent delegate to the United Nations during much of the Korean War. In January 1950, after the United Nations refused to grant China's seat to the newly-formed People's Republic of China, Malik announced a Soviet boycott of the U.N. Security Council, and did not return until August.

Ironically, the Soviet absence from U.N. deliberations left it unable to comment on, or veto, the U.N. decisions in June 1950 to help defend South Korea and to create a U.N. Command under the leadership of the United States. Through private conversations with U.S. officials, Malik kept lines of communication open between the Soviet Union and the United States. On June 23, 1951, he gave a radio address indicating the possibility of an armistice in Korea, which led to the start of talks less than three weeks later.

In October 1952, Malik replaced Andre Gromyko as the USSR's first deputy foreign minister, and in March 1953, after the death of Stalin, was appointed ambassador to the United Kingdom.

❑ *Georgi Malenkov* (1902-1988), a top leader in the Soviet hierarchy and a favorite of Stalin, assumed the posts of prime minister and first party secretary upon the death of his mentor in March 1953.

Immediately after Stalin died, Malenkov launched a "peace offensive" that led to the signing of the armistice agreement and the end of hostilities in Korea. Disputes between the United States and the Soviet Union, Malenkov said, could be "decided by peaceful means, on the basis of mutual understanding." There are also indications that the new Soviet leader directly asked the leadership of North Korea and China to end the war.

❑ *Mao Tse-tung* (1893-1976), chairman of both the government of the People's Republic of China and the Chinese communist party, was the ultimate policy maker for his country during the Korean War.

Mao probably learned of North Korea's plans to invade the south when he visited Stalin in Moscow in 1949. It is not likely that his permission was sought for the invasion and, still recovering from war and trying to consolidate his power, was not likely to have been enthusiastic about it. Nonetheless, when North Korea's army was smashed and U.N. forces began to advance on the Yalu, Mao saw the action as both an affront to international communism and a threat to the security of China's borders. He also believed that a victory against the forces of the United States, or even a stalemate, could immeasurably improve China's prestige internationally.

Mao's eldest son, Maj. Mao An-ying, was one of the Chinese volunteers who entered Korea in late 1950. He was killed in the first month of combat. Three months after the war ended, Mao met with Kim Il Sung in China. At this meeting, he not only forgave North Korea's war debt to his country, but granted it another 800 million Chinese dollars for postwar reconstruction. This generosity increased China's debt to the USSR and contributed to the growing rift between the two largest communist powers.

❏ *Pak Hon-yong* (1900-1955) was minister of foreign affairs and a vice-premier of North Korea when the Korean War began. In March 1950, at a secret meeting of North Korea's top leaders in Pyongyang, Pak reportedly spoke in favor of invading South Korea and promised that 200,000 South Korean communists would rise up to help the NKPA.

An anti-Japanese communist activist in Southern Korea in the 1920s and 1930s, Pak had established the Korean communist party and the Korean Communist Youth League in 1925. After World War II, Pak was one of the most logical and qualified choices to head the government of South Korea. Because of the U.S. opposition to communism, however, Pak was forced to move north and establish himself there.

Pak hoped to use his influence in the south to both aid the invasion forces and bolster his position in the government of a unified Korea. North Korea's failure to prevail in Korea, however, doomed Pak, and in 1955 the Kapsan faction tried, convicted, and executed him.

❏ *Joseph Stalin* (1879-1953), secretary general of the USSR's communist party from 1922 to 1953 and Soviet premier from 1941 to 1953, was the undisputed leader of the Soviet Union and the most powerful communist leader in the world during the Korean War.

In late 1949, Stalin received North Korean leader Kim Il Sung in Moscow to consider his plan for the invasion of South Korea. Ever cautious, Stalin likely conferred with Mao Tse Tung and had one more meeting with Kim before granting his approval for the operation. Stalin feared the possibility of direct confrontation between the Soviet Union and the United States, and publicly defined the war in Korea as a civil conflict in which the superpowers had no business. Secretly, he supported the communist war effort with men and materiel and favored the Chinese intervention, which he saw as serving Soviet interests in the Far East (like Acheson in the United States, Stalin saw Europe, rather than Asia, as the primary theater of interest to the superpowers).

Stalin died on March 5, 1953, and was succeeded by Georgi Malenkov as general secretary of the communist party of the USSR. His death brought about changes to Soviet foreign policy that almost certainly contributed to the completion of the Korean armistice agreement and the cessation of hostilities.

❑ *Valerian A. Zorin* succeeded Jacob A. Malik as the USSR's permanent delegate to the United Nations in October 1952. He served in this post for just six months, until April 1953, a month after Stalin's death, when he was replaced by Foreign Minister Andrei Y. Vyshinsky.

OTHER LEADERS

A number of political leaders unaffiliated with the superpowers or aggressor nations had an interest in the outcome of the Korean War. Some of these men were interested in ending the hostilities in Korea, while others hoped to see them continue as long as possible.

❑ *Chiang Kai-shek* (1887-1975), president of the Taiwan-based Republic of China, sought to influence U.S. policy toward Korea both prior to and during the war as a means to strengthen his position on mainland China.

Chiang gained control of the nationalist Kuomintang party in the 1920s and nominally unified China in 1928. A staunch anti-communist, he preferred to prosecute a civil war against the leftists rather than unite with them to drive the Japanese out of China. Nonetheless, in 1936 the two sides allied against Japan.

During World War II, Chiang called for Allied recognition of the Korean Provisional Government and its leader, Kim Ku, hoping to block assumption of power by either the communists or Syngman Rhee. In addition, in 1943 Chiang signed the Cairo Declaration, which called for the eventual independence of Korea. Despite these actions, however, Chiang was determined to assert Chinese dominion over Korea after World War II.

In 1949, Chiang and his forces lost control of China and fled to the island of Taiwan. Communist China was preparing to invade the island and crush

"Democratic" Asian leaders Chiang Kai-shek (at left) and Syngman Rhee were both vehemently opposed to the communist forces that divided their countries. They are seen here together during a meeting in South Korea.

the nationalists when war erupted in Korea. Truman ordered the U.S. 7th Fleet into the Straits of Taiwan, probably saving Chiang's regime from annihilation.

On June 27, 1950, after a U.N. call for multinational support for South Korea, Chiang offered 33,000 Nationalist troops, providing the United States would equip and transport them to Korea. This offer, thought by many to be insincere in the first place, was rejected by the United States for a variety of reasons, among them a shortage of equipment for U.S. troops, nationalist troops' poor record on the battlefield, and fears of bringing communist China into the conflict.

Chiang did all he could to prolong the war in Korea and used the conflict to strengthen his own position and to pressure the United States into signing a mutual defense treaty with his government.

❑ *Dag Hammarskjold* (1905-1961), a Swedish diplomat, replaced Trygve Lie as secretary general of the United Nations in April 1953. He assumed his role during the final months of the Panmunjom armistice talks, and had only a limited role in the finalization of an agreement. ·

❑ *Trygve Lie* (1896-1968), a Norwegian diplomat and the first secretary general of the United Nations, was instrumental in calling the U.N. Security Council into emergency session upon the invasion of North Korea and in gaining passage for the resolutions of June 25 and 27, which approved military assistance for South Korea.

After the mid-September 1950 Inchon Landing, Lie sought to end the war quickly and called for U.N.-supervised elections throughout the peninsula and for U.N. forces to forego crossing immediately into North

Korea. His plan was not approved, however, and the U.S.-backed resolution of October 15 allowed U.N. troops to cross the 38th parallel into North Korea.

Throughout the war, Lie mediated on the situation in Korea and continuously sought ways to end the fighting. Most of his attempts ended in failure, although a plan he proposed for discussion between military commanders likely reinforced Jacob Malik's activities and helped lead the start of the armistice negotiations.

In November 1950, the U.N. had passed a resolution extending Lie's term as secretary general for three years. His strong stand on the war and other issues had led to hostility from the Soviet Union and others at the United Nations, however, and he decided to step down in the summer of 1952, finally relinquishing his post in April 1953.

XII

ARMISTICE NEGOTIATIONS

"Peace, with justice and honor, is the best and most profitable of all possessions; but with shame and cowardice, it is the worst and most harmful of all."

—Polybius, *Histories, c. 125 B.C.*

I n the summer of 1951, once the conflict had bogged down into a stalemate not far from where it had begun, U.N. and communist military leaders agreed to begin discussing a negotiated settlement to the Korean War.

START OF NEGOTIATIONS

❑ During the first year of the war in Korea, the communists had refused U.N. efforts to discuss an armistice. After the Chinese spring offensives of 1951 failed to destroy U.N. forces and the lines of contact began to solidify, however, they became amenable to initiating talks. U.N. leaders, too, realized that they might not be able to concentrate the force, or be willing to suffer the casualties, necessary to break the Chinese defensive lines, which, like their own, were growing gradually stronger.

❑ On June 23, Soviet delegate to the United Nations Jacob Malik suggested that military representatives from each side begin negotiating a ceasefire, and they agreed.

❑ The United States instructed Gen. Matthew B. Ridgway, overall commander of the U.N. forces, to negotiate a military settlement to the conflict, but to avoid political subjects (e.g., future U.S. policy toward Nationalist China, reestablishment of the 38th parallel as the border between the two Koreas, or a place for communist China in the United Nations).

TALKS AT KAESONG

❑ On July 8, U.N. and communist military leaders met for the first time at a teahouse in Kaesong, the ancient capital of Korea. It was located in the communist zone of control, about 35 miles northwest of Seoul and just south of the 38th parallel. Plenary sessions began on July 10, with hopes high on both sides that the war could be brought to a swift conclusion.

❑ Gen. Matthew B. Ridgway selected U.N. naval commander Adm. C. Turner Joy to head the U.N. negotiating team. Together they chose the other four delegates: Maj. Gen. Henry I. Hodes (U.S. Army), Maj. Gen. Laurence C. Craigie (U.S. Air Force), Rear Adm. Arleigh A. Burke (U.S. Navy), and Maj. Gen. Paik Sun Yup (ROK Army).

❑ Gen. Nam Il, chief of staff of the North Korean People's Army and vice premier of the Democratic People's Republic of Korea, was chief delegate and the nominal leader of the communist delegation. His assistants were: Maj. Gen. Lee Sang Cho (NKPA), Maj. Gen. Chang Pyong San (NKPA), Gen. Teng Hua (Chinese People's Volunteers Army), and Maj. Gen. Hsieh Fang (Chinese People's Volunteers Army), who was in all likelihood the actual head of the communist negotiators.

❑ While the U.N. negotiating team was composed of highly proficient military men, none of them had substantial diplomatic or political experience. The communist negotiators, on the other hand, were all tough negotiators skilled in both political and military matters.

❑ Negotiations began slowly, taking two weeks to establish an agenda. Two points the communists pushed for initially, but which the U.N. negotiators were unwilling to budge on, were the withdrawal of all foreign military personnel from Korea, and the restoration of the 38th parallel as the border between North and Korea.

❑ Eventually, the communists agreed on four major agenda items, each of which was assigned to a subcommittee, so that discussion of them could proceed simultaneously, rather than one at a time. These were:

1) Adoption of the agenda

2) Establishment of a demilitarized zone

3) Creation of a military armistice commission and military observer teams to oversee fulfillment of the armistice terms

4) Disposition of prisoners of war

CHINA'S INFERIORITY COMPLEX

China was had long been considered a second-rate power by the West, and early on the U.N. delegation learned that the Chinese were very sensitive to issues of equality, protocol, and tradition, and reacted negatively to any perceived attempts by the U.N. delegation to demonstrate superiority. Indeed, the fact that the Chinese sat down as the equals of the Americans (and the superiors of the North Koreans) enhanced their international prestige and shifted the balance of power in Asia in their favor.

Communist delegates to the armistice talks had extensive military and political experience. From left to right are Chinese Gen. Hsieh Fang, Chinese Gen. Teng Hwa, North Korean Maj. Gen. Nam Il, and North Korean Gen. Chiang, pictured at Kaesong on July 16, 1951.

These facts make it is easier to understand why the Chinese felt obligated to treat the U.N. negotiators like suppliants and to engage in all manner of gamesmanship, even though an end to the conflict was in their best interests.

❏ For example, when one of the American delegates placed a small U.N. flag on the negotiating table at the start of the conference, the communists brought an even larger flag into the meeting. When the U.N. staff had a latrine built for their use, the communists constructed a much larger, brightly painted facility with landscaped surroundings. When the senior U.N. delegate began arriving at the meetings in a sedan, the communists obtained a car from the Soviet Union so that their senior delegate could arrive the same way.

❏ Once the agenda had been established, the Chinese used bluster, profanity, rudeness, and any other tactics that would gain them concessions or intimidate the U.N. delegation (although much of this was lost in the translation from Chinese or Korean). Once they had obtained all they could with these methods and were resolved to settling an issue, the communists would shift back to a civil, businesslike approach.

❏ It also became apparent that the communists would not accept U.N. proposals in their entirety. This led the U.N. delegation to deliberately insert errors into proposed agreements, knowing that once the communists found them they would be likely to leave the rest of the text untouched.

❏ The communists were also suspicious of U.N. attempts to reach quick compromises and offers of U.N. concessions that were not matched by demands for equivalent communist concessions.

❏ Another tactic used by the communists was waiting for the U.N. delegation to make a proposal. They would then accept the portions favorable to them, bargain for more and, when the U.N. delegation would not budge, tender a counter offer.

❏ During the bargaining sessions between the delegations, the Chinese consistently demonstrated that they were still willing to give ground on a point as long as they were arguing about it. Once they had settled on their final position, however, they declined to discuss it further.

❏ It soon became clear to the U.N. delegates that calmness, firmness, and patience were critical to dealing with the communists.

BREAKDOWN OF THE KAESONG TALKS

Soon after the negotiations began, both sides began to level charges that the other had violated the neutrality of the Kaesong meeting area.

❑ On August 4, a company of communist combat troops marched through the conference area in an apparent attempt to intimidate the U.N. negotiators. They responded by suspending the talks for five days, until the communists agreed not to repeat such blatant violations of the neutral zone.

❑ Stunned and unhappy at both the strong U.N. reaction to their violation of the Kaesong meeting area, and with the resulting negative publicity in the international media, the Chinese responded with a litany of complaints about U.N. violations of the zone.

❑ On August 23, the communists charged that U.N. warplanes had bombed the conference site. When the U.N. Command refuted these charges, the communists declared an indefinite suspension of the conference.

❑ In the meantime, liaison officers from both sides continued to meet to discuss ways to reduce future violations and agree on a more neutral site for continuation of the talks. They settled on Panmunjom, a village five miles west of Kaesong that, being on the line of contact rather than in the communist zone of control, was more easily accessible to both sides.

❑ While the talks lasted, both sides had taken the opportunity to reinforce their defensive positions. Most of the line of contact was above the 38th parallel at this time (slightly south of it in the west and well north of it along the east coast), and most U.N. leaders were opposed to launching a general offensive to take territory that might have to be returned under the terms of an armistice.

❑ U.S. 8th Army commander Gen. James Van Fleet, however, was concerned that his troops had lost their edge during the months of inactivity. These fears, along with a desire to keep pressure on the communists and incrementally improve his own defensive lines, prompted him to begin conducting limited offensive operations after the peace talks broke off.

❑ From late July through mid-October, U.N. ground forces conducted operations in the rough, hilly terrain in the middle of the peninsula, fighting battles at areas that became known as the Punchbowl, Bloody Ridge, and Heartbreak Ridge. While these operations were largely successful, the communist forces contested them vigorously, and U.N. units paid a heavy

U.N. delegates rest on the steps of the conference building during a break in the armistice talks at Kaesong in the summer of 1951. From left to right are U.S. Air Force Maj. Gen. Laurence C. Craigie, ROK Army Maj. Gen. Paik Sun Yup, U.S. Navy Vice Adm. C. Turner Joy, U.S. Army Maj. Gen. Henry I. Hodes, and Rear Adm. Arleigh Burke.

price in dead and wounded for the limited ground they took and the casualties they inflicted.

❏ Nonetheless, the limited offensives of the U.N. ground forces, reinforced with air and naval attacks, allowed them to gain the initiative, keep the enemy off balance, and ultimately persuade the communists to return to the conference table.

TALKS AT PANMUNJOM

On October 25, plenary sessions resumed at Panmunjom, where they would continue until the end of the war.

❏ Establishment of a military demarcation line and a demilitarized zone, agenda item two, had been on the table when the talks broke off, with the communist delegation insisting upon a restoration of the 38th parallel.

Chief U.N. Delegate C. Turner Joy had reacted to this by stating that, because the U.N. forces enjoyed both air and naval superiority in the conflict, the communists should be willing to give up more territory along the front.

❏ Each side flatly rejected the assertions of the other, and this mutual recalcitrance over the issue continued with the resumption of the talks and ultimately led both to drop their demands while continuing to reject those of their opponents. On November 27, the delegates agreed to accept the current line of contact as the line of demarcation.

❏ Although the U.N. delegation insisted that this line would remain valid for only 30 days, once it was established the communists showed a marked lack of interest in resolving the other agenda items and began to act as if the line had been permanently established and a ceasefire instituted.

AGENDA ITEM THREE: NEUTRAL NATION INSPECTORS

It was not until December 1951 that debate began on agenda item three, establishment of a military armistice commission to ensure that both sides complied with the terms of a ceasefire.

❏ Three basic points emerged during discussion of this item. These concerned who would be entrusted with compliance inspections behind the each side's lines; how much inspection would be allowed; and whether construction or repair of airfields would be permitted during the armistice.

❏ Eventually, the communists suggested that a number of neutral nations be selected to perform the inspections, but the U.N. negotiators adamantly refused to allow them to select the Soviet Union as one of these nations. Because the USSR played no official role in the Korean War, however, the U.N. pretenses for refusal sounded weak, and they finally settled on claiming that the proximity of the Soviet Union to the war zone might keep them from being impartial.

❏ While the communists had been opposed to inspections from the start, it was the U.N. delegation that proposed limiting inspections to specific points of entry and communication centers. The communists agreed to this, and the negotiators moved on to discussing how many inspection points there should be and where.

❏ Another impediment to resolution of Item Three was the U.N. insistence that construction or repair of airfields not be allowed during the armistice, in order to keep the communists from being able to establish bases of air operations in North Korea. Communist opposition to these efforts were resolute, however.

❏ Eventually, the communists withdrew their nomination of the Soviet Union as a neutral nation and the U.N. responded by dropping their insistence upon the airfield restrictions. The communists nominated Poland and Czechoslovakia and the U.N. nominated Sweden and Switzerland as members of the Neutral Nations Supervisory Commission.

❏ Finalization of Item Three included agreeing that 10 neutral nation teams would be assigned to each side, and that each would monitor five points of entry into the respective zone of control; that materiel and up to 35,000 troops per month could be replaced on a one-for-one basis; and that administration and supervision of the demilitarized zone, and violations of the armistice, would be handled by a Military Armistice Commission based at Panmunjom.

AGENDA ITEM FOUR: PRISONERS OF WAR

Once arrangements for Item Three had begun, discussion began on agenda Item Four, the repatriation of prisoners of war.

❏ Neither the United States nor North Korea had ratified the 1949 Geneva Convention on prisoners of war, but both delegations agreed to be bound by its provisions.

❏ Article 118 of the convention stated that prisoners of war should be returned immediately after cessation of hostilities. Nonetheless, problems arose early in discussions on the issue of repatriation and steadily increased as the talks continued.

❏ Trouble began in late December 1951 when the two sides exchanged lists of the prisoners. Those provided by the United Nations listed 132,000 military prisoners (20,00 of whom were Chinese) and 37,000 that they had reclassified as "civilian internees," which compared favorably with the communist claims of 188,000 personnel missing in action.

❏ Those provided by the communists, however, listed only about 11,500 prisoners (7,100 South Koreans and 4,400 U.N. personnel). These numbers did not mesh well with either earlier communist claims that they had taken 65,000 prisoners, or U.N. claims of 88,000 ROK and 11,500 U.S. troops missing in action.

❏ When the U.N. delegates insisted the communists explain this disparity, they claimed that they had released thousands of prisoners at the front after "reeducating" them. They also denied U.N. assertions that they had impressed South Korean civilians and POWs into the ranks of the North Korean People's Army and objected to the U.N. practice of screening prisoners and reclassifying as civilian internees those who claimed to have been forced into military service.

❏ Since mid-1951, U.S. military leaders had discussed the possibility that anti-communist prisoners of war were likely to be imprisoned or killed upon return to North Korean or Chinese control. They also realized that allowing prisoners to decide whether or not to be repatriated would be both humanitarian and offer U.N. forces propaganda opportunities.

❏ Nonetheless, U.N. negotiators had not broached this subject for a number of reasons, including fears that it might impede the quick and safe return of their prisoners and a realization that once the question of repatriation was raised, it would be difficult or impossible to withdraw it.

❏ What they hoped to do was convince the communists to agree to a one-for-one exchange and then, after all the U.N. prisoners had been returned in exchange for communists wishing to be repatriated, they could allow the remaining prisoners to decide whether to return or not. These hopes were dashed, however, by communist insistence of an all-for-all exchange of prisoners.

❏ A few days before the end of 1951, U.N. negotiators proposed that prisoners should be allowed to choose whether to return to their own forces or remain with the other side. They based this proposal on communist admissions that they had "reeducated" and released thousands of prisoners within their own lines and thus already endorsed the concept of voluntary repatriation. This tactic committed the U.N. delegation to the principal of voluntary repatriation.

❏ Not only did the communists reject the concept of voluntary repatriation, they denied any incongruity between this stance and their practice of reeducating prisoners and then impressing them into service as soldiers or laborers.

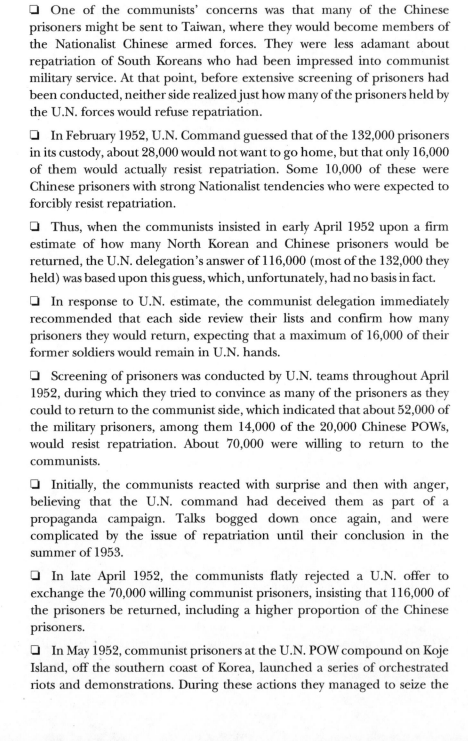

❏ One of the communists' concerns was that many of the Chinese prisoners might be sent to Taiwan, where they would become members of the Nationalist Chinese armed forces. They were less adamant about repatriation of South Koreans who had been impressed into communist military service. At that point, before extensive screening of prisoners had been conducted, neither side realized just how many of the prisoners held by the U.N. forces would refuse repatriation.

❏ In February 1952, U.N. Command guessed that of the 132,000 prisoners in its custody, about 28,000 would not want to go home, but that only 16,000 of them would actually resist repatriation. Some 10,000 of these were Chinese prisoners with strong Nationalist tendencies who were expected to forcibly resist repatriation.

❏ Thus, when the communists insisted in early April 1952 upon a firm estimate of how many North Korean and Chinese prisoners would be returned, the U.N. delegation's answer of 116,000 (most of the 132,000 they held) was based upon this guess, which, unfortunately, had no basis in fact.

❏ In response to U.N. estimate, the communist delegation immediately recommended that each side review their lists and confirm how many prisoners they would return, expecting that a maximum of 16,000 of their former soldiers would remain in U.N. hands.

❏ Screening of prisoners was conducted by U.N. teams throughout April 1952, during which they tried to convince as many of the prisoners as they could to return to the communist side, which indicated that about 52,000 of the military prisoners, among them 14,000 of the 20,000 Chinese POWs, would resist repatriation. About 70,000 were willing to return to the communists.

❏ Initially, the communists reacted with surprise and then with anger, believing that the U.N. command had deceived them as part of a propaganda campaign. Talks bogged down once again, and were complicated by the issue of repatriation until their conclusion in the summer of 1953.

❏ In late April 1952, the communists flatly rejected a U.N. offer to exchange the 70,000 willing communist prisoners, insisting that 116,000 of the prisoners be returned, including a higher proportion of the Chinese prisoners.

❏ In May 1952, communist prisoners at the U.N. POW compound on Koje Island, off the southern coast of Korea, launched a series of orchestrated riots and demonstrations. During these actions they managed to seize the camp commander and use him as a chip in negotiations for both concessions and admissions that communist prisoners had been treated inhumanely and had been coerced during screening. Even though these "admissions" were made under pressure and had no basis in fact, they allowed the communist armistice negotiators to seize the moral initiative during the months of mid-1952.

❏   After U.N. infantrymen were used to restore order in the camp, the U.N. Command conducted a more careful screening of the prisoners and then segregated those who wished to stay and those who wished to return into separate compounds.

❏   In July, U.N. delegates submitted a revised total of 83,000 prisoners willing to return to the communist side. This figure was obtained by including civilian internees in the list of POWs who would not resist repatriation. Once again, however, the communists rejected this total and insisted that larger number of prisoners, especially Chinese, be repatriated.

❏   With the talks going nowhere, both new U.N. commander Gen. Mark W. Clark and new chief negotiator Maj. Gen. William K. Harrison wanted to make a number of alternate proposals on the issue of repatriation and to demonstrate that they had reached their final position by suspending the armistice talks if the communists would not accept any of them.

❏   U.S. President Harry S. Truman approved this course of action, and on September 28, 1952, the U.N. delegation offered the communists three new proposals:

1. Prisoners held by both sides would be brought to the neutral areas on the line of demarcation and accounted for by the International Red Cross, after which they could choose to either be repatriated or remain with their captors;

2. Prisoners willing to be repatriated would be exchanged immediately. Those resisting repatriation would be brought to a neutral zone where they would be interviewed by neutral nation teams, after which they could decide whether to return to stay behind;

3. Prisoners willing to be repatriated would be exchanged immediately. Those unwilling to be repatriating would be transported to the neutral zone and freed, without any sort of screening or interviews, to go to whichever side they chose.

❏   The communists rejected all three of these proposals. This prompted the U.N. delegation, on October 8, 1952, to declare the armistice talks suspended until such time as the communists were willing to accept one of the new proposals or make a constructive one of their own.

SUSPENSION OF TALKS

During most of 1952, fighting along the line of contact had consisted mainly of limited offensives intended to take or keep advantageous pieces of terrain, to keep the enemy off guard, and to keep friendly forces from becoming complacent. U.N. leaders in particular wanted to avoid heavy casualties in exchange for objectives that might have to be relinquished under the terms of a ceasefire.

❑ Once the talks broke off a second time, U.N. Commander Gen. Mark Clark approved a number of larger offensives in the fall of 1952, mostly in the central sectors of the front. These offensives enjoyed only limited success, however, and were costly in terms of lives. The onset of winter ended further U.N. attempts to improve their defensive lines.

❑ During the suspension of talks, liaison officers continued to meet at Panmunjom throughout the end of the year and into 1953, mostly to deal with complaints and alleged violations of the conference area.

❑ In January and February 1953, after President-elect Dwight D. Eisenhower was inaugurated, the new Republican administration made several unsuccessful attempts to force the communists back to the bargaining table. These attempts included threats to utilize atomic weapons or expand the conflict—the very things for which Truman's administration had been criticized and Gen. MacArthur fired.

RESUMPTION OF TALKS

A break occurred on March 5, 1953, however, when Soviet Premier Joseph Stalin died unexpectedly. Even as his successors scrambled to consolidate their positions within the Soviet Union, they began to soften their stance toward the West, a shift that apparently spread to communist China and North Korea.

❏ In February 1953, Gen. Clark sent a routine communication to the communist military leaders proposing an exchange of sick and wounded prisoners (he did not expect it would be accepted). On March 28, 1953, however, the delegation both accepted the request and indicated that they were also willing to discuss repatriation of the other prisoners.

❏ On March 30, 1953, Chinese Foreign Minister Chou En-lai called for the resumption of plenary talks in mid-April, declaring that each side should turn over to a neutral nation commission those prisoners opposed to repatriation.

❏ When liaison officers met on April 6 to exchange lists of sick and wounded prisoners and arrange for their transfer, the talks were free of anger or recriminations and were conducted in businesslike manner.

❏ Operation Little Switch took place on April 20 at Panmunjom, when the U.N. returned 5,194 North Korean and 1,030 Chinese military prisoners and 446 civilian internees, and the communists returned 684 sick and wounded soldiers, among them 149 Americans.

❏ In the weeks after Little Switch, the U.N. and communist delegations addressed the final repatriation questions, including who would be responsible for the non-repatriates, how long they would be held, and what their final disposition would be if they remained unwilling to return home.

❏ While the U.N. Command had wanted Switzerland to head the Neutral Nations Repatriation Commission, the communists insisted India be a made a fifth member of the body and its chief. U.N. negotiators conceded this point on the condition that India provide all the necessary military and administrative personnel.

❏ China and North Korea also proposed that the non-repatriates be held by the neutral commission for six months while communist teams tried to convince them to return home. U.N. negotiators did not like this suggestion. After some discussion, the negotiators agreed on a 90-day period during which the communist teams could try to persuade the prisoners to come home, at a ratio not to exceed seven apologists for every 1,000 non-repatriates.

❏ Final disposition of those who still opposed being repatriated at the end of this three month period would be decided at a political conference after the signing of the armistice. If this conference failed to resolve their fate within 30 days of being convened, the non-repatriates would be declared civilians and allowed to seek residence in other countries.

SOUTH KOREAN OPPOSITION TO AN ARMISTICE

When armistice talks got back on track in April 1953, ROK President Syngman Rhee became alarmed at the prospect of an inconclusive peace and launched a strong public campaign calling for a decisive end to the war, promising that South Korea would continue to fight alone if forced to do so.

❏ South Korea could not wage or win a war against the communists without U.S. assistance. Rhee's words were thus more of an embarrassment than a obstacle to the peace process.

❏ South Korean reactions increased in May as the talks moved closer to a settlement, and crisis loomed when Rhee opposed the selection of India as head of the neutral nations commission and threatened to have Indian personnel shot if they set foot on South Korean soil.

❏ Part of Rhee's concerns were based on fears that the United States might not intervene if North Korea invaded the south following an armistice. At the end of May 1953, however, Eisenhower attempted to defuse the situation by offering South Korea a bilateral security treaty, even though he was reluctant to do so in the face of Rhee's public threats and pressure.

❏ Unfortunately, Rhee had exposed himself politically by rallying the South Korean people to this cause and now felt obligated to take some sort of action before accepting the American offer. On June 18, 1953, ROK camp guards, acting on Rhee's orders, allowed some 27,000 non-repatriates to escape. This action contravened the agreement that the negotiators had painstakingly worked out and threatened to derail the entire peace process. Most of the former prisoners quickly disappeared into the civilian population, and would have been difficult to recapture even with South Korean assistance.

❏ Although this unilateral action did cause an uproar, it also relieved some pressure from Rhee and led him to become more amenable to assurances of future U.S. military support. Despite his continued misgivings over the long term results of an indecisive peace, at the beginning of July Rhee agreed to stop trying to sabotage the conclusion of an armistice.

❏ While the communists made some political currency out of Rhee's actions, their reaction to them at the conference table was not excessive. They launched a series of offensives from May through mid-July in an attempt to snatch up as much territory as possible before conclusion of an armistice, and the resulting heavy ROK casualties may have cooled Rhee's ardor for war.

END OF THE WAR

Despite the inability of the U.N. Command to vouch for Rhee's actions once the armistice was signed, both sides were eager to finalize a truce, and in July the negotiators established a final line of demarcation and made final arrangements for the disposition of prisoners of war. (See Operation Big Switch in Chapter XIII, Prisoners of War and War Crimes.)

❑   On July 27, 1953, the opposing negotiators met at Panmunjom and each signed 18 copies of the armistice agreement, ending a war that had killed or wounded more than two million military personnel and ravaged two halves of a divided country.

❑   Within 12 hours of the signing, fighting ended along the entire front, the Korean War was over, and an uneasy peace that lasts to this day began.

XIII

PRISONERS OF WAR AND ATROCITIES

"So I am allotted months of emptiness, and nights of misery are apportioned to me. When I lie down I say, 'When shall I arise?' But the night is long, and I am full of tossing till the dawn. . . . My days are swifter than a weaver's shuttle, and come to their end without hope."

—Job 7:2-6, *Holy Bible*

Soldiers and civilians dependent upon the mercies of the other side were among those who suffered the most during the Korean War, from imprisonment, torture, and murder. To this day, more than half a century after the start of war, accusations of deceit and atrocity are still being leveled against the governments of both sides.

PRISONERS OF WAR

More than a quarter million military personnel from both sides endured incarceration as prisoners of war (POWs) during the three years of the conflict in Korea. Their treatment, actual numbers, and return have all contributed to one of the most emotional and tragic facets of the war, one that continues to haunt survivors of the conflict to this day.

❑   Most of those taken prisoner were captured during the first year of the war, as each side attacked and counterattacked across the 38th parallel and pockets of troops were overrun or cut off behind enemy lines. Once combat settled down into armed raids and limited offensives, fewer numbers of troops were taken prisoner.

❏ Neither side was prepared to adequately house or care for the great numbers of prisoners that they captured, and cultural differences certainly contributed to death and suffering among prisoners on both sides.

PRISONERS OF THE UNITED NATIONS

❏ In September 1950, the United States took charge of the all the communist prisoners held by the U.N. and ROK forces, and by 1951 was responsible for about 137,000 prisoners of war.

❏ U.S. mismanagement and naivete contributed to many of the problems that subsequently occurred amongst the prisoners in their custody, including underground political organizations, deaths, and rioting.

❏ It was important for America to try to win the hearts and minds of its prisoners, and its treatment of them was not only predominantly humane but actually better than what many of them had known under communism before the war. This treatment included vocational training, voluntary classroom instruction, and entertainment programs.

❏ Evidence of the success of these efforts is found in the large number of prisoners of war who subsequently refused to return to North Korea or China. Conditions in the U.N. camps was not ideal, however, and many prisoners perished there as a result of illness and other causes. Some 6,600 POWs died by December 1951.

❏ Had the communist prisoners been left in the charge of South Korea, however, which felt a great enmity toward the communist Koreans and did not share the liberal American need to win over its enemies to its own way of life, it is a certainty that far more of those prisoners would have died in imprisonment.

❏ Initially, most of the North Korean and Chinese prisoners were held in camps around Pusan, but in January 1951 most of them were transferred to compounds on Koje-do, a large island off the southeastern coast of Korea.

❏ These camps were overcrowded and underguarded, and it was not long before the communist prisoners organized into cells and began to exploit the weaknesses of their U.N. captors for propaganda purposes.

❏ Many of the communist leaders had experience as professional agitators and some of them were political officers who had deliberately allowed themselves to be captured in order to exert communist control over the other prisoners. Anti-communist prisoners organized as well, especially former Nationalist Chinese soldiers who had been impressed into the communist ranks after losing the Chinese Civil War.

❏ American camp administrators and guards found themselves increasingly incapable of controlling the violent political struggles between the various prisoner factions, which were encouraged not only by the communist government, but also by those of Nationalist China and the Republic of Korea.

❏ Confinement did not cut off the leaders of the communist prisoners from the outside world, and they managed to stay in contact with their leaders in the North Korean and Chinese armies through an underground network of spies and informers. Similarly, Nationalist Chinese and pro-Republic of Korea prisoners received orders and encouragement via Taiwanese and South Korean teachers and instructors.

❏ U.N. attempts to accurately screen prisoners to determine how many wished to be repatriated and how many preferred not to be were hampered by well-organized left-wing and right-wing groups, which did not hesitate to use even murder to coerce prisoners into following their orders.

❏ In May 1952, large-scale riots erupted in the Koje-do island compounds, during which communist prisoners captured the American camp commandant and held him hostage for several days until combat troops and a new commander were brought in to restore order. A number of prisoners were killed, both by agitators and the U.N. troops.

❏ Once the riots were quashed, the U.S. forces constructed a series of new compounds and segregated the prison population according to their politics, in order to reduce factional violence and allow the most troublesome groups to be more closely monitored.

PRISONERS OF THE COMMUNISTS

❏ North Korea moved its non-Korean prisoners—among them captured U.N. soldiers and civilians living in Korea who had been imprisoned after the war began—to camps along its northern frontier, many of them on the very banks of the Yalu River.

❏ Those captured in the first six months of the war suffered the most, especially as they were driven northward by the North Koreans, sometimes just hours ahead of the advancing U.N. troops. North Korean troops tended to treated prisoners harshly, and many died from exposure and exhaustion.

❏ North Korean troops also massacred many of the prisoners in their custody. For example, in October 1950, North Korean soldiers pulled 100 American prisoners off a train near Pyongyang, marched them to a clearing and told them they were to be fed, and then shot them.

❏ During the spring of 1951, the Chinese Communist Forces took control of the prisoner of war camps, and the arbitrary killings of prisoners largely came to an end. Indeed, China considered its treatment of U.N. prisoners of war rather humanitarian, in that they were given food, shelter, and medical care equivalent to that provided to criminals in Chinese prisons.

❏ Chinese camp administrators rigorously controlled their prisoners, however, and segregated them by nationality, rank, and race; forced them to participate in constant "re-education" and self-criticism sessions; and subjected them to severe, confined living conditions. The Chinese also subjected prisoners to grueling interrogations and attempted to obtain confessions from them—particularly of warmongering and biological warfare.

❏ Prisoners who tried to escape or who resisted communist control, especially by trying to organize or maintain the rank structure of their own military systems, were punished with revocation of their limited privileges, torture, and solitary confinement.

❏ Dealing with their communist captors was hard enough, but U.N. prisoners also lived with the threat of being caught in U.N. bombing raids against positions in North Korea.

❏ Most of the U.N. prisoners, especially Americans and Europeans, were completely unaccustomed to such limited amounts of food and debased conditions, and thousands died in captivity. Americans fared especially badly in the camps, and about 2,700 of the 7,140 U.S. prisoners officially acknowledged by the communists died while imprisoned.

REPATRIATION OF POWS

One of the major issues that hampered the conclusion of an armistice—and caused the war to drag on for two years longer than it might have otherwise—was the return of prisoners of war, a situation that was *complicated by the fact that about half the North Korean and Chinese prisoners did not wish to be repatriated.*

❏   In December 1951, about a year and a half after the war began, delegates to the armistice negotiations at Panmunjom began to discuss the release of POWs and exchanged lists of how many prisoners each held.

❏   United Nations lists indicated that they held a total of 159,000 prisoners of war. They had reclassified 37,000 of these prisoners, mostly those who claimed to be South Koreans impressed into military service by North Korea, as "civilian internees." This compared favorably with communist claims of 188,000 personnel missing in action.

❏   Communists lists, however, indicated that they held only about 11,500 prisoners—a mere 7,100 South Koreans and 4,400 U.N. personnel. These numbers did not mesh well with either earlier communist claims that they

Although conditions in U.N.-run prisoner of war compounds were far from ideal, they were immeasurably better than those in the communist-run camps. Thousands of North Korean and Chinese prisoners preferred to remain in U.N. custody than to be repatriated to their own countries.

had taken 65,000 prisoners, or the U.N. claims of 88,000 ROK and 11,500 U.S. troops missing in action.

❑ North Korea explained this disparity by claiming that they had "reeducated" and then released most of these men. A great number of them had also been impressed into military service, however, and some had been summarily executed. By subjecting Korean prisoners in its custody to these methods, North Korea ended up keeping relatively few of them incarcerated.

❑ By January 1952, the opposing sides agreed to exchange prisoners but immediately disagreed on how many should be repatriated.

❑ North Korea and China insisted upon an all-for-all exchange of prisoners, drawing upon provisions of the 1949 Geneva Convention as the basis for this demand. The United Nations Command, however, called for a one-for-one exchange of prisoners and eventually committed itself to the principal of not forcibly repatriating prisoners who did not wish to return to their original side.

❑ In April 1952, the U.N. armistice delegation proposed that prisoners under its control be screened to determine how many of them were willing to be returned, to which the communists tacitly agreed. At that point, the U.N. told the communists that it expected about 16,000 North Korean and Chinese prisoners to refuse repatriation. Discussions over the return of prisoners stalled, however, when the U.N. screening revealed only about 70,000 willing to return to the communists.

❑ Armistice talks dragged on throughout the rest of 1952 and into 1953, with the U.N. Command trying to keep the communists from losing interest in peace by harassing them with limited offensives, bombing raids, and implicit threats to use atomic weapons against the communists or expand the conflict beyond the peninsula.

❑ By March 1953, the United Nations and the communist powers had agreed to the formation of a neutral nations commission to oversee additional screening and disposition of non-repatriates.

❑ Most of the prisoners held by each side who wanted repatriation were returned to their respective sides in two operations, "Little Switch" and "Big Switch." In these exchanges, the U.N. forces returned a total of 82,493 communist prisoners, while the communists returned a total of 13,444 U.N. personnel.

❑ In early June 1953, the U.N. and communist armistice negotiators came to an agreement about the final arrangements for the return of prisoners of war. A few weeks later, ROK President Syngman Rhee tried to derail these arrangements by freeing some 27,000 non-repatriates that were being guarded by South Korean troops.

OPERATION LITTLE SWITCH

Conducted from April 20 to May 3, 1953, Operation Little Switch was primarily an exchange of sick and wounded POWs.

❑ In Operation Little Switch, the allies repatriated 5,194 North Korean and 1,030 Chinese military personnel, as well as 446 civilian prisoners, for a total of 6,670. The communists repatriated 684 sick and wounded U.N. troops. Among these were 149 Americans, 471 South Koreans, 32 British, 15 Turks, one Filipino, two Canadians, six Colombians, five Australians, one South African, one Greek, and one Dutch soldier.

❑ Both sides had agreed to Little Switch on April 11, during the armistice talks at Panmunjom. Several factors probably helped contribute to this agreement, including uncertainty in the communist bloc over Soviet policies following the death of Stalin in March 1953; initiatives in the United Nations and the International Red Cross in Geneva; and the indirect approach of U.N. Commander-in-Chief Gen. Mark W. Clark to Chinese Gen. Peng Dehuai and North Korean Premier Kim II Sung.

❑ Dissent surrounded the exchange, as it did everything concerned with the POW issue. Communist prisoners attempted to embarrass their U.N. captors by rejecting clothing and rations, while in the Western media sensational reports appeared claiming that the communists were still holding sick and wounded POWs, in spite of the exchange agreement.

❑ Worst of all, the issue that had prolonged the war for two years—that no communist POW would be forcibly repatriated by the U.N. forces—remained.

OPERATION BIG SWITCH

Conducted from August 5 to September 6, 1953, Operation Big Switch was supposed to be the final exchange of prisoners of war by both sides. Like its predecessor, Little Switch, Big Switch was marked by dissent over the issue of forced repatriation and, ultimately, by assertions of communist brainwashing and torture of allied POWs.

❏ In this operation, U.N. forces repatriated a total of 75,823 communist prisoners, among them 70,183 North Koreans and 5,640 Chinese. Among the North Koreans were 60,788 male POWs, 473 female POWs, 23 children, and 8,899 civilians; among the Chinese was one female POW.

❏ In Operation Big Switch, the communists repatriated 12,773 U.N. prisoners, among them 3,597 Americans, 7,862 South Koreans, 945 British, 229 Turks, 40 Filipinos, 30 Canadians, 22 Colombians, 21 Australians, 12 French, eight South Africans, two Greeks, two Dutchmen, one Belgian, one New Zealander, and one Japanese.

❏ On September 23, each side transferred its non-repatriates to the Neutral Nations Repatriation Commission in the demilitarized zone, more than 22,000 by the U.N. Command and some 359 by the communists, where they were to remain for 90 days.

❏ During this period the prisoners were urged to return home by representatives of their home countries. After most of the North Korean and Chinese non-repatriates ultimately rejected these arguments, the former were released in Korea and the latter were sent to Taiwan.

❏ Of those who did not wish to remain in South Korea or go to Taiwan, 628 ultimately changed their minds and accepted repatriation, 13 escaped or were missing, 38 died while held by the Indian Custodial Forces, and 86 went to India with the Indian Custodial Forces. By December 23, all of the prisoners held by the U.N. Command had been released in one way or another.

❏ Of the U.N. prisoners who had initially rejected repatriation, 325 Koreans, 21 Americans, and one Briton decided to remain with the communists. Of the others, eight South Koreans and two Americans accepted repatriation and two Koreans went with the Indian Custodial Force to India.

❏ Although the number of U.N. prisoners who refused to return home was minuscule compared to the thousands of POWs from North Korea and China who refused to return to their homelands, many American were shocked that any of their countrymen would decide to remain in a communist country.

❏ Various government commissions were formed to study this phenomena, and fingers were pointed at the state of discipline in the U.S.

Army. By 1955, a new code of conduct was adopted outlining how future American POWs should interact with their captors.

❏ Eventually, almost all the American defectors returned to their homeland. Today, all those who survive live in the United States, except for one who was accused of collaborating with the communists and compromising other prisoners. He has been refused entry into the United States and currently lives in Poland.

MISSING IN ACTION

Immediately after Big Switch, the U.S. government claimed that the communists had not returned all U.S. POWs and that there were 944 men who should have been accounted for, based on evidence that the communists would have known their fate. These men are some of the more than 8,000 U.S. personnel still listed as missing in action from the Korean War.

❏ In all likelihood, most of those 8,217 men were simply killed in action and their bodies unaccounted for. For half a century, however, the U.S. government has had evidence that the 944 prisoners who were not repatriated after the war had in fact been transported out of Korea and into China and the Soviet Union.

❏ Evidence of the fate of U.S. prisoners of war has been provided by a wide variety of sources, including contemporary U.S. intelligence reports and recent admissions by Russian government officials.

❏ For example, according to a Central Intelligence Agency information report from September 1952, titled "Location of Certain Soviet Transit Camps for Prisoners of War from Korea," at least four transit camps existed through which South Korean and American POWs were sent en route to the Soviet Union.

❏ "From December 1951 up to the end of April 1952, several railway transports of American and European (probably British) POWs were seen passing at intervals of 10 to 20 days through the Komi-Permyak National District in Northwestern Siberia," part of this report says. "The prisoners were clad in cotton-padded gray tunics and pants and wore civilian caps, so-called 'Sibirki' . . . They had no military insignia. They spoke among themselves in English, and they knew no other languages, except a few words of Russian."

❏ Even more stunningly, in 1991, during a trip to the United States, Russian President Boris Yeltsin announced that his nation had information about U.S. POWs from the Korean War. U.S. officials immediately explained away Yeltsin's comments and took no public steps to either confirm or deny them.

❏ To this day, family members of U.S. servicemembers who disappeared during the Korean War hold out hope that their loved ones might still be alive, or at the least that the dates and locations of their deaths might be learned and their remains returned.

WAR CRIMES

Episodes of atrocity marked the Korean War from its start, from the American prisoners of war summarily executed by North Korean soldiers during the summer of 1950 to Korean civilians who were reportedly gunned down in cold blood by U.S. troops. Most of these crimes of war took place in the first several months of the war, when emotions ran high on both sides.

❏ One of the first and most heinous instances of violence against civilians occurred in June 1950, when the North Korean forces overran Seoul, the ROK capital. When the U.S. Embassy personnel fled the city ahead of the communist advance, they left behind almost everything—including files listing the names and home addresses of its more than 5,000 South Korean employees. Many of those employees also fled Seoul. Every single one of those who did not was easily rounded up and exterminated by the North Korean soldiers.

❏ North Korean troops did not limit their murderous zealotry to South Korean civilians, and during the first months of the war U.S. troops discovered the remains of fellow soldiers who had been massacred. On August 17, U.S. troops moved onto Hill 303 near Waegwan, in South Korea, and were horrified to find 26 executed mortarmen of the 5th Cavalry Regiment, their hands bound with wire and their feet encrusted with blood. A number of other incidents of summary killings surfaced over the following months, including one in which 100 American prisoners of war were removed from a train moving into North Korea and shot by communist troops.

North Korean soldiers massacred many captured U.N. personnel early in the war; such incidents were probably initiated at a unit level and not dictated from above. Pictured are murdered troopers of the 5th Cavalry Regiment, 1st Cavalry Division, found near frontline areas in mid-August 1950.

❏ Even after they arrived at the communist POW camps, U.S. prisoners were not safe from the wrath of the North Korean soldiers. Harley Coon, a U.S. soldier captured during the first months of the war, remembers hearing shots from the prisoner enclosure next to his. Right afterward, a gun-wielding North Korean soldier came into Coon's shack. Before he could begin shooting, however, Chinese soldiers entered and led him out.

❏ Atrocities were not committed only by communist troops, however, and there are numerous accounts of violence perpetrated by ROK troops against North Korean civilians, and a number of accounts describing mostly isolated acts of brutality by U.S. troops against civilians. For example, in the summer and fall of 1951, after the U.N. forces crossed into North Korea and began moving toward the Yalu River, ROK troops routinely rounded up and executed suspected communists or guerrillas in captured villages. In August

1950, ROK Army officer Kim Ching-won had 50 North Korean soldiers beheaded.

❏ In his book *Colder Than Hell*, 1st Lt. Joseph R. Owen, a U.S. Marine Corps platoon leader, describes how one of his men took aim at an old man standing in front of his house and gunned him down in cold blood. Owen battered the man into submission, but did not take any further action against him.

❏ In another incident, journalist Stephen Barber, a reporter for the London *News Chronicle*, described how U.S. tank gunners machinegunned a committee of civilians led by old men who came out to welcome their liberators.

❏ Another British journalist, Reggie Thompson, whose reports were an indictment of a callous U.S. overuse of their firepower, wrote: "Every enemy shot released a deluge of destruction. Every village and township in the path of the war was blotted out. Civilians died in the rubble and ashes of their homes. Soldiers usually escaped."

❏ One particular incident, however, a massacre of South Korean civilians near the village of Nogunri, has overshadowed all other incidents from the Korean War in the American popular consciousness at the beginning of the 21st century.

NOGUNRI

In late 1999, nearly 50 years after it was alleged to have taken place, reports surfaced in the United States that U.N. air and ground forces had been ordered to attack and kill South Korean civilians.

❏ During the first months of the war, the young, scared, and inexperienced soldiers of the U.S. forces were being pushed back toward the Pusan Perimeter, harried not just by the advancing North Korean troops but also by pro-communist civilian guerrillas and communist troops in civilian garb.

❏ Some U.S. commanders authorized their soldiers to shoot at anything that looked like a threat during this desperate period, whether it was wearing civilian clothes or not. Such orders were generally not committed to writing and it is not clear just how high up the chain of command they originated, from individual company and battalion commanders or all the way up to the leaders of the 8th U.S. Army or the U.N. Command.

❏ Like so many episodes from the Korean War, there are many conflicting details and versions of an incident that happened near the South Korean village of Nogunri. All that is certain is that in late July 1950, soldiers of the 7th Cavalry Regiment (U.S. 1st Cavalry Division) fired upon a large group of civilians hiding under a railroad bridge outside of the village.

❏ According to survivors of the massacre at Nogunri, they had been attacked the previous day by U.N. jets, which had been strafing columns of refugees after apparently mistaking them for advancing North Korean troops, and were hiding under the bridge in order to escape further air attack. They say about 100 civilians were killed in those attacks.

❏ Troops of the 7th Cavalry Regiment's H Company, resting near Nogunri, recall receiving orders to prevent any civilians from crossing the U.S. line of retreat, in order to keep guerrillas from infiltrating U.S. units. Some of them also say they were fired upon from beneath the bridge.

❏ In any case, the 7th Cavalry troopers fired into the culvert over a period that might have been as long as three days, killing a large but unknown number of Korean refugees. Estimates begin at 100 dead and go as high as 300—the number claimed by survivors of the massacre who began seeking compensation from the U.S. and ROK governments in the late 1990s.

❏ Conflicting accounts have muddied attempts to determine just how many civilians died at Nogunri and whether any North Korean soldiers or guerrillas were among them. The credibility of at least one of the U.S. soldiers who says he took part in the massacre—Edward Daily, a veteran with a penchant for melodrama—is questionable because of doubtful claims he has made about his role in the Korean War.

❏ In September 1999, the U.S. Army Office of the Inspector General began conducting an official investigation to fully determine what happened at Nogunri. If true, the massacre at Nogunri will join the My Lai massacre of the Vietnam War as one of only two known mass killings of civilians by U.S. ground troops in the 20th century.

XIV

THE KOREAN WAR IN BOOKS, FILM, AND ON THE WEB

"The issues at stake in Korea were never clear. The people in Hollywood were as hard put as anyone to recognize the degree of American involvement, to understand the national goals, and identify who was the enemy."

—Paul M. Edwards, *A Guide to Films on the Korean War*

L ike those of other wars, the experiences and events of the Korean War have found expression in stories, films, and, most recently, on the World Wide Web.

BOOKS AND OTHER MEDIA

Events and experiences from the Korean War have inspired quite a number of novels, short stories, narratives, and novelizations based on actual events, and other works.

❏ Today, novelist James Michener is probably the best known author who has written widely about the Korean War, and a number of his books and stories were the basis for movies that use the conflict as their subject or backdrop. His works about the Korean War include *The Bridges at Toki-Ri*, *Sayonara*, and "The Forgotten Heroes of Korea," a short story he wrote for the *Saturday Evening Post*.

❏ Other novels written about the war include *Battle Hymn*, by Dean E. Hess, *Combat*, by Van Van Praag, *Hell's Outpost*, by Luke Short, *A Hill in*

Korea, by Max Catto, *The Hunters*, by James Salter, *The Intruder*, by Helen Fowler, *L'Hamecon*, by Vahe Katcha, *Love is a Many-Splendored Thing*, by Han Suyin, *The Manchurian Candidate*, by Richard Condon, *M*A*S*H*, by Richard Hooker (the pen name of authors H. Richard Hornberger and William Heinz), and *Melville Goodwin, U.S.A.*, by John P. Marquand.

❑   Short stories about the Korean War include "Bug Out," by James Warner Bellah, and "Case of the Blind Pilot," a short story written for the Saturday Evening Post by U.S. Navy Commander Harry A. Burns.

❑   A number of plays with Korean War themes were also written and produced, mostly in the years immediately following the war. One of the most notable of these was *Time Limit*, written by Henry Denker and Ralph Berkey, a courtroom drama about a U.S. Army officer accused of collaborating with the communists while held as a prisoner of war. It was made into a movie of the same name in 1957.

❑   Naturally, many of the authors who wrote about the Korean War had firsthand experience from the conflict. For example, James Salter was a U.S. Air Force pilot who flew F-86 Sabre Jets in Korea, and his first novel, *The Hunters*, was about aerial combat over the Korean Peninsula.

❑   North and South Korea have also produced many authors who have written about the Korea War. Such works reflect the Korean point of view of the war, as well as its politics, effects, and aftermath, and are not widely known outside of their countries of origin.

THE KOREAN WAR IN FILM

Between 1950 and 2000, nearly 100 feature films dealing with the war in Korea, to a lesser or greater extent, were produced for English language audiences. In addition, hundreds of documentaries and other specialized films have been produced.

❑   Some of the best Korean War films have been based on the experiences or writings of people with firsthand experience in Korea. Others reflect aspects of American life and philosophy, either during the war itself or when the film was made. (For example, M*A*S*H says as much about American attitudes toward the Vietnam War as it does about the Korean War.)

KOREAN WAR FILMS, 1951-2000

❏ While films about the Korean War have appeared steadily over the past 50 years, the bulk of them were made in the years during or immediately following the war (i.e., 59 in the 1950s, 14 in the 1960s, four in the 1970s, three in the 1980s, and just two in the 1990s). Some of them, such as *Big Jim MacClain* or *Heartbreak Ridge*, have a peripheral, rather than direct, connection with the Korean War. The films are as follows:

Afterburn (1992)
Air Cadet (1951; *Jet Men of the Air* in Great Britain)
All the Young Men (1960)
An Annapolis Story (1955; *The Blue and the Gold* in Great Britain)
Back at the Front (1952; aka *Willie and Joe Back at the Front*, *Willie and Joe in Tokyo* in Great Britain)
The Bamboo Prison (1955)
Battle Circus (1953)
Battle Flame (1959)
Battle Hymn (1957)
Battle Taxi (1955)
Battle Zone (1952)
Big Jim MacLain (1952)
The Bridges at Toko-Ri (1954)
Cease Fire (1953)
Collision Course (1975)
Combat Squad (1953)
Cry for Happy (1961)
Dragonfly Squadron (1954)
The Eternal Sea (1955)
Field of Honour (1986)
Fixed Bayonets (1951; originally *Old Soldiers Never Die*)
Flight Nurse (1953)
For the Boys (1991)
The Glory Brigade (1953)
The Great Imposter (1960)
Hell's Horizon (1955)
Hell's Outpost (1954)
Hell in Korea (1956; *A Hill in Korea* in Great Britain)

Hold Back the Night (1956)
The Hook (1962)
The Hunters (1958)
I Want You (1951)
Inchon (1981)
Iron Angel (1964)
Japanese War Bride (1952)
Jet Attack (1958; aka *Jet Squad*; in Great Britain as *Through Hell to Glory*)
Korea Patrol (1951)
Love is a Many-Splendored Thing (1955; aka *A Many-Splendored Thing*)
MacArthur (1977; aka *MacArthur, the Rebel General*)
The Manchurian Candidate (1962)
Marine Battleground (1966)
Marines, Let's Go! (1961)
Mask of Korea (1950; also known as *Gambling Hell*)
M*A*S*H (1970)
The McConnell Story (1955; *Tiger in the Sky* in Great Britain)
Men in War (1957)
Men of the Fighting Lady (1954)
Mission Over Korea (1953; *Eyes of the Skies* in Great Britain)
Mr. Walkie Talkie (1952)
My Son John (1952)
No Man's Land (1964)
The Nun and the Sergeant (1962)
One Minute to Zero (1952)
Operation Dames (1959; *Girls in Action* in Great Britain)
Pork Chop Hill (1959)
Prisoner of War (1954)
The Rack (1956)
The Reluctant Heroes (1971; also known as *The Egghead on Hill 656*)
The Rescue (1988)
Retreat, Hell! (1952)
Return from the Sea (1954)
Sabre Jet (1953)
Sayonara (1957)
Sergeant Ryker (1968; originally *The Case Against Paul Ryker*)
Sky Commando (1953)
Sniper's Ridge (1961)

Starlift (1951)
The Steel Helmet (1951)
A Step Out of Line (1971)
Strange Intruder (1956)
Submarine Command (1951)
Take the High Ground (1953)
Tank Battalion (1958; *The Valley of Death* in Great Britain)
Target Zero (1955)
Time Limit (1957)
Tokyo File 212 (1951)
Top Secret Affair (1957; *Their Secret Affair* in Great Britain)
Torpedo Alley (1953)
War Hunt (1962; aka *War Hero* and *War Madness*)
War is Hell (1964)
A Yank in Indo-China (1952; *Hidden Secret* in Great Britain)
A Yank in Korea (1951; *Letter from Korea* in Great Britain)
The Young and the Brave (1963)

BEST KOREAN WAR FILMS

❏ A dozen of the best films about the Korean War are described below. They cover a wide variety of themes, from gritty combat films produced during the war to films questioning why some American prisoners of war collaborated with the enemy.

❏ While this is a subjective listing, it is supported in many cases by academy awards, and all of these films are worth watching. There are many other worthwhile Korean War films, and interested readers are encouraged to make additional selections from the complete listing. Some of the video guides used to help compile this material may be of some use and are listed in the bibliography.

❏ *Battle Hymn* (1957. Directed by Douglas Sirk. Starring Rock Hudson, Don DeFore, Dan Duryea, Martha Hyer, Anna Kashfi). Based on a true story. Hudson plays the Reverend Dean Hess, a World War II veteran who, unable to cope with his peacetime role as a minister and family man, returns to service in the skies over Korea.

❏ *The Bridges at Toko-Ri* (1954. Directed by Mark Robson. Starring William Holden, Earl Holliman, Grace Kelly, Fredric March, Mickey Rooney,

Robert Strauss). Based on a novel by James Michener. This film portrays carrier-based U.S. Navy pilots flying missions against targets in Korea. Won an Oscar for special effects.

❏ *Field of Honour* (1986. Directed by Hans Scheersmaker. Starring Everett McGill, Ron Brandsteder, Hey Young Lee, Min Yoo, Dong Hyun Kim). This film, one of the few foreign-made movies about the war available in English, is about the experiences of a soldier from the Dutch Battalion who is left for dead after his unit is overrun by the Chinese.

❏ *The Manchurian Candidate* (1962. Directed by John Frankenheimer. Starring Frank Sinatra, Laurence Harvey, Janet Leigh, Angela Lansbury, Henry Silva, James Gregory, John McGiver, Leslie Parrish, Khigh Deigh). Based on a novel by Richard Condon. Capitalizing on the theme of Chinese brainwashing of U.S. prisoners, this film is about a Korean War hero who has been transformed into an unwitting political assassin.

❏ *Men in War* (1957. Directed by Anthony Mann. Starring Robert Ryan, Aldo Ray, Robert Keith, Vic Morrow, James Edwards, Scott Marlowe, Victor Sen Yung). Good action scenes distinguish this film about 24th Infantry Division and 1st Cavalry Division soldiers being driven south during the first months of the war.

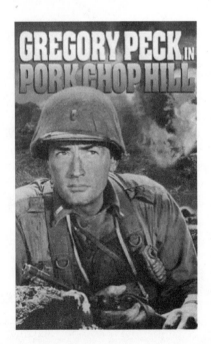

❏ *Men of the Fighting Lady* (1954. Directed by Andrew Marton. Starring Van Johnson, Walter Pidgeon, Louis Calhern, Dewey Martin, Keenan Wynn, Frank Lovejoy, Robert Horton, Bert Freed). Based on a pair of short stories, one by James Michener and the other by U.S. Navy Commander Harry S. Burns. An above-average film about the pilots and crew of an aircraft carrier operating off the coast of Korea.

❏ *Porkchop Hill* (1959. Directed by Lewis Milestone. Starring Gregory Peck, Harry Guardino, Rip Torn, George Peppard, James Edwards, Bob Steele, George Shibata, Biff Elliot, Woody Strode, Robert Blake, Norman Fell, Martin Landau, Bert Remsen, Harry Dean Stanton, Gavin Mcleod).

This film depicts one of the last bloodbaths of the Korean War, a seesaw battle over a worthless chunk of real estate that was fought out even as the negotiations at Panmunjom were being finalized. Based on the book by S. L. A. Marshall.

❏ *Retreat, Hell!* (1952. Directed by Joseph H. Lewis. Starring Frank Lovejoy, Richard Carlson, Russ Tamblyn, Anita Louise). This grim, powerful film depicts the experiences of a unit of U.S. Marines, starting with their deployment from the United States and culminating in their desperate withdrawal from the Chosin Reservoir during the November 1950 Chinese offensive.

❏ *Sayonara* (1957. Directed by Joshua Logan. Starring Marlon Brando, Ricardo Montalban, Miiko Taka, Miyoshi Umeki, Red Buttons, Martha Scott, James Garner). This film, which is set in occupied Japan against the backdrop of the Korean War, depicts a romance between an American pilot and a Japanese entertainer. It won Oscars for best supporting actor (Buttons), best supporting actress (Taka), and best art direction/set decoration. Based on yet another novel by James Michener.

❏ *Sergeant Ryker* (1968. Directed by Buzz Kulik. Starring Lee Marvin, Bradford Dillman, Vera Miles, Peter Graves, Lloyd Nolan, Murray Hamilton). Differing from combat-oriented films, this production focuses on the trial of a U.S. soldier accused of being a traitor and addresses the question of how repatriated prisoners who have been tortured or brainwashed should be treated.

❏ *The Steel Helmet* (1951. Directed by Samuel Fuller. Starring Gene Evans, Robert Hutton, Steve Brodie, James Edwards, Richard Loo, Sid Melton). This is the first film made about the Korean War, and is still considered by many to be the best. It was produced in a mere 12 days and completed just six months after the war began. *The Steel Helmet* focuses on a U.S. soldier who, wounded, left for dead, and cut off behind enemy lines, attempts to return to the American lines with the help of a young Korean boy.

❏ *Time Limit* (1957. Directed by Karl Maldin. Starring Richard Widmark, Richard Basehart, Dolores Michaels, June Lockhart, Rip Torn, Martin Balsam, Carl Benton Reid, James Douglas). This is a courtroom drama about the trial of a U.S. officer accused of collaborating with the enemy while in captivity in North Korea.

THE KOREAN WAR ON THE WORLD WIDE WEB

A large variety of World Wide Web sites are available with information about the Korean War, and many have been created or expanded because of the 50th anniversary of the conflict. Some of the best are listed below.

❏ KoreanWar.net (http://www.KoreanWar.net) is a nonprofit association dedicated teaching people about the Korean War, making information about it readily available, and interviewing as many veterans of the conflict as  possible. It has been officially recognized as an important resource by the U.S. Department of Defense, and has agreed to act as an official online companion to this book. KoreanWar.net offers regularly updated links to sites on these pages and many other appropriate sites as well.

❏ Run by the Canadian Department of Veterans Affairs, "Canadians in Korea" (http://www.vac-acc.gc.ca/historical/koreawar/korea.htm) details the experiences of the Canadian expeditionary force during the Korean War.

❏ Another worthwhile internet site it The Cold War International History Project (http://cwihp.si.edu/default.htm), which supports the release of historical materials by all of the governments involved in the Cold War and seeks to disseminate new information and perspectives on Cold War history emerging from previously inaccessible communist sources.

❏ The Coalition of Families of Korean & Cold War POW/MIAs (http://www.coalitionoffamilies.org) is an organization dedicated to accounting for the more than 8,200 American servicemen missing from the

Korean and Cold Wars, and strives to educate members of the government, media, and American public about issues related to their efforts.

❏ The Chinese Military Forum (http://www.anyboard.net/plaboard) is is dedicated to discussion and information about the armed forces of Communist China. Its content is not limited to the Korean War.

❏ The Chosin Few (http://home.hawaii.rr.com/chosin/Main.html) is the site of a membership organization for veterans of combat around the Chosin Reservoir during the first winter of the Korean War.

❏ The 50th Anniversary of the Korean War Commemoration Committee (http://korea50.army.mil) is the official, public access site for the Department of Defense commemoration of the 50th Anniversary of the Korean War.

❏ The Korean War (http://www.korean-war.com) contains detailed information about U.N. (U.S. and other allied) and communist forces that participated in the Korean War.

❏ A wealth of information about the Chinese People's Volunteers Army during the Korea War, from the communist point of view, can be found on The Korean War FAQ (http://centurychina.com/history/krwarfaq.html).

❏ The Korean War Veterans Association (http://www.kwva.org) is the official site of the primary membership organization for veterans of the Korean War.

❏ A National Park Service page, The Korean War Veterans Memorial (http://www.nps.gov/kwvm/index2.htm), describes the Korean War Veterans Memorial in Washington, D.C., which evokes the experience of the American ground troops in Korea through 19 stainless steel statues depicting a squad on patrol.

❏ The Korean War Veterans National Museum and Library (http://www.theforgottenvictory.org) site is a seven-gallery national museum dedicated to veterans of the Korean War under construction in Tuscola, Illinois.

❏ Living History Online (http://www.LivingHistoryOnline.com) in an online history magazine that boasts, in addition to feature articles and regular columns, comprehensive listings of Korean War reenactments, commemorations, and other events.

❏ The People's Korea (http://www.korea-np.co.jp./pk) is an official North Korean site contains information from the North Korean point of view and contains a number of excellent photographs. Its content is not exclusively related to the Korean War.

❏ Second   Squadron   SAAF   (Flying   Cheetahs)   in   Korea (http://ourworld.compuserve.com/homepages/RAllport/Korea.htm) is a site dedicated to the elements of the South African Air Force that flew for the U.N. Command during the Korean War.

❏ An even more focused site is the 13th Bomb Squadron Association (http://www.13thbombsquadron.org) is dedicated to telling the history of one U.S. Air Force bomb squadron during the Korean War, and includes oral histories and more than 500 photographs.

❏ U.S.-Korea 2000 Foundation (http://www.uskorea2000.org) is primarily dedicated to reaching out to those served in the "Forgotten War."

XV

FACTS AND FIGURES

"I am convinced of what I *know*. Everything else is hypothesis . . ."

—*Carl Jung, Psychology and Religion*

This section contains numerical, tabular, and statistical information about Korea, the 1950 to 1953 conflict, and the forces that participated in it. It is also a bit of a catch-all for material that does not fit neatly into any of the other chapters.

KOREA

By the time the Korean War began, society in North and South Korea had begun to diverge, the North becoming more monolithic, communist, and industrialized, and the South remaining more traditional and agrarian. Detailed economic and demographic data on North Korea for the war years is sketchy, while similar information on South Korea is much more readily available.

POPULATION

❑ About 30 million Koreans lived throughout the Korean Peninsula during the Korean War.

❑ South Korea's population in 1951 was estimated to be about 21 million, of whom more than one in six, about 3,700,000, were classified as refugees (more than 400,000 of whom had fled North Korea). The homes of about 400,000 of the South Korean refugees were destroyed during the war.

❑ Seoul, the capital of South Korea, had an estimated population of 715,572 in December 1952. In 1949, prior to the outbreak of war and the city changing hands four times, the population of the capital was estimated at 1,640,000. Pusan, the temporary capital of South Korea when Seoul was under enemy occupation, had an estimated population of 840,000 in 1952.

❑ North Korea's population in 1951 was estimated to be about 9 million, considerably less than half the population of South Korea. Pyongyang, the capital of North Korea, had an estimated population of 500,000 in 1952.

EDUCATION

Under the Japanese, most Koreans were denied any sort of state-sponsored education and what was offered was geared toward their role as a servitor people. For the most part, schools were segregated, with Korean and Japanese students attending separate institutions.

❑ In 1939, one-third of Korean children, or about 1,200,000, were enrolled in primary schools. In contrast, virtually all Japanese children living in Korea, or about 93,000, were enrolled. The same year, 62,000 Koreans and 34,000 Japanese were enrolled in secondary schools, professional schools, colleges, and Japanese-run Seoul Imperial University, many of the Koreans in agricultural training programs.

❑ There were many private schools throughout Korea, however, largely run by missionary organizations. For the most part, the Japanese were afraid to harass or curtail the activities of such groups, fearing negative international opinion. During the Japanese occupation, about a quarter of Koreans attended missionary high schools, as did 57 percent of those who attended college and 15 percent of those who attended professional schools.

❑ After the end of World War II, the educational system in Korea was completely reorganized. The U.S. military government supported these efforts in the south, distributing 15 million elementary school textbooks written in the native Hangul script.

❑ Compulsory elementary school education was established in South Korea in June 1950; the outbreak of the war the same month, however, prevented full implementation of this plan as scheduled. Students were offered 12 years of elementary and secondary education, with entrance to secondary institutions based on competitive examinations.

❏ In post-secondary education, an emphasis was placed on technical and scientific training, so that Koreans could take the place of the Japanese engineers who had left at the end of World War II.

❏ As of June 1, 1952, South Korea had 3,921 elementary schools with 2,525,369 students; 563 middle schools with 298,980 students; 321 high schools with 140,550 students; 49 colleges with 27,500 students; 17 normal schools with 20,240 students; seven technical schools with 1,350 students; 14 higher technical schools with 3,500 students; and 1,609 civic schools for adult education with 496,250 students.

❏ In 1948, the literacy rate in South Korea was reported at 70 to 80 percent for Hangul script, and significantly lower for Chinese ideographs.

RELIGION

Religion in Korea has had many foreign influences. Native religions included Sinkyo and Chondokyo, and those introduced by outsiders included Confucianism and Buddhism from China, Shintoism and various sects of Buddhism from Japan, and Christianity from Western missionaries.

❏ Sinkyo is a form of animistic nature worship, or shamanism. It is Korea's oldest religion and has played an important role in the culture and mores of its people since prehistoric times.

❏ Confucianism is second only to Sinkyo in its influence upon Korean culture. It was introduced to the peninsula in the 1st century A.D., and vied with Buddhism as a state religion until triumphing over it in 1392.

❏ Buddhism came to Korea in the 4th century A.D. from China and increased in popularity after the Japanese annexation. In 1938, there were an estimated 200,000 followers of Korean Buddhism and some 300,000 followers of Japanese Buddhism throughout Korea.

❏ Christianity spread in Korea primarily through schools run by missionary groups. In 1938, there were an estimated 500,000 Christians in Korea, more than half of them Protestants.

❏ Chondokyo, founded in 1959 by a religious figure named Choe, was an eclectic religion incorporating aspects of Shamanism, Confucianism,

Buddhism, and Christianity. According to some estimates, in the late 1920s there may have been as many as 2 million followers of Chondokyo throughout Korea. By 1947, however, there were about 73,000 in South Korea and an unknown number in the north.

❏ Shintoism flourished among Japanese colonists in Korea, but virtually disappeared after World War II. In 1938, there were 96,000 practitioners of Shinto, 21,000 of whom were Korean.

AGRICULTURE, FISHING, AND FORESTRY

During its occupation of Korea, Japan had cleared and irrigated land for agriculture, especially in the south, and built fertilizer factories, especially in the north (70 percent their output being used in the south). Japan used Korea as an imperial breadbasket, forcing it to export rice to Japan and import inferior grains for its own people.

❏ In 1952, some 15 million people in South Korea, about 60 percent of the population, were farmers. An average rural family farmed 2.5 acres, and one third of rural families farmed 1 acre or less.

❏ About a quarter of South Korea at this time, some 5,300,000 acres, was under cultivation. An additional 200,000 acres was used for orchards and mulberry trees, used in sericulture.

❏ South Korean agricultural production in 1951 included 56,300,000 bushels of rice; 15,100,000 bushels of barley, rye, and wheat; 4,300,000 bushels of soy beans; 500,000 bushels of other grains; 1,100,000 metric tons of vegetables; 68,000 tons of fruit; and 15,000 tons of tobacco.

❏ North Korean agriculture was less widespread but more diverse than in the south, and emphasized grains other than rice and greater fruit and vegetable production.

❏ At the end of 1951, South Korea had 393,000 work cattle; 780 dairy cattle; 20,000 goats; 17,000 horses; 719,000 poultry; 91,000 rabbits; and 1,000 sheep.

❏ In 1952, about 16 million acres of South Korea were classified as forest. During the previous decade, timber reserves were cut in half by warfare, indiscriminate cutting, and poor land management. In 1952, South Koreans used an estimated 3,500,000 cubic meters of firewood and 2,100,000 bags of charcoal.

❏ Fish and other seafood traditionally provided the majority of animal protein in the Korean diet. In the early 1950s, more than a million Koreans on both sides of the border were engaged in the fishing industry.

❏ In 1945, deterioration of the Korean fishing fleet and the withdrawal of large Japanese-owned boats reduced catches from Korean waters to 200,000 metric tons per year, about half of the average annual yield during World War II. Gains made in the fishing industry after the conflict were eliminated by the outbreak of the Korean War, and the 1952 yield was only 268,000 metric tons.

INDUSTRY

During their occupation of Korea, the Japanese began to develop specific industries in Korea, especially heavy industry in the north, to complement its own industrial base. By the time the war began in 1950, North Korea was considerably more industrialized than the south and controlled most of the peninsula's mineral resources.

❏ South Korean industries included textiles and food processing. After being cut off from the north by the opposing occupation forces, South Korea found its light industry inadequate to meet local needs.

❏ North Korea's most important industries included cement, chemicals, electrical power, iron and steel, and machinery. At the end of World War II, the capacities of these industries was reduced from damage inflicted by departing Japanese technicians and from theft of equipment by Soviet forces.

❏ Textiles comprised South Korea's most important manufacturing industry during the Korean War, with cotton textiles accounting for about 80 percent of total textile output. In 1952, textile production totalled 2,200,000 pounds of cotton yarn, 43,200,000 yards of cotton sheeting, 16,000,000 square yards of rayon, 2,700,000 square yards of silk, and 434,000 square yards of woollen and worsted cloth.

❏ Other goods manufactured in South Korea in 1952 included 21,688,000 pairs of rubber shoes, 320,000 bicycle tires, 36,224 metric tons of cement, 10,866 metric tons of paper, and 3,140 metric tons of coke.

❑ Mineral production for South Korea in 1952 included 575,906 tons of anthracite; 10,832 metric tons of copper ore; 619 kilograms of gold; 14,812 metric tons of graphite; 17,420 metric tons of iron ore; 1,766 metric tons of kaolin; 378 metric tons of lead ore; 2,255 metric tons of lignite; 7,416 metric tons of manganese; 12.7 metric tons of molybdenum; 1,000 metric tons of nickel; 80,677 metric tons of peat; 755 metric tons of pyrites; 191 kilograms of silver; 3,789 metric tons of tungsten; and 1,014 metric tons of zinc ore.

❑ Mineral resources available in North Korea exceeded those in the south, and included coal, copper, graphite, iron ore, lead, magnesite, pyrites, tungsten, and zinc.

❑ In the late 1940s, lightly industrialized South Korea was able to produce only 30 to 40 percent of its electrical power needs; the balance was provided by plants in North Korea. In May 1948, North Korea cut off the supply of power to the south, which was eventually able to fulfill its needs by using U.S.-provided power barges and constructing domestic facilities. In 1952, South Korean electrical production totalled 635 million kilowatt hours.

TRADE

Prior to the end of World War II, Korea was under Japanese occupation and almost all of its trade was with other countries within the empire. For example, in 1939, 97 percent of Korean exports were to countries controlled by Japan, and 89 percent of its imports were from those countries.

❑ In 1952, South Korea had a trade deficit of $28,700,000. Major imports totalled $53,700,000 and included chemicals, fertilizer, and rice. Major exports, more than 20 percent of which went to Japan, totalled $25,500,000 and included tungsten and other minerals. In addition, the Republic of Korea received aid from the United Nations and the United States totalling $154,400,000.

❑ In the years prior to and during the Korean War, most of North Korea's trade was with the People's Republic of China and the Soviet Union.

TRANSPORTATION AND COMMUNICATIONS

Under the Japanese occupation, railroads became the most important mode of transportation in Korea and Japanese companies provided the country's shipping requirements. By the time the Korean War began, however, neither North or South Korea had a modern transportation infrastructure.

❏ During its occupation of Korea, Japan built an extensive rail network to connect Sinuiju and Pusan, cities at the northern and southern ends of the country, for military—rather than economic—purposes. Prior to World War II, Japan built, with U.S. technical supervision, some 3,500 miles of standard-gauge track (4 feet 8.5 inches).

❏ After the outbreak of the Korean War, the U.N. Command controlled, operated, and maintained most of the railroad system in South Korea. From April 1, 1951, to March 31, 1952, South Korean railroads carried 28,404 passengers and 10,050,417 metric tons of freight. In February 1953, South Korea had 439 operating and 144 non-operating locomotives.

❏ In 1945, Korea had an average of 0.17 miles of roads and highways per square mile (as compared with 4.5 miles in Japan). By 1952, there were only 21,000 miles of roads on the peninsula, the primary highways linking Pusan with Sinuiju and Hunyung with Mokpo. Almost all the roadways were hard packed dirt and gravel, except for streets in Seoul and Pusan and a 20-mile stretch of highway from Seoul to Inchon, which were paved.

❏ On January 1, 1950, South Korea had 9,700 trucks, 2,600 automobiles, 1,500 taxicabs, and 1,000 buses.

❏ As early as 1929, Japan had encouraged air transportation in Korea through subsidies to Japanese firms. All of them pulled out of Korea at the end of World War II, and by 1953 the only commercial airline operating out of the Republic of Korea was Korean Air Transport, which flew to Hong Kong, Taipei, and Tokyo.

❏ Before the outbreak of the Korean War, U.S.-based carrier Northwest Airlines provided international service to Seoul. During the war, it shifted its service to Pusan.

❏ Waterborne transportation was also important in Korea for a variety of reasons, including the lack of east-west highways and railroads, the country's mountainous interior, and large coastal population centers.

❑ At the end of World War II, Japan withdrew most of its ships from Korean waters, leaving behind older vessels totalling about 15,000 tons. In 1953, South Korea had a mere eight ocean-going vessels, most of them antiquated, and a coastal fleet with a cargo capacity of 42,000 tons.

❑ In 1949, South Korea had 38,000 telephone lines, 50,000 telephone stations, and 175 telegraph stations, all owned and operated by the government.

❑ Until December 1949, international communications services in South Korea were provided by the Radio Corporation of America, after which the government took control of them. On January 11, 1952, the Republic of Korea's service was granted admission into the International Telecommunications union.

FINANCE

Prior to the end of World War II, Korea's only bank was the Bank of Chosen, under the direct control of the Japanese Ministry of Finance. In South Korea, it continued to operate as the Bank of Chosen until 1950, when it was reorganized as the Bank of Korea. In North Korea, it was reorganized as the North Korean Central Bank.

❑ As of June 30, 1952, the Bank of Korea had assets and liabilities of 1,712,402 million *won* (or about $285,000,000 in U.S. currency).

❑ In February 1953, the official foreign exchange rate for South Korean currency was 6,000 *won* to $1.00 U.S., while the black market exchange rate was about 27,000 *won* to $1.00 U.S.

❑ For the fiscal year ending March 31, 1952, the Republic of Korea had a budget that provided for expenditures and receipts of 1,564,000 million *won*. For fiscal year 1952-1953, the Republic of Korea had a budget that provided for expenditures of 2,319,086 million *won* and receipts of 3,341,585 million *won*.

❑ In 1953, in an effort to control inflation, the government of South Korea retired the *won* and issued a new currency, the *hwan*, establishing an exchange rate of 100 won to 1 *hwan*.

U.N. MILITARY CONTRIBUTIONS

A total of 20 countries, including the United States and South Korea, committed naval, air, and ground units to the U.N. war effort in Korea. Three countries—Australia, Canada, and the United States—contributed forces from all three of their major services.

❑ Some 5,720,000 Americans served in the U.S. armed forces during the Korean War. About 1,789,000 of them, more than 31 percent, served in the Korean theater of war. Numbers in the following section do not necessarily reflect maximum or minimum contributions, simply the numbers in Korea at various points during the war (e.g., in the case of ground forces, on June 30, 1951, a year after the war began; on June 30, 1952; and on July 31, 1953, four days after the armistice was signed).

U.N. NAVAL FORCES

U.N. naval forces consisted almost entirely of vessels from the United States, South Korea, and Great Britain. Denmark's naval contribution was a single hospital ship.

❑ From June 1950 to July 1953, a total of four battleships, eight cruisers, and about 80 destroyers were active in the waters around the Korean peninsula. At various times during the war, 16 aircraft carriers were also active around Korea (13 U.S., two British, and one Australian), and navy and marine aircraft from those carriers flew more than 255,000 sorties.

❑ The United States had 186 ships committed to the war in Korea in mid-1951, 195 ships committed in mid-1952, and 261 ships committed at the end of the war in mid-1953.

❑ South Korea had 34 ships committed to the war in mid-1951, 67 ships in mid-1952, and 76 ships in mid-1953.

❑ Australia, Canada, Colombia, Denmark, the Netherlands, New Zealand, Thailand, and the United Kingdom also contributed to the U.N. naval forces, committing a total of 36 ships during the period January to October, 1952. Most of these vessels, 22 of them, were sent by the United Kingdom. Australia sent four of them, Canada three, New Zealand two, Thailand two, and Colombia, Denmark, and the Netherlands one each.

U.N. AIR FORCES

Air squadrons from five nations flew in defense of the Republic of Korea during the Korean War.

❑ The United States had 58 Air Force, Navy, and Marine Corps air squadrons committed in June 1951, 67 air squadrons committed in June 1952, and 66 air squadrons committed on July 31, 1953.

❑ South Korea did not have any combat squadrons in 1950. After the war began, the United States began to train South Korean pilots, which produced one ROK squadron by late 1951, two in 1952, and three in 1953.

❑ Australia, Canada, and South Africa each had a single air force squadron committed at each of the three sample periods.

U.N. GROUND FORCES

Numbers of U.N. personnel present at three points during the Korean War appear below. Medical contributions of the various neutral nations that did not send combat troops are also listed here.

❑ By the end of the war, U.N. ground forces consisted of nearly 1 million personnel. In mid-1951, this strength was 554,577; by mid-1952 it was 678,051; and on July 31, 1953 it had risen to 932,539.

❑ South Korea provided the greatest number of allied troops. In June 1951, there were 273,266 ROK soldiers, in June 1952 there were 376,418 ROK soldiers, and by the end of July 1953, there were 590,911.

❑ After the Republic of Korea, the United States committed the greatest number of ground troops to the war in Korea, including U.S. Marine Corps and U.S. Navy personnel assigned to U.S. Army commands. At the end of June 1951, there were 253,250 U.S. troops on the ground in Korea; in June 1952 the number was 265,864; on 31 July, 1953, there were 302,483 U.S. troops in Korea.

❑ Australia had 912 troops committed in mid-1951, 1,844 troops committed in mid-1952, and 2,282 troops committed at the end of the war, on July 31, 1953.

❏ Belgium had 558 troops committed in mid-1951, 579 troops committed in mid-1952, and 900 troops committed at the end of the war, on July 31, 1953.

❏ Denmark had 100 medical personnel committed from March 1951 through August 953.

❏ Luxembourg had 44 troops committed from November 1950 until late 1953.

❏ Canada had 5,403 troops committed in mid-1951, 5,155 troops committed in mid-1952, and 6,146 troops committed on July 31, 1953.

❏ Columbia had 1,050 troops committed in mid-1951, 1,007 troops committed in mid-1952, and 1,068 troops committed on July 31, 1953.

❏ Ethiopia had 1,153 troops committed in mid-1951, 1,094 troops committed in mid-1952, and 1,271 troops committed on July 31, 1953.

❏ France had 738 troops committed in mid-1951, 1,185 troops committed in mid-1952, and 1,119 troops committed on July 31, 1953.

❏ Great Britain had 8,278 troops committed in mid-1951, 13,043 troops committed in mid-1952, and 14,198 troops committed on July 31, 1953.

❏ Greece had 1,027 troops committed in mid-1951, 899 troops committed in mid-1952, and 1,263 troops committed on July 31, 1953.

❏ India had 333 medical troops committed in mid-1951, 276 medical troops committed in mid-1952, and 70 troops committed on July 31, 1953.

❏ Italy had no personnel committed in mid-1951, 64 medical personnel committed in mid-1952, and 72 medical personal committed on July 31, 1953.

❏ Netherlands had 725 troops committed in mid-1951, 565 troops committed in mid-1952, and 819 troops committed on July 31, 1953.

❏ New Zealand had 797 troops committed in mid-1951, 1,111 troops committed in mid-1952, and 1,389 troops committed on July 31, 1953.

❏ Norway had 79 medical personnel committed in mid-1951, 109 medical personnel committed in mid-1952, and 105 medical troops committed in July 1953.

❏ Philippines had 1,143 troops committed in mid-1951, 1,494 troops committed in mid-1952, and 1,496 troops committed on July 31, 1953.

❑ Sweden had 162 medical personnel committed in mid-1951, 148 medical personnel committed in mid-1952, and 154 medical troops committed in July 1953.

❑ Thailand had 1,057 troops committed in mid-1951, 2,274 troops committed in mid-1952, and 1,294 troops committed on July 31, 1953.

❑ Turkey had 4,602 troops committed in mid-1951, 4,878 troops committed in mid-1952, and 5,455 troops committed on July 31, 1953.

CASUALTIES

Casualty statistics from the Korean War vary, depending on who has tabulated them. The following figures are drawn from a number of mostly official U.S. sources. In many cases, North Korean, Chinese, and Soviet figures differ markedly. Casualty totals include dead, wounded, and missing personnel.

More than 33 thousand U.S. personnel were killed, wounded, or missing in action during the Korean War. Pictured is Pfc. Thomas Conlon (21st Infantry Regiment, 24th Infantry Division), who was wounded while crossing the Naktong River during the breakout from the Pusan Perimeter.

❏ United States casualties during the Korean War included 33,651 personnel killed in action, 103,284 wounded in action, 8,184 missing in action, and 7,140 prisoners of war. An additional 20,617 U.S. military personnel died worldwide from all causes during the Korean War.

❏ Of the 7,140 U.S. prisoners of war, 2,701 of them died in captivity—a staggering 37.8 percent; 4,418 returned to the United States; and 21 refused repatriation.

❏ U.S. Army casualties totalled 109,958: 27,704 dead (19,334 killed in action), 79,526 wounded in action, 4,442 missing in action, and 6,656 prisoners of war. In addition to those men killed in action, 1,930 wounded died, 3,778 of the missing were declared dead, and 2,662 prisoners of war died.

❏ U.S. Navy casualties totalled 2,087: 458 dead (279 killed in action), 1,599 wounded in action, 174 missing in action, and 35 prisoners of war. In addition to those killed in action, 2,501 wounded soldiers died, 5,127 of the missing in action were declared dead, and 2,701 prisoners of war died.

❏ U.S. Marine Corps casualties totalled 28,205: 4,267 dead (3,308 killed in action), 24,281 wounded in action, 391 missing in action, and 225 prisoners of war.

❏ U.S. Air Force casualties totalled 1,841: 1,200 dead (379 killed in action), 379 wounded in action, 859 missing in action, and 224 prisoners of war.

❏ South Korea suffered a total of 238,656 military casualties (about 47,000 killed, 183,000 wounded, and 8,656 prisoners of war) and about 1 million civilian casualties.

❏ North Korea suffered a total of 630,723 military casualties (about 520,000 killed or wounded and 110,723 prisoners of war). Like South Korea, North Korea also suffered about 1 million civilian casualties.

❏ China suffered a total of 381,374 military casualties: about 360,000 killed or wounded and 21,374 prisoners of war.

❏ Australia's casualties were 1,332: 261 killed, 1,034 wounded, and 37 missing in action or taken prisoner.

❏ Canada's casualties were 1,543: 294 killed, 1,202 wounded, and 47 missing in action or taken prisoner.

❏ Great Britain's casualties were 4,286: 686 killed, 2,498 wounded, and 1,102 missing in action or taken prisoner.

❏ New Zealand's casualties were 102: 22 killed, 79 wounded, and 1 missing in action.

❏ Casualties for the other U.N. nations present in Korea totalled 9,997: 1,931 killed, 6,484 wounded, and 1,582 missing in action or taken prisoner.

❏ Total U.N. casualties were 17,260, including 3,194 killed, 11,297 wounded, and 2,769 missing in action or taken prisoner.

U.N. COMMANDERS

Leadership of the overall U.N. Command and of the major commands subordinate to it changed throughout the Korean War.

COMMANDERS-IN-CHIEF OF THE U.N. COMMAND

Tensions between North and South Korea have remained high since the termination of hostilities in 1953. Indeed, since that time, a United Nations presence there has always been deemed necessary. U.N. troops under the command of a U.S. commander are stationed in South Korea today, and will be for the foreseeable future.

All of the following commanders were U.S. Army generals ("four star"), except for MacArthur, who was a general of the army ("five star"). Those with a (D) after their name were deceased as of January 2000.

Gen. Douglas MacArthur (D):   July 23, 1950 to April 11, 1951
Gen. Matthew B. Ridgway (D):   April 11, 1950 to May 12, 1952
Gen. Mark W. Clark (D):   May 12, 1952 to October 7, 1953
Gen. John E. Hull (D):   October 7, 1953 to April 1, 1955
Gen. Maxwell D. Taylor (D):   April 1, 1955 to June 5, 1955
Gen. Lyman L. Lemnitzer (D):   June 5, 1955 to July 1, 1957
Gen. George W. Decker (D):   July 1, 1957 to June 30, 1959
Gen. Carter B. Magruder (D):   July 1, 1959 to June 30, 1961
Gen. Guy S. Meloy Jr. (D):   July 1, 1961 to July 31, 1963
Gen. Hamilton H. Howze (D):   August 1, 1963 to June 15, 1965
Gen. Dwight E. Beach: June 16, 1965 to August 31, 1966
Gen. Charles H. Bonesteel (D):   September 1, 1966 to September 30, 1969
Gen. John H. Michaelis (D):   October 1, 1969 to August 31, 1972

Gen. Donald V. Bennett:	September 1, 1972 to July 31, 1973
Gen. Richard D. Stilwell (D):	August 1, 1973 to October 8, 1976
Gen. John W. Vessey Jr.:	October 8, 1976 to July 10, 1979
Gen. John A. Wickham Jr.:	July 10, 1979 to June 4, 1982
Gen. Robert W. Sennewald:	June 4, 1982 to May 31, 1984
Gen. William J. Livsey:	June 1, 1984 to June 24, 1987
Gen. Louis C. Menetrey:	June 25, 1987 to June 25, 1990
Gen. Robert W. Riscassi:	June 26, 1990 to June 14, 1993
Gen. Gary E. Luck:	June 15, 1993 to July 8, 1996
Gen. John H. Tilelli Jr.:	July 9, 1996 to December 10, 1999
Gen. Thomas A. Schwartz:	December 10, 1999 to present

COMMANDING GENERALS OF THE 8TH U.S. ARMY

Four U.S. Army generals commanded the 8th U.S. Army during the Korean War. All were U.S. Army lieutenant generals ("three star"). I Corps commander Maj. Gen. Frank W. Milburn served as acting commander of the 8th U.S. Army after Gen. Walker was killed in an accident until Gen. Ridgway arrived in Korea. Gen. Van Fleet was promoted to full general on August 1, 1951, and Gen. Taylor was promoted to full general on June 23, 1953.

Lt. Gen. Walton H. Walker:	July 13, 1950 to December 23, 1950
Lt. Gen. Matthew B. Ridgway:	December 26, 1950 to April 14, 1951
Lt. Gen. James A. Van Fleet:	April 14, 1951 to 11 February, 1953
Lt. Gen. Maxwell D. Taylor:	February 11, 1953 until the end of the war

COMMANDING GENERALS OF THE U.S. I CORPS

Five U.S. Army major generals ("two star") commanded the U.S. I Corps during the Korean War. Kendall was promoted to lieutenant general on September 16, 1952.

Maj. Gen. John B. Coulter:	August 2, 1950 to September 11, 1950
Maj. Gen. Frank W. Milburn:	September 11, 1950 to July 19, 1951
Maj. Gen. John W. O'Daniel:	July 19, 1951 to June 29, 1952

Maj. Gen. Paul W. Kendall: June 29, 1952 to April 11, 1953
Maj. Gen. Bruce C. Clarke: April 11, 1953 through the end of the war

COMMANDING GENERALS OF THE U.S. IX CORPS

*Eight U.S. Army or Marine Corps major generals commanded the U.S.
IX Corps during the Korean War. Gen. Moore died on February 23 of
injuries sustained in a helicopter accident. Gen. Hoge was promoted to
lieutenant general on June 3, 1951. Gen. Jenkins was promoted to lieutenant
general on November 8, 1952.*

Maj. Gen. Frank W. Milburn: August 10, 1950 to September 12, 1950
Maj. Gen. John B. Coulter: September 12, 1950 to January 31, 1951
Maj. Gen. Bryant E. Moore: January 31, 1951 to February 23, 1951
Maj. Gen. Oliver Smith (U.S.M.C.): February 24, 1951 to March 5, 1951
Maj. Gen. William F. Hoge: March 5, 1951 to December 24, 1951
Maj. Gen. Willard G. Wyman: December 24, 1951 to July 31, 1952
Maj. Gen. Joseph P. Cleland: July 31, 1952 to August 9, 1952
Maj. Gen. Reuben E. Jenkins: August 9, 1952 through the end of the war

COMMANDING GENERALS OF THE U.S. X CORPS

*Four U.S. Army major generals commanded the U.S. X Corps during
the Korean War, starting with MacArthur's protege Edward. M. Almond.
White was promoted to lieutenant general on November 7, 1952. Maj. Gen.
I. P. Smith served as acting commander from July 10 to 12, 1952; Maj. Gen.
David L. Ruffner served as acting commander from August 12 to 14, 1952;
Maj. Gen. Joseph P. Cleland served as acting commander from April 1 to 7,
1953.*

Maj. Gen. Edward M. Almond: August 26, 1950 to July 15, 1951
Maj. Gen. Clovis E. Byers: July 15, 1951 to December 5, 1951
Maj. Gen. Williston B. Palmer: December 5, 1951 to August 12, 1952
Maj. Gen. I. D. White: August 15, 1952 through the war

COMMANDING GENERALS OF THE FAR EAST AIR FORCE (FEAF)

All three of the officers commanding the Far East Air Force were U.S. Air Force generals. Gen. Partridge served as acting commander of FEAF for a month, in between the commands of generals Stratemeyer and Weyland. Weyland was promoted to lieutenant general on July 28, 1951, and then to full general on July 5, 1952.

Lt. Gen. George E. Stratemeyer: April 26, 1949 to May 21, 1951
Lt. Gen. Earle E. Partridge: May 21, 1951 to June 1, 1951
Maj. Gen. O. P. Weyland: June 1, 1951 through the end of the war

COMMANDING GENERALS OF THE 5TH AIR FORCE

During the Korean War, five U.S. Air Force generals commanded the 5th Air Force, the main component of the Far East Air Forces.

Lt. Gen. Earle E. Partridge: October 6, 1948 to May 21, 1951
Maj. Gen. edward J. Timberlake: May 21, 1951 to June 1, 1951
Maj. Gen. Frank F. Everest: June 1, 1951 to May 30, 1952
Lt. Gen. Glenn O. Barcus: May 30, 1952 to May 31, 1953
Lt. Gen. Samuel E. Anderson: May 31, 1953 through the end of the war

COMMANDERS OF THE FAR EAST NAVAL FORCES

Both of the commanders of the Far East Naval Forces were U.S. Navy vice admirals.

Vice Adm. C. Turner Joy: August 26, 1949 to June 4, 1952
Vice Adm. R. P. Briscoe: June 4, 1952 through the end of the war

COMMANDERS OF THE U.S. 7TH FLEET

Four U.S. Navy admirals commanded the U.S. 7th Fleet during the war.

Vice Adm. Arthur D. Struble: May 6, 1950 to March 28, 1951
Vice Adm. H. H. Martin: March 28, 1951 to March 3, 1952
Vice Adm. R. P. Briscoe: March 3, 1952 to May 20, 1952
Vice Adm. J. J. Clark   May 20, 1952 through the end of the war

CHIEFS OF STAFF OF THE REPUBLIC OF KOREA ARMY

Four ROK generals served as chief of staff of the ROK armed forces during the Korean War. Chae Byung Dok was demoted after the North Korean invasion and was killed at the Battle of Hadong on July 26, 1950.

Maj. Gen. Chae Byung Dok: April 10, 1950 to June 30, 1950
Lt. Gen. Chung Il Kwon: June 30, 1950 to June 23, 1951
Maj. Gen. Lee Chong Chan: June 23, 1951 to July 23, 1952
Lt. Gen. Paik Son Yup: July 23, 1952 to May 5, 1953

PLENARY MEMBERS OF THE ARMISTICE NEGOTIATIONS

Negotiations to conclude an armistice and thus an end to the Korean War began July 10, 1951, and were conducted by high-ranking members of the opposing military forces.

U.N. COMMAND DELEGATES

Many of the members of the U.N. delegation also had other jobs during the Korean War. For example, Vice Adm. C. Turner Joy was commander of the Far East Naval Forces. Service affiliation of the delegates is given after their names.

U.S. DELEGATES

Vice Admiral C. Turner Joy (U.S.N.):   July 10, 1951 to May 22, 1952
Maj. Gen. Henry Hodes (U.S.A.):   July 10, 1951 to Dec. 17, 1951

Rear Adm. Arleigh A. Burke (U.S.N.):   July 10, 1951 to Dec. 11, 1951
Maj. Gen. Laurence C. Craigie (U.S.A.F.):   July 10, 1951 to Nov. 27, 1951
Maj. Gen. Howard M. Turner (U.S.A.F.):   Nov. 27, 1951 to July 5, 1952
Maj. Gen. Claude B. Ferenbaugh (U.S.A.):   Dec. 17, 1951 to Feb. 6, 1952
Rear Adm. Ruthven E. Libby (U.S.N.):   Dec. 11, 1951 to June 23, 1952
Lt. Gen. William K. Harrison Jr. (U.S.A.):   Feb. 6, 1952 to July 27, 1953;
Brig. Gen. Frank C. McConnell (U.S.A.):   May 22, 1952 to April 26, 1953
Brig. Gen. Joseph T. Morris (U.S.A.F.):   July 5, 1952 to April 26, 1953
Brig. Gen. Ralph M. Osborne (U.S.A.):   June 23, 1952 to July 27, 1953
Brig. Gen. Edgar E. Glenn (U.S.A.F.):   April 25, 1953 to June 20, 1953
Brig. Gen. George M. Finch (U.S.A.F.):   June 20, 1953 to July 27, 1953

ROK DELEGATES

Maj. Gen. Paik Son Yup (ROK Army):   July 10, 1951 to Oct. 24, 1951
Maj. Gen. Lee Hyung Keun (ROK Army):   Oct. 24, 1951 to Feb. 6, 1952
Maj. Gen. Yu Jai Hyung (ROK Army):   Feb. 6, 1952 to May 28, 1952
Brig. Gen. Lee Han Lim (ROK Army):   May 28, 1952 to April 26, 1953
Brig. Gen. Choi Duk Shin (ROK Army):   April 26, 1953 to May 16, 1953

NORTH KOREAN AND CHINESE COMMUNIST DELEGATES

As with the members of the U.N. delegation, many of the communist delegates to the armistice talks held other positions during the Korean War, and all were members of either the North Korean People's Army or Navy or the Chinese People's Volunteer Army. For example, Lt. Gen. Nam Il also served as chief of staff of the North Korean People's Army.

NORTH KOREAN DELEGATES

Lt. Gen. Nam Il (NKP Army):   July 10, 1951 to July 27, 1953
Maj. Gen. Lee Sang Cho (NKP Army):   July 10, 1951 to July 27, 1953
Maj. Gen. Chang Pyong San (NKP Army): July 10, 1951 to Oct. 24, 1951
Maj. Gen. Chung Tu Hwan (NKP Army):   Oct. 24, 1951 to April 28, 1952
Rear Adm. Kim Mon Wu (NKP Navy):   April 28, 1952 to August 11, 1952

Maj. Gen. So Hui (NKP Army):   August 11, 1952 to April 26, 1953
Maj. Gen. Chang Chun San (NKP Army): April 26, 1953 to May 25, 1953
Adm. Kim Won Hu (NKP Navy):   May 25, 1953 to June 17, 1953
Maj. Gen. Kim Dong Hak (NKP Army):   June 17, 1953 to July 27, 1953

CHINESE DELEGATES

Gen. Teng Hua: July 10, 1951 to Oct. 24, 1951
Maj. Gen. Hsieh Fang: July 10, 1951 to April 26, 1953
Gen. Pien Chang-wu: Oct. 24, 1951 to April 26, 1953
Gen. Ting Kuo-yu: April 26, 1953 to July 27, 1953
Maj. Gen. Tsai Cheng-wen: April 26, 1953 to May 27, 1953

WELL-KNOWN KOREAN WAR VETERANS

A number of well-known people served in the armed forces during the Korean War, including actors, astronauts, professional athletes, and members of Congress. Some of the best known are listed below.

CELEBRITIES

Quite a few celebrities served in the armed forces during the Korean War, in both the U.S. and other allied units.

❑ These included comedian Bob Newhart; actor Clint Eastwood (who missed his troop transport to Korea and was sent to the brig as a result); astronauts John Glenn and Buzz Aldrin (as combat pilots); baseball legend Ted Williams, (who was also a pilot and served as John Glenn's wingman); actor Ed McMahon; actor Regis Philbin; British actor Michael Caine (who served in the Commonwealth forces); actor Jamie Farr (who played Cpl. Klinger in the Korean War television series M*A*S*H), and actor James Garner.

MEMBERS OF CONGRESS

Many Korean War veterans have served as elected officials since the end of the war. As of 1999, several active members of Congress had served in the U.S. armed forces during the conflict in Korea, including the following.

❏ Representative Bill Archer (Republican, Texas) served in the Air Force from 1951 to 1953.

❏ Representative Michael Bilirakis (Republican, Florida) served in the Air Force from 1951 to 1955.

❏ Senator John H. Chafee (Republican, Rhode Island) served in the Marine Corps from 1942 to 1945 and from 1951 to 1952.

❏ Senator Ben Nighthorse Campbell (Republican, Colorado) served in the Air Force from 1951 to 1953.

❏ Representative John Conyers (Democrat, Michigan) served in the Army National Guard from 1948 to 1952, in the Army from 1952 to 1953, and in the Army Reserve from 1953 to 1957.

❏ Representative Sam Johnson (Republican, Texas) served in the Air Force from 1951 to 1979.

❏ Representative Charles B. Rangel (Democrat, New York) served in the Army from 1948 to 1952.

❏ Representative Floyd D. Spence (Republican, South Carolina) served in the Navy Reserve from 1947 to 1952, in the Navy from 1952 to 1954, and in the Navy Reserve from 1954 to 1985.

❏ Senator John Warner (Republican, Virginia) served in the Navy from 1944 to 1946 and in the Marine Corps from 1950 to 1952.

PAY RATES FOR U.S. ENLISTED PERSONNEL

Monthly pay rates for enlisted personnel in the U.S. armed services was revised less than a year before the outbreak of the Korean War, by the Career Compensation Act of October 12, 1949. (Note: Army rank for each pay grade is shown in parentheses.):

Grade	Army Rank	First Two Years	Highest Pay in rank
E-1	Recruit	$80.00	$ 95.00
E-2	Private	$82.50	$120.00
E-3	Private 1st Class	$95.55	$147.00
E-4	Corporal	$117.60	$191.10
E-5	Sergeant	$139.65	$227.85
E-6	Technical Sergeant	$169.05	$249.90
E-7	Master Sergeant	$198.45	$294.00
	First Sergeant		

❑ Basic pay increased by five percent for each two-year increment up to 22 years, subject to the maximum pay available for each rank. Only personnel in grade E-7 continued to receive increases after this, at 26 and 30 years.

❑ All grades received a subsistence allowance of $45 a month if they had no dependents. Grades E-5 through E-7, and grade E-4 with more than seven years in service received a subsistence allowance of $67.50 a month if they had one or more dependents (e.g., a spouse or child).

MUNITIONS

Massive amounts of ammunition were expended by both sides during the war:

❑ A Soviet-made MiG-15 fighter jet was loaded with 80 rounds of ammunition for each of its two 23mm NS-23 cannon and 40 rounds of ammunition for its 37mm N-37 cannon. Rate of fire for these weapons was 14 rounds per second for the 23mm gun, and seven rounds per second for the 37mm gun.

❑ Projectiles from the NS-23 weighed 0.44 pounds and those from the N-37 weighed 1.62 pounds; all had a muzzle velocity of 2,264 feet per second. Soviet munitions experts calculated that eight hits by 23mm projectiles or two hits by 37mm shells were, on average, sufficient to shoot down a U.S. B-29 bomber.

❑   U.S. warplanes tended to be armed with .50 caliber machine guns, which were not nearly as effective in air-to-air combat as the guns mounted on the Soviet-made aircraft. Each of the American guns, which had a muzzle velocity of 2,750 feet per second, could fire 20 rounds per second (120 for all six), each of which weighed 1.17 ounces.

❑   This inadequacy was pointed to by the amount of ammunition that frequently had to be expended in order to sufficiently hit and kill an enemy jet. For example, Lt. Col. Bruce Hinton, the first U.N. pilot to shoot down a MiG-15 in aerial combat, used nearly 1,500 rounds of ammunition in his attack against the enemy plane. MiGs were also sturdy aircraft, and frequently returned from combat with up to 50 bullet holes in them.

❑   Throughout the course of the war, U.N. warships fired more than 4 million rounds of ammunition from their guns, ranging in size from 3-inch to 16-inch.

❑   During the Battle of Bloody Ridge (August 18-September 5, 1951), the U.S. Army's 15th Field Artillery Battalion set a record among American units by firing 14,425 artillery shells in 24 hours.

CHRONOLOGY

"One cannot begin a conversation with the end, or a war with a peace treaty, or life with death. Willy-nilly, actively or passively, one must await the given time; one cannot skip a single moment."

—Franz Rosenzweig, *The New Thinking*

olitical interaction between the United States and Korea began in 1882, with the signing of the Korean-American Treaty of Friendship and Commerce. Major events prior to and following the Korean War are reflected on the following timeline. The Korean War began with the June 1950 invasion of South Korea and concluded with the July 1953 cease fire that ended the fighting.

1943

❏ December 1: Korean independence is promised in the Cairo Declaration, agreed to by the United States, Great Britain, and Nationalist China.

1945

❏ August 8: The Soviet Union declares war on Japan and deploys troops for the occupation of Korea.

❏ August 11: The United States and Soviet Union agree to divide Korea into zones of military occupation at the 38th parallel.

❏ September 2: Japan surrenders, ending World War II.

❑ September 8: U.S. troops arrive in Korea to occupy the southern half of the country.   .

❑ December 21: The formula for Korean unification is spelled out in the Moscow Agreement.

1946

❑ May 8: After failing to agree on how to execute the Moscow Agreement, the joint Soviet-American Commission adjourns.

1948

❑ August 15: The Republic of Korea is established in the U.S.-occupied southern half of the peninsula.

❑ September 9: The Democratic People's Republic of Korea is established in the Soviet-occupied northern half of the peninsula.

❑ December 12: A United Nations resolution recognizes the Republic of Korea as the only legitimate government on the peninsula, calls for the withdrawal of both U.S. and Soviet forces, and establishes the U.N. Commission on Korea.

1950

❑ January 12: In a speech at the National Press Club in Washington, D.C., U.S. Secretary of State Dean Acheson excludes Korea from the U.S. sphere of strategic interest.

❑ June 25: War erupts when the northern Korean Democratic People's Republic sends 90,000 soldiers, two-thirds of its 135,000-man army, across the 38th parallel into the southern Republic of Korea. Decrying this action, the U.N. Security Council calls for an end to North Korea's aggression.

❑ June 27: The United Nations asks its members to go to the assistance of the Republic of Korea. President Harry S. Truman deploys the U.S. Navy's 7th Fleet to the waters near Taiwan in order to contain the conflict in Korea and prevent it from spreading throughout Asia.

❑ While providing security for Americans evacuating Korea, an F-82 of the U.S. Air Force's 68th "All-Weather" Squadron shoots down a North Korean Yak fighter, scoring the first air victory of the war. U.S. planes shoot down two more enemy aircraft in the same battle.

❑ June 28: North Korean forces capture the South Korean capital of Seoul and all but destroy the lightly-armed Republic of Korea (ROK) army.

❑ June 29: Eighteen B-26 "Invader" light bombers of the Fifth Air Force's 3rd Bombardment Group attack Heijo Airfield, outside of the North Korean capital of Pyongyang, shooting down one Yak fighter and destroying 25 enemy aircraft on the ground.

❑ June 30: President Truman orders U.S. ground forces into Korea.

❑ July 1: Task Force Smith, the first U.S. infantry unit deployed for the Korean War, arrives in Korea from Japan. It is commanded by Lt. Col. Brad Smith and consists of 406 infantrymen of the 1st Battalion, 21st Infantry Regiment (24th Infantry Division) and 134 artillerymen of Battery A of the 52nd Field Artillery Battalion.

❑ July 2: USS *Juneau* helps ROK forces destroy three of four attacking North Korean torpedo boats near Chumunjin in the waters off of Korea's east coast.

❑ July 5: **Battle of Osan.** In the first U.S. ground action of the war, Task Force Smith engages and delays advancing NKPA units, suffering heavy casualties in the process.

❑ July 5-August 4: U.N. forces fight to delay the communist advance, but are driven steadily southward toward the port city of Pusan.

❑ July 6: Fifty-seven Army nurses arrive in Pusan and help set up a hospital for wounded personnel. Two days later, 12 of them move forward to Taejon with an army medical unit.

❑ July 7: Seeing the need for the forces of its members nations to have unified leadership, the United Nations creates the United Nations Command, to be headed by U.S. General Douglas MacArthur and headquartered in Japan.

❑ August 4: U.N. forces establish the Pusan Perimeter, a box-shaped area in the southeastern corner of Korea.

❑ August 4-September 16: Some 84,478 troops of the U.S. Army's 1st Cavalry Division, 2nd, 24th, and 25th Infantry Divisions, and the 1st Provisional Marine Brigade, help to defend the Pusan Perimeter.

❑ August 5-19: **First Battle of Naktong Bulge.**

❑ August 27-September 15: North Korean forces desperately try to implode the Pusan Perimeter in the heaviest fighting of the war, to that time.

❑ September 1-5: North Korean forces launch the Naktong Offensive.

❏ September 15: **Inchon Landing** (Operation Chromite). U.S. and allied forces land U.S. Marines and U.S. Army troops at Inchon on Korea's west coast, not far from Seoul and deep in the rear of the North Korean forces besieging Pusan.

❏ September 15-26: **Liberation of Seoul**. Driving inland from Inchon, U.S. and allied forces lay siege to Seoul and, after heavy fighting, recapture it on September 26.

❏ September 16-27: **Breakout from Pusan**. Four divisions of the U.S. Eighth U.S. Army—the 1st Cavalry Division and the 2nd, 24th, and 25th Infantry Divisions—break out of the Pusan Perimeter.

❏ September 19-October 1: U.N. forces trap most of the the North Korean People's Army (NKPA) between the U.S. Eighth Army, driving north from Pusan, and the U.S. X Corps, centered on Seoul. North Korea's forces are decimated and forced to retreat.

❏ October 7: U.N. forces cross the 38th Parallel into North Korea. The United Nations sanctions the destruction of the People's Democratic Republic of Korea and the reunification of the country.

❏ October 12: Chinese Communist Forces (CCF) cross the Yalu River into Korea.

❏ October 15: General MacArthur and President Truman meet at Wake Island for a brief, half-day conference.

❏ October 19: U.N. Forces capture Pyongyang, the North Korean capital.

❏ October 20: Some 2,860 paratroopers of the 187th Airborne Regimental Combat Team take part in the first airborne operation of the war, jumping into Sukchon and Sunchon north of Pyongyang. Working with ground forces driving north, they kill or capture about 6,000 North Koreans.

❏ October 25: Chinese Communist Forces (CCF) enter the Korean War and launch their first phase offensive.

❏ October 26: After reembarking at Inchon, X Corps lands at Wonsan on Korea's east coast. ROK troops, however, have already advanced 50 miles up the peninsula beyond this point.

❏ November 1950: U.N. units drive retreating North Korean troops before them and approach the Yalu River, which forms the border with China. The end of the war appears to be within sight.

❏ November 1: CCF units ambush the 1st Cavalry Division at Unsan.

❏ November 8: U.S. government authorizes the Korean Service Medal.

❑ November 8-26: U.S. Navy warplanes and Far East Air Force (FEAF) B-29 bombers attack Yalu River bridges in an attempt to keep Chinese Communist Forces from crossing into North Korea and joining in the battle against the allied ground forces.

❑ November 10-26: U.N. forces, separated by the Taebak Mountains, advance north toward the Yalu River, Eighth Army in the west and X Corps in the east.

❑ November 24: MacArthur's "final offensive" begins.

❑ November 25-December 15: CCF units counterattack allied forces moving north toward the Yalu, including the 1st Marine Division and the U.S. Army's 1st Cavalry Division and 2nd, 3rd, 7th, 24th, and 25th Infantry Divisions.

❑ November 25: CCF units attack the Eighth Army along the Chongchon River.

❑ November 26-December 1: Chinese units defeat the U.S. 2nd and 25th Divisions (Eighth Army) along the Chongchon River, forcing them to retreat.

❑ November 27-December 10: **Battle of Chosin Reservoir**. CCF units hit the Marine 1st and Army 7th Divisions (X Corps) at Chosin Reservoir, forcing them to retreat toward the port city of Hungnam. Completely encircled by the communists, the marines fight their way southeastward from Koto-ri in one of the most desperate and bloody actions of the war.

❑ December 22: Eighth Army commander General Walton H. Walker is killed in a traffic accident; he is replaced by General Matthew B. Ridgway.

❑ December 24: About 105,000 U.S. and ROK military personnel and 100,000 Korean refugees flee the besieged city of Hungnam by boarding ships or through evacuattion by Navy aircraft to warships waiting off the coast.

1951

❑ January 1-15: CCF Third Phase Offensive. Enemy forces totaling 500,000 men drive U.N. forces 50 miles south of the 38th Parallel.

❑ January 4: Comunist forces capture Seoul for the second time.

❑ January 14-15: U.N. forces consolidate their lines along the 37th parallel, in South Korea.

❑ January 25: U.N. forces reassume their offensive.

❑ February 1: **Battle of the Twin Tunnels.** A U.N. force composed of the 23rd Infantry Regiment (2nd Infantry Division), 347th Field Artillery Battalion, and the French Battalion engages several CCF regiments, killing at least 1,300 Chinese soldiers. Also, the United Nations votes to end the conflict in Korea by "peaceful means."

❑ February 13-14: Communist forces counterattack during the U.N. offensive.

❑ February 13-15: **Battle of Chipyong-ni.** In this first mass assault by the Chinese, 18,000 troops smash into a multinational force that includes the 23rd Infantry Regiment (2nd Infantry Division), the 37th Field Artillery Battalion, Battery B of the 82nd Antiaircraft Artillery Battalion, the 1st Ranger Company, and the French Battalion. Despite the ferocity of the attack, the allied forces stop the advance of the communists.

❑ February 16, 1951-July 27: **Siege of Wonsan.** A U.N. blockade and escort force designated Task Force 95 blockades Wonsan Harbor. This blockade eventually lasts an incredible 861 days, the longest effective siege of a port in U.S. Naval history.

❑ February 17-March 17: U.N. forces continue their offensive northward.

❑ March 7-April 4: **Operation Ripper.** Seven U.S. divisions—U.S. Army 1st Cavalry Division, 2nd, 3rd, 7th, 24th, and 25th Infantry Divisions, and the 1st Marine Division—succeed in recapturing Seoul on March 18, and drive communist forces back across the 38th parallel.

❑ March 23: **Operation Tomahawk.** In this second-largest airborne operation of the war, 120 C-119 and C-46 transport aircraft drop 3,437 paratroopers of the 187th Regimental Combat Team near Munsan-ni.

❑ April 11: President Truman fires General MacArthur. General Ridgway is promoted to overall command of the U.N. forces, and General James Van Fleet is given command of Eighth Army.

❑ April 12: More than 40 MiG-15s attack a B-29 formation and shoot down two bombers in this first major aerial duel of the conflict. Eleven of the MiGs are destroyed in the battle, seven of them by B-29 gunners.

❑ April 22-29: **Chinese First Spring Offensive.** In what is the largest single battle of the war, Communist Chinese forces launch their spring offensive with 27 divisions, a total of 250,000 men, against five U.S. Army divisions (2nd, 3rd, 7th, 24th, 25th).

❑ April 30: CCF is forced to break contact with U.N. forces.

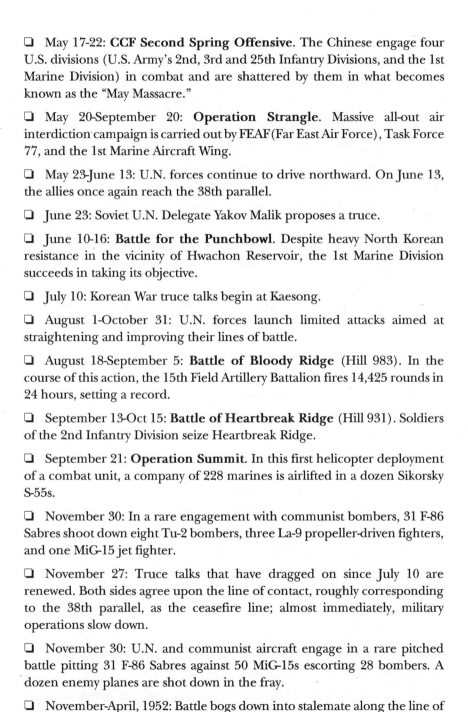

❏ May 17-22: **CCF Second Spring Offensive.** The Chinese engage four U.S. divisions (U.S. Army's 2nd, 3rd and 25th Infantry Divisions, and the 1st Marine Division) in combat and are shattered by them in what becomes known as the "May Massacre."

❏ May 20-September 20: **Operation Strangle.** Massive all-out air interdiction campaign is carried out by FEAF (Far East Air Force), Task Force 77, and the 1st Marine Aircraft Wing.

❏ May 23-June 13: U.N. forces continue to drive northward. On June 13, the allies once again reach the 38th parallel.

❏ June 23: Soviet U.N. Delegate Yakov Malik proposes a truce.

❏ June 10-16: **Battle for the Punchbowl.** Despite heavy North Korean resistance in the vicinity of Hwachon Reservoir, the 1st Marine Division succeeds in taking its objective.

❏ July 10: Korean War truce talks begin at Kaesong.

❏ August 1-October 31: U.N. forces launch limited attacks aimed at straightening and improving their lines of battle.

❏ August 18-September 5: **Battle of Bloody Ridge** (Hill 983). In the course of this action, the 15th Field Artillery Battalion fires 14,425 rounds in 24 hours, setting a record.

❏ September 13-Oct 15: **Battle of Heartbreak Ridge** (Hill 931). Soldiers of the 2nd Infantry Division seize Heartbreak Ridge.

❏ September 21: **Operation Summit.** In this first helicopter deployment of a combat unit, a company of 228 marines is airlifted in a dozen Sikorsky S-55s.

❏ November 30: In a rare engagement with communist bombers, 31 F-86 Sabres shoot down eight Tu-2 bombers, three La-9 propeller-driven fighters, and one MiG-15 jet fighter.

❏ November 27: Truce talks that have dragged on since July 10 are renewed. Both sides agree upon the line of contact, roughly corresponding to the 38th parallel, as the ceasefire line; almost immediately, military operations slow down.

❏ November 30: U.N. and communist aircraft engage in a rare pitched battle pitting 31 F-86 Sabres against 50 MiG-15s escorting 28 bombers. A dozen enemy planes are shot down in the fray.

❏ November-April, 1952: Battle bogs down into stalemate along the line of contact, as peace discussions drag on at Panmunjom.

1952

❏ April 2: Allied forces begin screening communist POWs. Riots begin at the POW camp on Koje-do.

❏ May 7: Communist POWs on Koje-do capture the camp commandant, Brigadier General Francis T. Dodd.

❏ May 12-June 12: Brigadier General Haydon Boatner quashes the riots on Koje-do. General Mark Clark replaces General Matthew Ridgway at FECOM.

❏ May 25: Nine tanks of the 245th Tank Battalion, 45th Infantry Division, launch an attack against North Korean-held Agok, in retaliation for three raids against the American division's sector.

❏ June-October: Truce talks deadlock over the question of repatriation of POWs. There is a stalemate along the line of contact, punctuated by several hill battles, including White Horse Mountain.

❏ June 6-14: **Operation Counter**. 45th Infantry Division soldiers launch a series of attacks in the vicinity of Old Baldy (Hill 266) in order to establish 11 patrol bases. A pair of CCF battalions fiercely counterattack the 2nd and 3rd Battalions of the 180th Infantry Regiment holding Outpost Eerie on Hill 191, but are unable to dislodge them.

❏ July 17-August 4: **Battle for Old Baldy** (Hill 266).

❏ July 23: FEAF and Navy planes launch massive air strikes against North Korea's hydroelectric power grid, causing an almost complete blackout for more than two weeks. Results of strikes extend into northeast China, which loses nearly 25 percent of its electrical requirements.

❏ August 29: **Largest air raid of the Korean War**. Aircraft from FEAF and offshore aircraft carriers launch 1,403 bombing sorties against Pyongyang, the largest one-day raid of the entire war.

❏ September 1: **Largest all-Navy raid**. A total of 144 planes from three aircraft carriers destroy the North Korean oil refinery at Aoji.

❏ September 17-24: CCF troops besiege the 65th Infantry Regiment (3rd Infantry Division), holed up in Outpost Kelly.

❏ October 8: Truce talks at Panmunjom deadlock and are recessed.

❏ October-November: Communist forces put heavy pressure on ROK forces holding the center of the battle line.

❏ October 9-July 1953: **"Cherokee" Airstrikes**. The 7th Fleet launches a bombing campaign against front line enemy supply facilities.

❏ October 14-25: **Operation Showdown/Battle of Hill 598 (Sniper Ridge).** The 7th Infantry Division battles the Chinese near Kumhwa, the right leg of the Iron Triangle.

❏ October 26-28: **Battle of the Hook.**

❏ November: India makes a proposal in the United Nations concerning POW repatriation.

❏ November 3: Soldiers of the 2nd Battalion, 160th Infantry Regiment (40th Infantry Division), holds Hill 851, Heartbreak Ridge area, against communist assault.

❏ December: President-elect Eisenhower fulfills a campaign pledge to visit Korea. U.N. forces intensify psychological warfare against the communists. Stalemate continues, broken up by hill battles.

❏ December 25: **Battle of T-Bone Hill.** The 38th Infantry Regiment (2nd Infantry Division) repels Chinese forces during an intense battle.

1953

❏ January: Stalemate and hill battles continue.

❏ January 25: **Operation Smack.** Elements of the 31st Infantry Regiment (7th Infantry Division) assault Spud Hill.

❏ February 11: General Maxwell D. Taylor replaces General James Van Fleet as commander of Eighth Army.

❏ February 22: The U.N. Command once again proposes an exchange of sick and wounded POWs.

❏ March 5: Soviet Premier Josef Stalin dies, sparking disaffection in the USSR's satellite states and a struggle for power in the Kremlin.

❏ March 17: Chinese forces assault Hill 355 (Little Gibraltar), held by the 9th Infantry Regiment (2nd Infantry Division).

❏ March 23-24: The 32nd Regiment (7th Infantry Division) assumes control of the Old Baldy/Pork Chop Complex, relieving the 31st Infantry Regiment (7th Infantry Division).

❏ March 26-30: Chinese forces suffer the loss of a regiment during a heavy attack against outposts at the Nevada cities (Vegas-Reno-Carson) held by the 5th Marine Regiment.

❏ March 28: The Communists agree to the POW exchange proposed by the U.N. Command.

❑ March 30: Chinese Foreign Minister Chou En-lai indicates that the communist powers will agree to the Indian POW proposal made to the United Nations the previous November. Peace talks resume at Panmunjom.

❑ April 16-18: **Battle of Pork Chop Hill.** The 17th and 31st Infantry Regiments of the 7th Infantry Division suffer heavy casualties in a see-saw battle over a strategically insignificant chunk of territory.

❑ April 20-26: **Operation Little Switch.** U.N. and communist forces exchange sick and wounded POWs, among them 149 Americans.

❑ April 27: Plenary sessions resume at Panmunjom.

❑ May: While truce details are negotiated at Panmunjom, savage fighting continues along the static battle line.

❑ May 13: **Raid on Toksan Dam.** In the first of a two-week series of attacks against North Korean irrigation systems, F-84s of the 58th Fighter-Bomber Wing attack and destroy a major dam. Floodwaters immerse five miles of valuable rice crops and wash out several miles of highways and railroad tracks.

❑ June 4: The Communists finally agree, for all practical purposes, to the U.N. truce proposals.

❑ June 15: A record for offensive sorties flown from an aircraft carrier in a single day is set when USS *Princeton* launches 184 sorties. Also on this day, Navy and Marine Corps aircraft fly a total of 910 sorties, the highest combined number flown during a single day of the Korean War.

❑ June 25: CCF forces launch massive attacks against ROK divisions. Walter S. Robertson begins the "little truce talks" with Syngman Rhee in order to obtain ROK acceptance of the armistice.

❑ June 30: FEAF F-86 Sabres shoot down 16 MiGs, the largest number shot down in a single day.

❑ July 6-10: After five days of heavy fighting, the 7th Infantry Division is ordered to evacuate its defensive positions on Pork Chop Hill.

❑ July 7: The Republic of Korea agrees to the cease fire terms.

❑ July 13-20: **Battle of Kumsong River Salient.** In this last communist offensive, the CCF launches a six-division attack, directed in part against the 3rd, 40th, and 45th Infantry Divisions of the U.S. IX Corps. During the fighting, the 187th Regimental Combat Team is attached to 2nd Infantry Division.

❏ July 24-26: In the final episode of U.S. ground combat, a 3,000-man communist force launches an assault against the "Boulder City" area of the Berlin Complex, held by the 1st and 7th Marine Regiments. Combat on Hills 111 and 119 are the final Marine ground actions of the war.

❏ July 27: An F-86 Sabre shoots down an enemy transport near the Manchurian border, the last air kill of the war.

❏ July 27: **Armistice.** North Korea, China, and the United States sign an armistice, ending the fighting in Korea. This fails, however, to bring about a permanent peace and to date the Republic of Korea and the Democratic Peoples' Republic of Korea have not signed a peace treaty.

❏ September 4: Indian neutrals begin screening and repatriating communist POWs at Freedom Village, near Panmunjom.

❏ September 6: **Operation Big Switch.** The last American POWs are repatriated.

ACRONYMS AND MILITARY TERMS

"Excuse me sir, seeing as how the VP is such a VIP, shouldn't we keep the PC on the QT? 'Cause if it leaks to the VC, he could end up an MIA, and then we'd all get put on KP."

—Robin Williams, *Good Morning Vietnam*

A large variety of abbreviations and acronyms were used in military and government documents, speech, and correspondence during the Korean War. Most of those that follow were official U.S. military acronyms; others are unofficial but were common or were used by foreign countries, such as HMCS for His Majesty's Canadian Ship. Explanatory information is given in some cases.

❑ AAA: anti-aircraft artillery.

❑ Abn: airborne.

❑ A/C: aircraft. Used by pilots in mission reports.

❑ ACSI: Assistant Chief of Staff for Intelligence.

❑ ADCOM: Advance Command and Liaison Group in Korea.

❑ ADF: automatic direction finder. A type of equipment used on jet aircraft.

❑ Adm.: admiral

❑ Admin: administration/administrative.

❑ AFF: Army Field Forces.

❑ AFFE: Army Forces, Far East.

❑ AN: annex.

❑ AP: armor-piercing. Type of cannon round used by direct fire artillery pieces and tanks against armored vehicles.

❑ API: armor-piercing incendiary. Type of ammunition used by fighter aircraft. In the oxygen poor stratosphere, however, where much jet-to-jet combat took place, such ammunition damaged but often failed to ignite struck aircraft.

❑ APU: auxiliary power unit. A jet aircraft component.

❑ Armd: armored.

❑ Arty: artillery.

❑ AU: Army unit.

❑ B: bomber (e.g., B-29 "Superfortress").

❑ BAR: Browning automatic rifle. The primary squad-level fully automatic weapon used by U.S. infantry forces in Korea.

❑ BCT: battalion combat team. An infantry battalion reinforced with other elements and capable of operating independently. Such units were employed by some U.N. nations (e.g., the Philippines). A typical BCT might consist of three infantry companies, one tank company, one reconnaissance company, and one artillery battery.

❑ Bde: brigade.

❑ Bn: battalion. An combat unit consisting of about 1,000 men, further divided into five or more companies.

❑ BOQ: bachelor officers quarters. Living quarters for single officers or those unaccompanied by their families.

❑ Br: branch.

❑ Cav: cavalry.

❑ CCF: Chinese Communist Forces.

❑ CCP: Chinese Communist Party.

❑ CG: commanding general.

❑ CIA: Central Intelligence Agency.

- ❏ CinC: commander-in-chief.

- ❏ CINCFE: Commander-in-Chief, Far East.

- ❏ CINCPAC: Commander-in-Chief, Pacific.

- ❏ CINCPACFLT: Commander-in-Chief, U.S. Pacific Fleet.

- ❏ CINCUNC: Commander-in-Chief, United Nations Command.

- ❏ CINFO: Chief of Information.

- ❏ CMS: constructive months service.

- ❏ Cmte: committee.

- ❏ CNO: Chief of Naval Operations.

- ❏ Co.: company. A unit consisting of 100 to 200 soldiers, further divided into three or more platoons.

- ❏ CofS: Chief of Staff.

- ❏ Comd: command.

- ❏ COMNAVFE: Commander, U.N. Naval Forces, Far East.

- ❏ Conf: conference.

- ❏ Cong: Congress.

- ❏ Corresp: correspondence.

- ❏ CPVA: Chinese People's Volunteers Army.

- ❏ CONUS: Continental United States.

- ❏ DA: Department of the Army.

- ❏ DA-IN: incoming message.

- ❏ DCofS: Deputy Chief of Staff.

- ❏ Dept: department.

- ❏ DF: Disposition Form.

- ❏ Div: Division.

- ❏ DMZ: demilitarized zone.

- ❏ DPRK: Democratic People's Republic of Korea (North Korea).

- ❏ ECA: Economic Coordination Administration.

- ❏ EDC: European Defense Community.

- ❏ En: Enemy. Used by pilots in flight reports.

❑ Engr: Engineer.

❑ EUSAK: Eighth U.S. Army in Korea. Used only for the forces operating in-theater during the war.

❑ F: fighter (e.g., F-86 "Sabre").

❑ FA: field artillery.

❑ FAC: forward air controller. A fighter pilot on the ground or in an observation aircraft who directs friendly air attacks against enemy ground targets.

❑ FEAF: Far East Air Forces.

❑ FEAMCOM: Far East Air Material Command.

❑ FEC, FECOM: Far East Command.

❑ G-1: personnel section of a divisional or higher staff.

❑ G-2: intelligence section of a divisional or higher staff.

❑ G-3: operations section of a divisional or higher staff.

❑ G-4: logistics section of a divisional or higher staff.

❑ G-5: civil affairs section of a divisional or higher staff.

❑ GCA: ground controlled approach. A system of radar-guided instrument flight used for landing aircraft in inclement weather.

❑ GCI: ground controlled intercept. Use of ground based radar to steer fighter aircraft toward targets or an airbase under conditions of limited visibility.

❑ GCM: gold-colored metal. Used in describing buttons, insignia, etc.

❑ GHQ: general headquarters.

❑ GI: government issue. Common slang name for an American soldier.

❑ HBT: herringbone twill, a type of cloth used in U.S. military uniforms.

❑ HE: high explosive. A type of ammunition used by tanks and artillery primarily for use against personnel.

❑ HEAT: high explosive, anti-tank.

❑ Hist: history, historical.

❑ HMCS: Her/His Majesty's Canadian Ship.

❑ HQ: Headquarters.

❏ HVAP-T: high-velocity armor piercing-tank. A type of tungsten-cored ammunition used by allied armored forces.

❏ HVSS: horizontal volute spring suspension. A tank suspension system that entered service in December 1944 on the M-4A3E8 Sherman.

❏ ICRC: International Committee of the Red Cross.

❏ Inf: infantry.

❏ Instr: instructions.

❏ Intel: intelligence.

❏ Interv: interview.

❏ IRO: International Refugee Organization.

❏ J-1: Joint Staff personnel section.

❏ J-2: Joint Staff intelligence section.

❏ J-3: Joint Staff operations section.

❏ J-4: Joint Staff logistics section.

❏ J-5: Joint Staff civil affairs section.

❏ Jato: jet assisted takeoff. Accomplished with attached rockets that could be jettisoned once in flight.

❏ JCS: Joint Chiefs of Staff.

❏ Jnl: journal.

❏ JP: jet propellant (fuel).

❏ JSPOG: Joint Strategic Plans and Operations Group.

❏ KATCOM: Korean Augmentation Troops, Commonwealth.

❏ KATUSA: Korean Augmentation to the U.S. Army.

❏ KCOMZ: Korean Communications Zone.

❏ KIA: killed in action.

❏ KMAG: Korean Military Advisory Group; United States Military Advisory Group to the Republic of Korea.

❏ KMT: Kuomintang party.

❏ KSC: Korean Service Corps.

❏ kts: knots, nautical miles. A nautical mile is equal to 1.1515 statute miles.

❏ LST: landing ship, tank.

❑ M: model, as in "M1952 body armor."

❑ MAAG: Military Assistance Advisory Group.

❑ MAC: Military Armistice Commission.

❑ MASH: Mobile Army Surgical Hospital.

❑ M&S: maintenance and supply group.

❑ MDAP: Mutual Defense Appropriations Program.

❑ MGMC: Multiple Gun Motor Carriage. Designation for the U.S. antiaircraft systems consisting of multiple machineguns mounted on a modified armored vehicle chassis (e.g., the Quad 50, the Dual 40).

❑ MIA: missing in action.

❑ MiG: family of Soviet-made jet aircraft. A contraction of "Mikoyan-Gurevich," the names of the aircraft's two primary developers.

❑ MIS: Military Intelligence Service.

❑ MLR: main line of resistance (i.e., the line of battle between the opposing forces).

❑ MP: military police.

❑ MQ: model quartermaster.

❑ MSA: Mutual Security Act.

❑ MSR: main supply route. Primary roads and highways used as lines of movement and supply for military units. Usually used in conjunction with an identifying name or number, such as MSR Red 7.

❑ NATO: North Atlantic Treaty Organization.

❑ NAVFE: U.S. Navy, Far East.

❑ NCO: noncommissioned officer. Enlisted ranks such as corporal, sergeant, etc., attained through experience and time and service, rather than a commission.

❑ NKPA: North Korean People's Army.

❑ nm: nautical miles (e.g., "The Thunderjets were a mere 60nm from the site of combat.").

❑ NNRC: Neutral Nations Repatriation Commission.

❑ NNSC: Neutral Nations Supervisory Commission.

❑ NPRJ: National Police Reserve Japan.

❑ NSC: National Security Council.

❑ OCA: Office, Comptroller of the Army.

❑ O-Club: officers club.

❑ OD: olive drab.

❑ OG: olive green.

❑ Opnl: operational.

❑ Opns: operations.

❑ ORO: Operations Research Office.

❑ PIR: Periodic Intelligence Report.

❑ Plng: planning.

❑ POR: Periodic Operations Report.

❑ POW: prisoner of war.

❑ PPS: Policy Planning Staff.

❑ PRC: People's Republic of China (communist China).

❑ PSP: pierced steel planking. Perforated plates of steel that could be laid on the ground and interlocked to create airfield runways on otherwise unsuitable terrain, such as loose sand.

❑ PX: post exchange.

❑ QMCTC: Quartermaster Corps Technical Committee.

❑ RAAK: Resist America Korea Movement.

❑ RandR, R&R: rest and recuperation, rest and rehabilitation.

❑ Rcd: record.

❑ RCT: regimental combat team.

❑ Regt: regiment.

❑ ROC: Republic of China (nationalist China).

❑ ROK: Republic of Korea (South Korea).

❑ ROKA: Republic of Korea Army.

❑ RON: remain overnight.

❑ ROTC: Reserve Officer Training Corps.

❏ S-1: personnel section of a battalion staff, responsible for personnel management, administration, morale, and discipline.

❏ S-2: military intelligence section of a battalion staff, responsible for collecting, interpreting, and disseminating tactical information.

❏ S-3: operations section of a battalion staff, responsible for planning military operations and training.

❏ S-4: logistics section of a battalion staff, responsible for unit supply, maintenance, and transportation plans.

❏ SANACC: State-Army-Navy-Air Force Coordinating Committee.

❏ SCAP: Supreme Commander for the Allied Powers.

❏ Sec: section. A unit within an office.

❏ sec.: section (of a document).

❏ Secy: Secretary (of Defense, the Army, etc.).

❏ Sess: session.

❏ SGS: Secretary of the General Staff.

❏ SUC: stand-up collar, used to describe a feature of some U.S. military uniforms.

❏ T: test. Used to describe items undergoing testing, as in "T-1952 body armor."

❏ TAC: Tactical Air Command.

❏ TAG: The Adjutant General.

❏ TDY: temporary duty.

❏ Teleconf: telephone conference.

❏ TF: task force.

❏ TO&E: table of organization and equipment. U.S. Army tables that showed the allotment of troops, weapons, and equipment at every level of command, from company through corps.

❏ T.O.T.: time on target. Projected attack time on targets for fighter or bomber attacks.

❏ UN: United Nations.

❏ UNC: United Nations Command.

❏ UNCOK: United Nations Commission on Korea.

❏ UNCMAC: UN Command Military Armistice Commission.

❏ UNCURK: United Nations Commission for the Unification and Rehabilitation of Korea.

❏ UNKRA: United Nations Korean Reconstruction Agency.

❏ UNRC: United Nations Reception Center.

❏ UNRRA: United Nations Relief and Rehabilitation Administration.

❏ UNTCOK: United Nations Temporary Commission on Korea.

❏ US: United States.

❏ USAF: United States Air Force.

❏ USAAF: United States Army Air Force.

❏ USAFIK: United Nations Armed Forces in Korea.

❏ USARPAC: U.S. Army, Pacific.

❏ USMA: United States Military Academy.

❏ USMC: United States Marine Corps.

❏ USSR: Union of Soviet Socialist Republics.

❏ WAC: Women's Army Corps.

❏ WAF: Women in the Air Force.

❏ WIA: wounded in action.

❏ WSB: War Stabilization Board.

❏ ZI: Zone of the Interior (i.e., the continental United States).

SELECT BIBLIOGRAPHY

Almanac of Naval Facts. United States Naval Institute, 1964.

Angelucci, Enzo. *The Rand McNally Encyclopedia of Military Aircraft, 1914 to the Present.* The Military Press, 1990.

Avery, Derek, ed. Cross, Robin, Fitzsimons, Bernard, Humble, Richard, and Lloyd, Mark. *History of the United States Fighting Forces.* Chevprime Limited, 1989.

Brady, James. *The Coldest War: A Memoir of Korea.* Pocket Books, 1990.

Bunge, Frederica M., ed. *North Korea: A Country Study.* Foreign Area Studies, The American University, 1981.

Chamberlain, Peter and Ellis, Chris. *The Sherman: An Illustrated History of the M4 Medium Tank.* Arco, 1969.

Crow, Duncan and Icks, Robert J. *Encyclopedia of Tanks.* Chartwell Books Inc., 1975.

Cumings, Bruce. *War and Television.* Verso, 1992.

Davis, Ray. *The Story of Ray Davis.* Research Triangle Publishing, 1995.

Edwards, Paul M. *A Guide to Films on the Korean War.* Greenwood Press, 1997.

Evans, Douglas K. *Sabre Jets Over Korea: A Firsthand Account.* Tab Books Inc., 1984.

Ezell, Edward Clinton. *Small Arms of the World: A Basic Manual of Small Arms.* Stackpole Books, 1983.

Fehrenbach, T. R. *This Kind of War: The Classic History of the Korean War.* Brassey's, 1998.

Ferrell, Robert H. *Harry S. Truman: A Life.* University of Missouri Press, 1994.

Forty, George. *At War in Korea.* Bonanza Books, 1985.

Foss, Christopher F. *Artillery of the World* (Revised Edition). Charles Scribner's Sons, 1976.

Halliday, Jon and Cumings, Bruce. *Korea: The Unknown War.* Pantheon Books, 1988.

Hermes, Walter O. *United States Army in the Korean War: Truce Tent and Fighting Front.* Office of the Chief of Military History, 1988.

Hoare, James and Pares, Susan. *Conflict in Korea: An Encyclopedia.* ABC-CLIO, 1999.

Hoffschmidt, Edward M. and Tantum, William H. IV, eds. *U.S. Military Vehicles, World War II.* WE, Inc., 1970.

House, Jonathan M. "Toward Combined Arms Warfare: A Survey of 20th Century Tactics, Doctrine, and Organization." Combat Studies Institute, August 1984.

Hunnicutt, R. P. *Pershing: A History of the Medium Tank T20 Series.* Feist Publications, 1971.

Jessup, John E. *An Encyclopedic Dictionary of Conflict and Conflict Resolution, 1945-1996.* Greenwood Press, 1998.

Knox, Donald. *The Korean War: Pusan to Chosin; An Oral History.* Harcourt, Brace, Jovanovich, 1985.

Maltin, Leonard. *Leonard Maltin's 2000 Movie and Video Guide.* Signet, 1999.

Matray, James I., ed. Historical Dictionary of the Korean War. Greenwood Press, 1991.

Mao Tse-Tung. *Quotations from Chairman Mao Tse-Tung.* Foreign Languages Press, 1966.

Milsom, John. *Russian Tanks, 1900-1970; The Complete Illustrated History of Soviet Armoured Theory and Design.* Galahad Books, 1970.

Naval Orientation. Bureau of Naval Personnel, 1961.

Orgokiewicz, Richard M. *Armoured Forces: A History of Armoured Forces and their Vehicles.* Arco Publishing Company, Inc., 1970.

Owen, J. I. H., ed. *Brassey's Infantry Weapons of the World, 1950-1975.* Bonanza Books, 1979.

Price, Scott T. "The Forgotten Service in the Forgotten War: The U.S. Coast Guard's Role in the Korean Conflict." U.S. Naval Institute Press, 2000.

Robertson, William Glenn. "Counterattack on the Naktong, 1950." Combat Studies Institute, December 1988.

Rosignoli, Guido. *Army Badges and Insignia Since 1945* (Book One). MacMillan Publishing Co. Inc., 1973.

Savada, Andrea Matles and Shaw, William, eds. *South Korea: A Country Study.* Federal Research Division of the Library of Congress, 1992.

Shores, Christopher. *Fighter Aces.* Hamlyn Publishing Group Ltd., 1975.

Smith, Digby. *Army Uniforms Since 1945.* Blandford Press, 1980.

Spick, Mike. *The Complete Fighter Ace: All the World's Fighter Aces, 1914-2000.* Stackpole Books, 1999.

Stanton, Shelby. *U.S. Army Uniforms of the Cold War, 1948-1973.* Stackpole Books, 1998.

Stanton, Shelby. *U.S. Army Uniforms of the Korean War.* Stackpole Books, 1992.

Stokesbury, James L. *A Short History of the Korean War.* Quill, 1988.

Toland, John. *In Mortal Combat: Korea, 1950-1953.* William Morrow and Co. Inc., 1991.

White, William Lindsay. *The Captives of Korea: An Unofficial White Paper on the Treatment of War Prisoners.* Charles Scribner's Sons, 1957.

INDEX

Aces, 42-45; Canadian, 44; Chinese, 44; North Korean, 44; Soviet, 36, 44-45; U.S., 42-43

Acheson, Dean, 204, 288

"Active defense," 21

Agok, 24

Agriculture, 266

Air Force, ROK, 122

Air Force, U.S., 33, 51; Fifth, 34; Thirteenth, 34; Twentieth, 34

Air forces, communist, 36-37, 156-157, 163

Air operations/support, 9, 18, 23, 37-38

Air raids/strikes, 6, 8, 24, 27-28, 55-57, 294, 296, largest, 294, Toksan Dam, 296

Air-to-air combat, 39-45, 76, first all-jet, 39

Air-to-ground combat, 38

Air war, 33-50

Aircraft, 45-50, 80; allied, 46-49; attack, 20, 29, 46, 50; bomber, 45-48; communist, 49-50; fighter, 46-50; jet, 36, 38-39, 45-46, 48-50, 52; piston-driven, 36, 38-39, 45, 47-48, 50; reconnaissance, 46, 57; transport, 39, 46-47

Aircraft carriers, 8, 34, 51-52, 56, 59-62

Airfields, 8, 35-36, 53

Almond, Edward M., 8, 17, 204

Amphibious operations, 8-10, 65, 80

Amphibious warfare vessels, 8, 64-65

Andong, 15, 36, 41

Antiaircraft weapons, 25, 174-175

Aoji, 56

Armistice/armistice negotiations, 23, 27, 29, 31, 38, 69, 74, 223-237, 297; Agenda Item 3, 229-230; Agenda Item 4, 230-234; at Kaesong, 224-227; at Panmunjom, 228-229; communist

delegation, 225-226; South Korean opposition, 236-237; suspension, 234; U.N. delegation, 224

Armored vehicles, U.N., 171-177; antiaircraft armored vehicles, 174-175; armored personnel carriers, 175; tracked landing vehicles, 176-177

Army, ROK, 8, 10-12, 14, 18, 21, 25-28, 71, 83, 115-120; 1st Division, 10; 2nd Division, 27; 5th Division, 75; 6th Division, 20; 8th Division, 18; 9th Division, 25; III Corps, 17; corps, 83

Army, U.S., 81-105; organization, 81-82

Army Air Forces, U.S., 34

Arrowhead Hill, 27

Artillery, 2, 6, 18, 20, 23-26, 28-31, 177-179; coastal, 8, 56

Atomic weapons, 52, 185-186, 224

Australia, 128-129; air forces, 33, 128; aircraft, 46; ground forces, 74, 128-129; naval forces, 53, 72

Awards, 202; Korean Service Medal, 290

B-26 Marauders, 46

B-29 Superfortresses, 41, 47

Battles: *Bloody Ridge*, 22-24, 77, 293; *Bowling Alley*, 6; *Bunker Hill*, 25; *Chipyong-ni*, 16, 18, 292; *Chosin Reservoir*, 12, 291; *Heartbreak Ridge*, 22, 77, 293; *Hoengsong*, 16; *Hook*, 295; *Kum River*, 4; *Kumsong River Salient*, 30, 296; *Naktong Bulge (First)*, 6, 289; *Naktong Bulge (Second)*, 6; *Notch*, 4; *Old Baldy*, 294; *Osan*, 3-4, 289; *Pork Chop Hill*, 30-31, 296; *Punchbowl*, 293; *Taejon*, 4; *Taeusan*, 22; *T-Bone Hill*, 295; *Twin Tunnels*, 16, 292; *White Horse Hill*, 25-27

Battleships, 51-52, 59-61

Belgium / Belgian forces, 129-130
Berlin Complex, 30
Bloody Ridge, 22-24, 71
Books and literature, 253-254
Bradley, Omar Nelson, 204
Brady, James, 1
Briscoe, Robert Pearce, 204
"Bugging out," 14

C-54A Skymaster, 47
Canada, 130-132; air forces, 44,
    130-131; ground forces, 74, 130-132;
    naval forces, 53, 72, 130-131
Capitol Building, ROK, 71
Casualties, 3-4, 6, 9-10, 12, 14, 16,
    18-20, 23-24, 26, 28-29, 35, 56-57, 91,
    92, 94, 96, 97, 99, 100, 102, 103, 104,
    108, 110, 111; allied, 129, 130, 132,
    133, 135, 137, 138, 140, 141, 142, 143,
    144, 145, 146, 147, 148; frostbite, 12;
    illness, 12; mines, 55
Cates, Clifton Bledsoe, 204-205
Chae Byung Dok, 205
Changjin Reservoir, 71, 73
Chaeryong Plain, 70
Cheju Island (Cheju-do), 70-71
Chiang Kai-shek, 220-221
China, 10-11, 21, 36, 53-54, 70, 75, 78
China Sea, 57
Chindong, 78
Chinese First Spring Offensive, 20-21,
    161-162, 292
Chinese People's Volunteers Army /
    Chinese forces, 11-12, 14-18, 20-21,
    25-28, 30-31, 55, 72, 74, 78, 156-163,
    290-291; tactics, 162-163
Chinese Second Spring Offensive, 21,
    162, 293
Chinnampo, 53, 72
Chipyong-ni, 17-18, 72
Chochiwon, 4
Choi Yong-kon, 216-217
Chonan, 4
Chonggodo, 10
Chorwon, 23, 25, 74, 77

Chosin, 37
Chosin Reservoir, 11-12, 71-73
Chou En-lai, 217, 235
Chuksan, 55
Chumunjin, 53
Chung Il-kwon, 205
Civil War, vii
Clark, Mark Wayne, 205-206, 234-235
Climate, Korean, 70-71
Coast Guard, ROK, 57
Coast Guard, U.S., 57-59
Cold War, vii
Colombia / Colombian forces, 30,
    132-133
Collins, Lawton Joseph, 206
Commonwealth Brigade, 27th, 74
Commonwealth Division, 1st, 20,
    147-148
Communications, 269-270
Corps, U.S., 17, 83, 86-89; I Corps,
    16-17, 83, 86-87; IX Corps, 17, 20,
    25-27, 83, 87-88; X Corps, 7-11,
    17-18, 20, 54-55, 73, 77-78, 80, 83-85,
    88-89
Cruisers, 8, 51-53, 59-62

Dean William F., 4, 84, 206
Demilitarized Zone, 23, 31, 69, 73, 77
Denmark/Danish personnel, 149
Destroyers, 8, 51-52, 62
Detachment X, 3
Divisions, U.S., 12, 89-103; *2nd Infantry
    Division,* 6, 10, 12, 14, 18, 21, 23,
    27-28, 83, 92-93; *3rd Infantry
    Division,* 12, 19, 25, 30-31, 83, 93-95;
    7th Infantry Division, 8-12, 18, 25,
    27-28, 30, 71, 79, 83, 95-96; *24th
    Infantry Division,* 3-4, 6, 10, 12, 18-19,
    83-84, 97-98; *25th Infantry Division,*
    4, 6, 10, 12, 19, 26, 30, 83-84, 98-100;
    40th Infantry Division, 83, 100-101;
    45th Infantry Division, 24-25, 28, 77,
    83, 101-103
DMZ, See Demilitarized Zone
Dogfights, 34, 38-45

Dulles, John Foster, 207

Education, 264-265
8th U.S. Army, 7, 9-10, 14, 16, 19-21, 27,
   31, 76-78, 82-86, 215
Equipment, 14, 18; body armor,
   194-195; heavy, 14; helmets, 193-
   194; individual, 192-193
Eisenhower, Dwight David, 207, 234,
   236
Ethiopia / Ethiopian forces, 133-134
EUSA, See 8th U.S. Army

F-4U Corsairs, 38, 48
F-9F2 Panthers, 40, 46
F-80 Shooting Stars, 39-40, 46, 48-49
F-82 Twin Mustangs, 39, 48
F-84 Thunders, 40, 46
F-86 Sabres, 35, 40-41, 44, 46, 50
Farm Line, 73
Far East Air Force, See FEAF
FEAF, 34-35, 37-39, 41, 56, 82-83,
   184-185
Fechtler, William Morrow, 207
Fencheng, 36
Films, 254-260, best, 257-260
Finance, 270
First (1st) Cavalry Division, 4, 6, 10, 12,
   18, 73, 83-84, 90, 290
Fishing, 266-267
Flamethrowers, 23, 28
Forestry, 266-267
Formosa, 73
France / French forces, 16, 18, 27,
   134-135
Frigates, 62
Fusen, 37

Geographical sites, 71-80
Great Britain, 135-137, 287; air forces,
   34, 135; ground forces, 74, 135-137;
   naval forces, 51-52, 135
"Great Pohang Guerrilla Hunt," 15
Greece/Greek forces, 137-138
Grenades, 23, 28, 31, 163, 168-170

Ground war, 1-31; phases, 1-2; *U.N.
   defensive*, 2-7; *U.N. offensive*, 2, 7-11;
   Chinese intervention, 2, 11-14; *First
   U.N. counteroffensive*, 2, 15-19;
   Chinese spring offensives, 2, 20-21,
   U.N. counteroffensive, 2, 21-24;
   Second Korean winter-spring, 2,
   24-25; *Korean summer-fall 1952*, 2,
   25-28; *Third Korean winter*, 2, 28-29;
   Korean spring-summer 1953, 2, 29-31
Hadong, 4
Hagaru-ri, 12
Hamhung, 11
Hammarskjold, Dag, 221
Han River, 16-18, 70, 73-74
Harriman, 207-208
Heartbreak Ridge, 23
Helicopters, 52, 55
Hills: *111*, 31; *119*, 31; *303*, 73; *314*, 73;
   812, 28
Hoengsong, 16-17
Hoeryong, 40
Huichon, 73
Hungnam, 12, 14, 55-56, 66, 73, 80
Hyesanjin, 12, 79

Ilyushin Il-10, 50
Imjin River, 14, 73-74
Inchon, 7-10, 17, 54, 62, 74, 76, 78, 84,
   154, 290
Inchon Landing, 7-9, 54, 65, 74, 84, 154,
   290
Industry, 267-268
India/Indian forces, 138, 235-236
Invasion of South Korea, 2
Iron Triangle, 22-23, 27, 74
Italy/Italian personnel, 149
Itazuke Air Base, 3, 74
Iwon, 10

Jamestown Line, 22
Jane Russell Hill, 27-28
Japan, 35, 54-55, 69-71, 73-74, 79, 83,
   287; guerrilla activity against, 76, 151
Joint Task Force 7, 8

Journalists, 74
Joy, C. Turner, 74, 208

Kaesong, 74, 224-225
Kansas / Kansas-Wyoming Line, 19-20, 22, 74, 76, 161
Kapyong, 20, 74
KATCOM, 125
KATUSA, 122-124
Kim Chaek, 38
Kim Il Sung, 152, 217-218
Kim Suk Won, 208
Kimchon, 38
Kimpo Airfield, 9, 17, 154
Kojo, 56
Korean Augmentation to the U.S. Army, see KATUSA
KoreanWar.net, 260
Kosong, 56
Koto-ri, 12
Kozhedub, Ivan, 36
Kum River, 70, 75
Kum River Line, 4
Kumhwa, 23, 27, 74
Kunu-ri, 12, 14, 75
Kuomintang (Chinese Nationalists), 78
Kwangfu, 75
Kynonju, 75
Kyosen, 37

Leaders, communist, 216-220; neutral, 220-222; U.S. / ROK, 203-216
Lie, Trygve, 221-222
Little Gibraltar (Hill 355), 28
LORAN stations (LORSTA), 58
Luxembourg/Luxembourg platoon, 139-140

MacArthur, Douglas, 4, 8, 11-12, 17, 20, 54, 80, 82, 209
Machine guns / automatic weapons, 23, 28, 39, 82
Malenkov, Georgi, 218
Malik, Jacob A., 218, 223
Manchuria, 36, 38, 41, 75-76, 79-80

Mao Tse-tung, 158, 218-219
Maps, 5, 13, 32, 41
Marines, ROK, 8, 120-121
Marines, U.S., 8-9, 80, 105-112, 120; *aviation units*, 38; *1st Marine Aircraft Wing*, 111; *1st Marine Division*, 8-12, 15, 18, 30, 54, 73, 83, 109-111, 120; *1st Provisional Marine Brigade*, 6, 38, 105-108; *Marine Air Group 33*, 38, 107-108; *pilots*, 34, 38, 42-43, 48, 57; *provisional units*, 111-112
Marhsall, George C., 209-210
Masan, 15
May Massacre, 21
Medal of Honor, 44
Medical detachments, U.N., 148-150
MiG Alley, 33, 40-41, 76
MiG-15s, 35-36, 38, 40-41, 43-44, 46, 49-50, 76
Military Advisory Groups, U.S., 112-113
Military Sea Transportation Service, 59
Mines, 10, 54-55, 63
Minsweeping operations, 54
Miryang, 76
Missiles, 39
Missing in Action (MIA), 247-248
Missouri Line, 22
Mountains: *Chirri Massif*, 70; *Halla*, 70; *Paektu*, 70; *Sobaek*, 70, 78; *Taebak*, 70, 78
Muccio, John Joseph, 210,
Munsan-ni, 19
Mustangs, (aircraft) P-51/F-51, 38, 47-48

Naktong River, 6, 70, 76, 78
Nampo, 72
Naval Command Far East Blockade and Escort Force, 83
Naval forces, communist, 157, 164
Naval warfare, 51-68; U.N. Operations, 52-57, 72
Navy, ROK, 57, 122
Navy, U.S., 51-68, 72; 7th Fleet, 52-53; pilots, 38, 42-43, 48, 57
Netherlands/Netherland forces, 140-141

Neutral nations commission, 235-236
Nevada Cities, 30
New Zealand, 141-142; ground forces, 74, 141-142; naval forces, 53, 141-142
No Name Line, 20-21, 76, 162
Nomenclatures, 165-166
Nogunri, 250-251
North Korean People's Army / North Korean forces, 1-10, 15, 21, 23, 28, 30, 38, 76, 78, 84, 151-157
Norway/Norwegian personnel, 149

Oklahoma National Guard, 28
Old Baldy (Hill 266), 24-25, 30, 77, 294
Ongjin Peninsula, 77
Operations, U.N./U.S., *Big Switch*, 245-246, 297; *Chromite*, 7-9; *Clam-Up*, 24-25; *Commando*, 22; *Counter*, 24, 294; *Dauntless*, 19; *Detonate*, 22; *Hudson Harbor*, 186; *Killer*, 18-19; *Little Switch*, 235, 296; *Nomad*, 22; *Piledriver*, 22-23; *Polar*, 22; *Ripper*, 19, 292; *Roundup*, 17-18; *Rugged*, 19; *Showdown*, 27-28, 295; *Smack*, 28-29, 295; *Saturate*, 37; *Strangle*, 37, 292; *Summit*, 293; *Thunderbolt*, 16; *Tomahawk*, 19, 114, 292; *Wolfhound*, 15-16
Osan, 3-4, 10, 16, 77, 84
Outposts: *Berlin*, 30; *Bruce* (*Hill 148*), 25; *East Berlin*, 30; *Harry*, 30; *Kelley*, 25

Pace, Frank J., 210-211
Paik Sun Yup, 211
Pak Hon-yong, 219
Panmunjom, 27, 29, 71, 74, 77, 227-228, 234-235
Partisan Infantry, U.N., 125
Partridge, Earle E., 34
Pepelyaev, Eugeny, 36
Philippines/Filipino forces, 57, 143
Photographs/pictures, 7, 11, 15, 22, 26, 30, 35, 49, 53, 58, 63, 72, 75, 79, 83, 86, 88, 90, 92, 93, 95, 97, 98, 100, 101,

109, 116, 121, 123, 133, 136, 139, 146, 152, 155, 156, 158, 174, 177, 181, 184, 190, 191, 194, 214, 215, 221, 225, 228, 243, 249, 258, 259, 260
Pike's Peak, 27
Pilots, 39; *Australian*, 47; *Chinese*, 37, 40; *North Korean*, 37, 40; *South Korean*, 47; *Soviet*, 36-36, 39, 44-45; *U.S.*, 40-44, 48
Pohang, 15
Population, Korean, 263-264
Pork Chop Hill (Hill 234), 24, 30-31, 77
Prisoners of war (POWs), 235-237, 239-247; *Big Switch*, 245-246; *communist-held*, 241-242; *Little Switch*, 235, 245; *repatriation*, 29, 235-237, 242-247; *U.N.-held*, 240-241, 294
Punchbowl, 71, 77, 293
Pusan, 2, 4, 6, 10, 76-78, 84, 154-155
Pusan Perimeter, 4, 6-7, 10, 38, 76, 78, 84, 154, 290; breakout from, 10, 78, 290
Pyongtaek, 4
Pyongyang (capital), 10, 53, 56, 70, 72, 74, 78
Pyongyang (village), 23

Railroads, 35, 37-38, 269
Rangers, 113-114; *1st Company*, 18; *2nd Company*, 19; *4th Company*, 19
Refugees, 14, 263-264
Regiments, U.S. Army Infantry, *9th*, 23, 28; *14th*, 26; *15th*, 30; *17th*, 12; *19th*, 4; *21st*, 3, 10; *23rd*, 16, 18; *31st*, 12, 27, 30; *32nd*, 12, 30; *34th*, 4; *38th*, 28; *65th*, 25; *179th*, 24, 28
Regimental Combat Teams, 83, 103-105; *5th*, 30, 83, 103; *187th*, 19, 83, 104-105, 114, 290
Regiments, U.S. Marine, *1st*, 8; *5th*, 8, 28, 30, 106; *7th*, 25, 31
Religion, Korean, 265-266
Ridgway, Matthew B., 14-18, 20, 212, 223-224

Rivers, 70
Rockets, 34, 38

Sandy Hill, 27
Sanju, 78
Sea of Japan, 70, 78
Seoul, 1-2, 7-10, 14-20, 72-73, 78, 85,
    154, 290
Sherman, Forrest P., 211
Ships / vessels: *ammunition*, 67;
    auxiliary, 59-60, 65-68; *cargo*, 66;
    Coast Guard cutters, 57-59; *command
    ships*, 59; *designations*, 59-60;
    hospital, 67-68; *minesweepers*, 54-55,
    60, 63-64; *North Korean*, 53; *oilers*,
    67; *patrol*, 60; *repair*, 67; *support*, 51;
    tenders, 66; *torpedo boats*, 53;
    transport, 63, 66, 73; *tugboats*, 60,
    66-67; *types*, 60-68
Ships, combatant / war, 8, 12, 51-52, 73,
    80; *amphibious warfare*, 59, 64-66;
    small / specialized, 62-65
Sinuiju, 10, 38
Smith, Charles B., 3
Sniper Ridge, 31
Snook Hill, 24
Sondong, 15
Songjin, 56
Sorties, 34, 57
South Africa/South African air forces,
    33, 143-144
Soviet Union/Russia, 36-37, 52, 54,
    69-70, 76, 287; *pilots*, 36-37, 39-40,
    44-45
Soyang River, 21
Special U.S. military units, 112-114
Spud Hill, 29
Stalin, Joseph, 219-220
Straits of Korea, 15, 70, 78
Straits of Taiwan, 52
Struble, Arthur, 52
Submarines, 52, 60
Suiho, 37
Sunchon, 78
Supplies/supply lines, 9, 14, 20, 59, 64,
    84, 154
Suwon, 16-17, 78
Sweden, Swedish personnel, 150
Syngman Rhee, 71, 211-212

38th parallel, 9, 14, 16, 18-19, 69, 73-74,
    77, 79, 287-288, 290
Taedong River, 70, 72
Taegu, 2, 73, 84
Taejon, 4, 84
Taiwan, 73, 78
Tanks, 6, 25, 29, 35, 82, 172-174; *T-34*, 3,
    183
Task Force 77, 53, 56
Task Force 90, 56
Task Force Faith, 12
Task Force Smith, 3-4, 10, 74, 77, 84, 289
Taylor, Maxwell D., 31
T-Bone Hill, 28
Terrain, Korean, 70
Thailand / Thai forces, 144-145
Tokyo, 79
Trade, 268
Transportation, 269-270
Trench warfare, 24, 31
Triangle Hill, 25, 27-28
Truman, Harry S., 3-4, 20, 33, 51-52, 80,
    82, 213, 234, 236, 288-289
Tumen River, 70, 79
Tupolev Tu-2, 47, 50
Turkey/Turkish brigade, 145-147

Uisong, 15
Ungok, 28
Uniforms, communist, 199; *branch
    insignia*, 201-202; *rank insignia,
    Chinese*, 200-201
Uniforms, U.N., 197-198
Uniforms, ROK, 195; *branch insignia*,
    196-197; *rank insignia*, 195-196
Uniforms, U.S., 187-191; *insignia*,
    191-192
United Nations, 2-4, 74, 222; military
    contributions, 271-274
U.N. Command, 29, 79, 82

United States Ships (USS), 59-68;
  Benevolence, 68; *Brush,* 55; *Juneau,*
  53; *Lewis,* 56; *Magpie,* 55; *Mansfield,*
  54; *Missouri,* 54, 59, 61; *Partridge,*
  55; *Pirate,* 55; *Pledge,* 55; *Princeton,*
  56; *Sarsi,* 55; *St. Paul,* 56; *Toledo,* 53;
  Valley Forge, 53; *Walke,* 55
Utah Line, 19

Vandenberg, Hoyt S., 213
Van Fleet, James, 20, 27, 214, 227
Vehicles, 14, armored, 2, 18, 171-177,
  183-184
Vladivostok, 40

Wake Island, 79-80, 210
Walker, Walton H., 14, 84, 215, 216
War Crimes, 248-251
Weapons, communist, 179-185; *armored
  vehicles,* 183-184; *artillery,* 184-185;
  grenades / explosives, 181-182; *heavy
  weapons,* 182-183; *small arms,*
  179-181
Weapons, U.S. / U.N., 166-179; *armored
  vehicles,* 171-177; *artillery,* 177-179;
  grenades / explosives, 168-170; *heavy
  weapons,* 170-171; *small arms,*
  166-168
White Horse Hill (Hill 395), 25-27
Wolmi-do, 8, 54, 62, 80
Wonju, 17-18
Wonsan, 10, 55-56, 80, blockade, 56, 292
World War I, 24, 33
World War II, vii, 8, 34-36, 40, 42-45,
  47-48, 51-52, 64, 69, 76, 80, 83
World Wide Web, 260-262
Wyoming Line, 22

Yak fighters, 39
Yalu River, 10, 12, 21, 41, 70, 73, 75-76,
  79-80, 290
Yang-yang, 74
Yechon, 4
Yellow Sea, 70, 80
Yongdok, 78

Yudam-ni, 12

Zone of the Interior, 80
Zorin, Valerian, 220